HITLER'S PRE-WAR POLICY AND
MILITARY PLANS
1933–1939

E. M. ROBERTSON

Hitler's Pre-War Policy and Military Plans 1933–1939

LONGMANS

LONGMANS, GREEN AND CO LTD
48 GROSVENOR STREET, LONDON W1

*Associated companies, branches and representatives
throughout the world.*

© E. M. ROBERTSON 1963
First published 1963

PRINTED IN GREAT BRITAIN BY
SPOTTISWOODE, BALLANTYNE AND CO. LTD.
LONDON AND COLCHESTER

CONTENTS

Abbreviations

AW   *Ausbildungswesen*
DBFP   Documents on British Foreign Policy
DGFP   Documents on German Foreign Policy
IMT   International Military Tribunal
NCA   Nazi Conspiracy and Aggression
ND   Nuremberg Documents
OKH   *Oberkommando des Heeres*
OKL   *Oberkommando der Luftwaffe*
OKW   *Oberkommando der Wehrmacht*
RIIA   Royal Institute of International Affairs

A map of Europe appears on pp. 146–7

Preface

The genesis of this study is a monograph completed in the Cabinet Office Historical Section in 1955. It was based principally on official German documents, the majority of which had not then been published. As explained in the Note on Sources, which precedes the Bibliography, references to any still unpublished material cannot be given in the text. Work on this study has been continued since then at Trinity College, Dublin, later at the Institut für Zeitgeschichte, Munich, and at the University of Edinburgh.

I owe a great debt to Professor Norman Gibbs of All Souls College, Oxford, for permitting me to read a draft of the early chapters of his forthcoming volume on Grand Strategy, 1933 to September 1939, in the official military histories of the Second World War, as well as monographs prepared for him by Miss E. Streatfield. My thanks are also due to Sir James Butler, the Editor of the military histories, to the late Mr. A. B. Acheson, Mr. B. Melland, Dr. G. W. S. Friedrichsen in Washington, Mr. A. Sefi and Mr. W. Todhunter, all of the Cabinet Office, for the pains they have taken to help me in various ways; to the Honourable Margaret Lambert and Mr. K. H. M. Duke, respectively British Editor-in-Chief and Joint Editor of Documents on German Foreign Policy, to Mr. R. Wheatley, now U.K. Editor-in-Chief of Documents on German Foreign Policy (German edition), to Miss A. C. Johnston, formerly of the Foreign Office Library, to Commander M. G. Saunders, R.N. and Mr. A. J. Lawson of the Admiralty, all of whom have given me great assistance with the German Foreign Ministry, Military and Naval Archives in Great Britain and the United States.

In the later phases of the work the library staffs both at Trinity College, Dublin, and the Institut für Zeitgeschichte have offered me every facility. My thanks are also due to the late Professor Sir Charles Webster, Professor Robert Waite of Williams College, U.S.A., Professor Geoffrey Barraclough of the Royal Institute of International Affairs, and Mr. John Ehrman for reading an earlier draft and encouraging me to persevere. Finally, I am greatly indebted to Professor W. Medlicott of the London School of Economics and to Professor B. D. Horn and Mr. V. Kiernan of the University of Edinburgh for reading the completed draft, and Mrs. A. Orr for helping me with the index.

I also wish to acknowledge the permission of the Controller H.M. Stationery Office to quote from publications issued by the British Government.

Belfast 1963   E.M.R.

Introduction

Before embarking on any one dramatic venture Hitler had to balance the risks and make sure which of the Great Powers were likely, and which not likely, to intervene against Germany. Was his information factually correct, or did he owe his early triumphs to unforeseen circumstances? The general aim of this study is to answer questions such as these, and to establish the relationship between Hitler's foreign policy and military planning. It will be seen how Hitler used a revolutionary movement for the purpose of rearmament and territorial expansion; how railway time-tables on occasions forced him to postpone or to advance the date of some intended military action.

The documentary foundation for an inquiry of this kind seems impressive.[1] *Mein Kampf*, Hitler's public speeches, affidavits used during the Nuremberg trials and a host of memoirs by German statesmen had already been exploited by historians before publication of the bulk of the official documents.[2] It is even claimed that 'every detail of Hitler's political activity' is 'historically established'.[3] There is no foundation for this extravagant claim. The recently published documents, and those still in the official archives or in private collections, are not merely adding to our store of knowledge, but forcing us to change our entire perspective. Nevertheless, despite the accumulation of evidence, few documents, at least for the earlier part of the period covered by this study, bring us face to face with the reality of the situation. An explanation for this is to be found mainly in Hitler's attitude to evidence about himself.

Hitler was never destined to write his memoirs, nor, after the manner of a Frederick the Great or a Bismarck, to address posterity

---

[1] For a most interesting discussion on the historiography of the Second World War, see an article by Professor Desmond Williams in *Historical Studies;* 1, Papers read to the second Irish conference of Historians (Bowes and Bowes, 1958) editor, Professor Desmond Williams.

[2] The first three volumes of DGFP(C) 1933–37, see bibliography, appeared between 1957 and 1959. This series is not yet complete.

[3] See Trevor-Roper's introduction to *Hitler's Table Talk*. Weidenfeld & Nicolson, 1953. A. J. P. Taylor does not make such sweeping claims, *Origins of the Second World War.*

with the words *Ecce Homo*. It is thus difficult for us to play the role of the detective; to point out the errors and distortions of his life's work and, in so doing, to uncover the authentic portrait of the man himself. Contemporary records, at least for the period between 1933 and 1938, are also inadequate. In these years Hitler kept no diary, wrote few private letters or memoranda, and was not given to the Kaiser's practice of making marginal comments on official correspondence. Unlike his brother dictator, Mussolini, he was even denied the services of an adoring biographer. It might be contended, as Hitler himself claimed, that everything he did he said he was going to do in *Mein Kampf*, and that there is thus less need to explain in detail each episode in the unfolding of the story.[1] Admittedly, Hitler's contemporaries—especially outside Germany—were slow in reading the book. Here was an extremely useful guide to the operations of its author's mind—his phobias and disillusionments, his dreams into the future: that Germany was able again to become a Great Power and make a new bid for world power, lends a certain prophetic plausibility to Hitler's savage outbursts. But the historian must be careful, for the book, which is discussed more fully below,[2] contains no political programme to be systematically worked out in advance; it must not be used as an infallible framework of reference with which to test and explain Hitler's later acts. As Konrad Heiden remarks: 'Far too much has been read into the so-called foreign policy chapters. . . . No statesman is in a position to indicate ten years in advance what he is going to do later. . . .'[3] The essential parts of the book do not deal with foreign policy or military geography but with race, political education, the building of a political force at home. The decisive point is that Hitler's ideas were capable of realization, which is due not merely to a hidden diabolic genius on his part to which he gave expression in *Mein Kampf*, but to some fundamental unsoundness in the Europe of his day.

(Hinsley)

Besides *Mein Kampf*, Rauschning's conversations shed light, as Bullock suggests, on Hitler's general attitude. But even this work,

---

[1] Part I of *Mein Kampf* was published in 1925; Part II, with chapters XIII and XIV on foreign policy, two years later. It is described in Bullock, *Hitler, A Study in Tyranny*, Odhams, 1952, pp. 109–10 and pp. 286–91 and in *The World in March 1939* (RIIA), pp. 321–2. Page references below are to the Murphy edition (Hurst & Blackett, 1939).

[2] See p. 2.

[3] *Der Führer*, Victor Gollancz, 1944, p. 226 and Bullock, *Hitler*, ibid., p. 346.

though fresh and lively, is no contemporary record and provides few clues to why Hitler on any given occasion acted when he acted.[1]

But no statesman can dispense with the written word altogether. It is an integral part of the apparatus of government, and if Hitler on many crucial occasions failed to put on record what he really thought, some written order had to be issued on what he wanted done. Although he disliked formal Cabinet meetings with minutes, and preferred to speak with his lieutenants in unrecorded conversations in which discussion was limited to some specific topic demanding a practical decision, there were times when he had to allow his policy to come up for review before a restricted audience. Certain of his listeners, for instance, General Liebmann, Colonel Hossbach, Ulrich von Hassell and, later, General Halder, could not be prevented from making some unofficial record of the proceedings, and a few highly valuable documents have survived. It is known exactly what Hitler told his generals on his future aims immediately before and after assuming power. Minutes of those Cabinet meetings, presided over by Hitler, prove just how much continuity there was in German foreign policy until the end of 1934, after which they were no longer regularly kept. Many of Hitler's conversations with his own diplomats, on the eve of the reoccupation of the Rhineland, are so graphically recorded that posterity can watch the stages by which the decision was made, despite certain gaps, almost in slow motion.

The primary sources enable us to view the scene from a few well placed but separate vantage points, but they are insufficient in number to keep under constant observation the changes Hitler had been adopting; an order might be released, but no document found accounting for radical amendments made to it before it was put into effect.[2] The picture presented is also one-sided. Whereas von Blomberg and von Reichenau, of the Defence Ministry, and von Neurath and von Bülow, of the Foreign Ministry, kept comparatively careful records of their conversations with Hitler and with each other, Göring, Goebbels, Hess, Röhm, von Ribbentrop, Rosenberg, Frank and Habicht, the men to whom Hitler would speak his mind more freely, have not served future historians generously.

[1] *Hitler Speaks*, Thornton Butterworth, London, 1939.
[2] E.g. changes made to Hitler's original proposals on Future German Policy after the reoccupation of the Rhineland in March 1936, see Chapter 8.

Hitler had evolved no central system for co-ordinating policy, and allowed his subordinates a considerable measure of freedom within their own spheres. There was much overlapping in the work of the respective hierarchies, an endless number of feuds, which he personally at some stage or other had had to settle. Figuratively speaking, it is thus necessary to be constantly on the move from one office to another. At certain vital junctures, for instance at the end of 1937, a party organization interfered in important negotiations and, having won Hitler's approval, deflected them from their previous course. Sometimes, in order to find the source of instructions sent to a certain German Embassy, it is necessary to abandon the search among the Foreign Ministry files and to turn up a military directive or intelligence report. Diplomats, too, were themselves often deliberately kept in the dark, and the suggestions they made, frequently turned down. Indeed they were not, as was the practice in some foreign services, allowed to correspond directly with one another; all their despatches had to go straight to Berlin, where anything relevant was extracted and circulated to whomever it strictly concerned.

The Military Archives are even more confusing. Soldiers were discouraged from taking an active interest in what could be broadly described as 'current affairs'. After Hitler had consolidated himself in power they were to be given information or pass it on to their subordinates only when it was strictly necessary for the fulfilment of their duties.[1] With work rigorously departmentalized, inter-service rivalry was rife. The existence of an Armed Forces High Command, over and above those of the three individual Services, only added to duplication of work, confusion and jealousy and was not, as Captain Cyril Falls has correctly observed, to prove anything like so effective as the British practice of inter-Service committees.[2]

The character of the documents for the beginning and for the end of the period under review corresponds with changes Hitler made in the administration.

Before the death of Hindenberg in August 1934 Hitler is portrayed as the head of the *Executive* with his ministers as his uneasy

---

[1] See the decisions taken at the end of Hitler's staff conference of 23 May 1939. See p. 172.

[2] See the Preface by Captain C. Falls to *The German General Staff* by Görlitz.

colleagues, whom he sought to overrule. After the reshuffle of appointments early in 1938 Hitler was to all intents and purposes the *Executive* of the Nazi State, with his former ministers either deposed or reduced to ciphers. General Beck could thus not stop Hitler, he could only write memoranda; a diplomat like Ulrich von Hassell could not counsel; as his diary shows, he could only conspire. In proportion as the resistance in Germany was driven underground the documents pertaining to it belong more to literature than history, revealing what Hitler meant rather than what he did.[1] But there are gains as well as losses. No sooner had Hitler effectively silenced his generals and diplomats than he himself became less embarrassed about what posterity would think of him. His adjutant, Schmundt, and his chief of staff, Halder, appointed in 1938, put more on record than their more out-spoken predecessors, Hossbach and Beck. In July 1941 at the apogee of his power Hitler allowed his table talk to be recorded; soon afterwards verbatim minutes of his staff conferences were made.[2]

New documents are slowly making their way into learned periodicals and general publications; for the present the sheer bulk of the evidence is more than enough to keep historians busy. It is hoped that more of the non-German archives will soon become a hunting ground for the research worker. Until such a time our historical perspective for the years before the Second World War will remain one-sided and *Germanocentric*.

[1] Their value as commentary has yet to be exploited, and it is the opinion of the author that Dietrich Bonhöffer's analysis of the modern tyrant is by far the most profound statement on Hitler yet attempted. See *Ethics*, pp. 11–14, SCM Press 1955.

[2] Trevor-Roper, op. cit. See also *Hitler Directs his War*, selected and annotated by F. Gilbert, Oxford University Press, New York, 1950.

CHAPTER 1

Hitler's Originality

Historians for some years will continue to debate whether Hitler's advent to power meant a greater degree of continuity or of change in German policy, and will ask whether he succeeded in doing things beyond the dreams of Weimar statesmen, or whether he threw to the winds all moral restraints and launched out on something entirely new. Hitler most certainly introduced a radically new temper into German political life; he gave inspiration to a succession of events which were moving so fast, that not only outsiders but even his closest collaborators, did not know quite what to expect next.[1] To argue either for or against the thesis that Hitler carried Stresemann's policy to its logical conclusion may therefore well be a wasted effort. Rather it should be asked whether Hitler had a valid alternative, and if so, whether it was supported by his own official advisors in the Foreign and Defence Ministries.

The classical conception of foreign policy whereby the world situation was reviewed at regular intervals and seen as an ordered system, in which the movements of even the smallest part had some significance for German policy, was utterly alien to Hitler. Hitler seldom looked more than one move ahead; and the view that he had tried to put into operation a programme, carefully formulated in advance, is quite untenable—indeed, had he done so he would have rendered the task of future historians immeasurably easier. Hitler, instead, regarded diplomacy as the continuation of the *struggle for power* inside Germany, and the years of experience, gained from street brawls, polemical warfare and mob oratory, had made up for his lack of a professional training: indeed it had fitted him better for penetrating into the mind of his own people and for winning mass support. That he could, with equal skill, so often apprehend and successfully exploit the weaknesses of foreigners, despite his notoriously absurd ideas about them and

---

[1] This is conspicuously evident from predictions made by von Neurath, his Foreign Minister, at a Cabinet Meeting of 7 April 1933, see p. 11.

1

despite his tactical blunders, is frankly astonishing. This can only be given some partial explanation on the assumption that the tensions and antagonisms prevailing in the Europe of his day in some way reflected those fatal divisions, social and political, inside Germany itself.

In the early years of his apprenticeship, when the interests of foreign policy were still subordinate to those of winning absolute power and of restoring military sovereignty inside Germany, Hitler's declamations at cabinet meetings on his future aims bear a distinct resemblance to those he so clumsily made in *Mein Kampf*. In the course of time, however, the circumstances in which Hitler tried to realize his ideas as well as the ideas themselves, changed, and hence *Mein Kampf* gradually loses its value as the criterion for testing Hitler's political principles.

Its main theme need only be summarized here. Since it was written in prison Hitler could afford to be more frank than in his public speeches. Here he gave full vent to the revenge theme, and proved that he too had mastered long words and scientific jargon. In it Hitler addressed himself to the Germany of his day: he looked to the past rather than to the future, and demonstrated how German history ought to have happened. He threw into high relief the things which alienated him from the older Germany, and in so doing brought to consciousness the frustrated hopes and inarticulate longings of his own generation. He realized that more was to be gained by exploitation of the feeling of shame than of national pride; of anti-war psychosis than the glory of arms. In this respect he showed greater insight than those who continued to follow in the steps of Generals von der Goltz and von Bernhardi. In certain passages Hitler allowed his antagonism to the old school of German nationalists to assume command. He was an Austrian; they were Prussian. Unlike them he resolutely refused to admit that the territorial limits, which Bismarck had fixed, should ever be regarded as permanent. It was not enough to redress the injustices of defeat and return to the *status quo ante bellum*. Hitler completely repudiated the view that Germany should regain her pre-1914 frontiers, for this would bring about no substantial reduction in strength of her former antagonists. A nation's strength should be measured only in relation to that of the existing Powers, not in terms of what it had itself been in the past. Hitler also, with special reference to the South Tyrol, inveighed against the so-called patriots, who merely showed a sentimental solicitude for those Germans whose homes were now outside the Fatherland. If Germany laid claim to all the straggling pieces that were lost, and continually protested and nagged on their behalf, she would infuse new life into the old coalition of her antagonists. The nucleus of the Reich must first be made strong, 'for in strength alone resides the right of possession'. The new Germany should not only embrace the whole racial community, but acquire food-producing areas and strategic frontiers. Above all Hitler regarded it as a sacred duty never to allow two first-class military Powers to establish themselves on Germany's borders. It will be seen that with these ideas no actual or ultimate *status quo* could be acknowledged: each neighbour had to be overthrown in turn before she became too strong. Indeed, Papen's comment that it was on the limitless character of her aims that Germany ran aground is a fitting epitaph to Hitler's Reich.[1]

The general direction of German expansion was in Hitler's mind historically determined: it lay, not in internal colonization or in overseas trade, but in the food-producing areas in the Baltic States and the Ukraine. But the military danger came from the West. France, whether under a Bourbon, Jacobin, Napoleonic, Bourgeois-Democrat, Clerical-Republican or Red Bolshevist regime, would always strive to extend her frontier to the Rhine and would remain Germany's implacable foe. While Britain was only opposed to Germany as a *World Power*, France was opposed to her as a *Power*. Germany could not break French encirclement by diplomacy alone: she had first to prove herself *bündnisfähig*, an ally whose support meant something. The mere possession of an army or an armaments industry would not in itself serve this purpose. The whole nation had first to dedicate itself to its true destiny and to speak with one voice. Other powers would then try to realize their aspirations in accord with her. Alliances must have a specific, not a general aim, and Hitler declared that defensive treaties, which in the inter-war years were still the fashion, were without meaning or sense. They clogged freedom of action, and would merely commit Germany to support national interests which were not her own; and by provoking other powers into forming rival groups they would inevitably defeat their own ends. If, for example, Germany, as was widely suggested at the time, were to align herself

[1] ND: 3300-PS NCA.Supp. A.

3

with Soviet Russia, a power universally feared, France would have little difficulty in enlisting allies against her. If, on the other hand, she made common cause with such powers as Britain and Italy, which were still at least nominally associated with France, this danger would not arise.

In *Mein Kampf* Hitler took a long-distance view of German foreign policy, and a later work published in 1961 and written almost certainly in 1928, amounts to little more than a reiteration of the old themes, with a lengthier discussion on co-operation with Italy and the problem of South Tyrol.[1] Of more practical interest is a letter by Hitler of 2 December 1932 to Colonel Walter von Reichenau, chief of staff of Military District (Wehrkreis) I, East Prussia. Reichenau had first met Hitler in April 1932, through an intermediary Pastor Ludwig Müller, Chief Chaplain to Military District I, the notorious ecclesiastic who later became leader of the German Christian Movement and Reich Bishop. Reichenau had evidently formed a favourable impression. But in the absence of his chief, General von Blomberg (then acting as head of the German military delegation at the Disarmament Conference at Geneva) he was left with the tricky task of defending East Prussia against a possible Polish attack. He had evidently cautioned Hitler in an earlier letter, so far not found, to exercise some discipline in this exposed province over his unruly followers.

Hitler replied on 2 December.[2] He began with a criticism of the Reichswehr's Eastern policy of friendship with Russia. His objections to it are not markedly different from those in *Mein Kampf*, except that whereas in *Mein Kampf* he complained that Russia would be of little value as an ally because she had no motor industry, she had now, after the introduction of the First Five Year Plan in 1928, her own manufactures. This might account for an ambiguous statement Hitler made about economic co-operation with Russia ruining Germany's export trade. Otherwise the turgid ungrammatical style and the stock phrases are the same. Hitler also urged, as he had done in *Mein Kampf*, closer ties with Britain and Italy.

[1] *Hitler's Zweites Buch*, published by the Institut für Zeitgeschichte in Munich and edited by A. L. Weinberg, 1961.

[2] Reichenau's letter to Schleicher of 1 April 1932 can be found in *Nachlass, Schleicher*, Bd 19 fol. 49 (*Bundesarchive Koblenz*). Hitler's letter of 2 December to Reichenau is published, together with a commentary by Dr. Thilo Vogelsang, in the *Vierteljahrshefte für Zeitgeschichte*, October 1959.

Hitler's main preoccupation in his letter to Reichenau was Germany's relations with France. He argued that since Russia's strength was growing France considered that the value of Poland as an ally was deteriorating. She would accordingly either attempt to divert Russian strength to the Far East, and so relieve pressure on Poland, or allow her alliance with Poland to lapse and encourage Russia to take her place. He was referring to an improvement in Franco-Russian relations; a non-aggression pact had been concluded on 29 November 1932. France, however, despite her agreement with Russia, had not lost her alliance with Poland, and Hitler regarded the Russo-Polish Non-Aggression Pact, signed on 25 July 1932, as a noteworthy French success.[1] It was proof that France could by the power of the purse exert leverage on both Poland and Russia. Germany was thus once more confronted with the dreaded spectre of encirclement. Nothing, he believed, was more desirable for France, than for a 'third party' to take the first step in a move against Germany. A French-inspired attack by Poland would for instance, be the immediate result of an attempted restoration of the Hohenzollerns. Hitler also strongly condemned Germany's insistence on theoretical *equality of status in armaments* which was soon to be granted by the heavily armed powers at the Disarmament Conference in Geneva.[2] It would mean that France, having failed to veto Germany's claim, would seek a pretext for a preventive war at that highly critical juncture, after *equality of status* was accorded to Germany, but before actual progress in rearmament had been made.[3] East Prussia would be lost immediately, and Germany's prospects of general resistance he thought, quite hopeless. Her weakness was due less to the slow progress in technical rearmament than to the total disinclination of the German people, 'thanks to their spiritual, moral and political collapse,' to bear arms. Having pointed out how at the recent election over half the aggregate vote was cast

---

[1] A conciliation convention had also been concluded between Russia and Poland on 23 November 1932; see Beloff, *The Foreign Policy of the Soviet Union*, Vol. I, pp. 20–3.

[2] See p. 21.

[3] Hitler again on 3 February 1933, see below, expressly warned his military staffs that the most dangerous moment would arise when the armed forces were in the process of expansion. 'It will then', he declared, 'be seen if France has statesmen; if it's yes, she will not allow us time but will fall on us (presumably with her eastern satellites).'

for those parties which were inclined towards pacifism, Hitler put forward his own ideas on how to create a new military consciousness. He ridiculed as 'just childish' the view, held by certain generals, that false political doctrine could be rooted out by military training. Marxism, which in 1914 had just been an idea, had now in fact 'conquered a gigantic part of the world' and Germans, particularly from the interior, were even less psychologically prepared for war. In his view para-military formations were useless. 'The very moment' they were despatched to the front as 'nothing more nor less than untrained cannon fodder, the red mob would break loose at home'. In comparison the year 1918 would be 'child's play'. Failing complete national regeneration 'all talk of "equality of status and rearmament" is superficial idle chatter'. Hitler attacked the government of Schleicher and warned Reichenau that the army's job was technical rearmament, not propaganda; *'for neither the police nor army has destroyed, and still less created, a world view'*.

Hitler concluded with a five-point programme, the aim of which was: (a) the complete eradication of Marxism in all its forms; (b) the inward regeneration of Germany; (c) increased technical rearmament; (d) exploitation of all the energies of the population for defence; (e) legal recognition from the rest of the world of the new situation after it had already come into existence.[1] Significantly Hitler did not mention the subject of *Lebensraum*. Its practical realization lay in the distant future after Germany had built up a new army and had established a springboard for attack.

Hitler had not however abandoned the ideas of *Mein Kampf*. In an address to prominent members of the High Command on 3 February 1933, a few days after his appointment as Chancellor, he asked: 'How is political power to be used after it has been won?' He stated earlier in his talk that since Germany's living space was too small, the only radical solution of her economic problems in

[1] How far Hitler undermined the authority of Schleicher by contacts with Blomberg and his staff cannot be determined. While there was certainly full agreement between them on the issue of actual equality of status in armaments, no contract seems to have been drawn up. Hitler's letter contained threats rather than promises, and he left no doubt that unless he were given power in full measure Germany's vital interests would be undermined by his unruly followers. His letter suggests that he was still regarded by the generals as the 'enfant terrible' who had to be brought under control. Hence the impression which Bullock conveys, op. cit., p. 225, that Blomberg had been courted by the Nazis in advance, may be mistaken.

the future lay in rural colonization and not in increased exports. He expressed his preference, therefore, for the 'conquest of new *Lebensraum* in the East and its ruthless Germanization'.[1]

Mein Kampf, Hitler's second book, and his exchanges with his generals, make it possible in a summary fashion to relate his original intentions to the actual unfolding of his policy. Where, we must ask, did his originality lie? Hitherto, according to Namier, the law of odd and even numbers, was taken as axiomatic: any given power would make common cause with its opponents' opponent.[2] But Hitler with a singleness of purpose aimed his offers, not at France's potential enemies, which his immediate predecessors had done, but at her allies. He succeeded because he alone knew where the inherent weakness of the French security system lay. Whereas it was a fixed principle of French policy to resist every increase of German strength, others only feared it in certain directions and in limited quantities. Poland was averse to German expansion in the North-East, but might be kept quiet if Germany confined her claims to Czechoslovakia and Austria. For a short time Italy was prepared to challenge Germany, but only when a specified area was threatened. Britain, too, feared Germany in the air, but within certain limits might be prepared to accept expansion of German strength on land and sea. France had a host of allies, but none was entirely dependable: by implication they had each made some provision which would enable them to withhold support. Wherever France restrained them he could give them a free hand. France could thus be forced to transfer her favours continually until the system which she had been at such pains to establish was rent asunder.

Hitler's success in disarming the suspicion of those who were pledged, or who were about to pledge themselves, to support France can largely be attributed to his skill in using arguments

[1] Notes on the meeting were taken by Lieutenant-General C. Liebmann, later Commandant of the War Academy. His papers are at present held by the Institut für Zeitgeschichte at Munich. Some of them have been published in the *Vierteljahrshefte für Zeitgeschichte* (October 1954), together with a commentary by Dr. Thilo Vogelsang on *Neue Dokumente zur Geschichte der Reichswehr, 1930–1933*. See also Wheeler-Bennett. *The Nemesis of Power*, pp. 289–91, where Admiral Raeder's account of the meeting is discussed, in his *Mein Leben*, Vol. I, p. 280.

[2] It is well summed up in Nietzche's dictum: 'In politics it is not your neighbour but your neighbour's neighbour who is your fellow creature.' See also Namier, *Vanquished Supremacies*, Hamish Hamilton, 1958, p. 170.

best calculated to appeal to their suspicions and fears. Whereas Mussolini's bellicose outpourings were intended to remove any doubts that the Italians had no stomach for war, Hitler knew how to whip up a warlike spirit at home without giving his more gullible listeners abroad the impression that war was his aim.[1] In 'pep' talks he used the indicative rather than the imperative. 'Germans! you are not second rate ... you are a strong nation if you yourselves wish to be strong.' With more pity than reproach he exhorted them not to dream 'of justice in the stars', but to throw themselves together into 'the great melting-pot of the nation'. While foreigners in general were reminded that there would be no 'hurrah patriotism' and that he only came to free his country from the chaos of Communism, the Anglo-Saxon world in particular was asked to conform with Wilsonian political morality; it was reminded that Germany only demanded equality of status in the name of 'right and reason'.[2] If Germany's grievances were redressed—and Hitler dwelt on them more tediously than a Celtic bard in a dirge—Germany would destroy the last machine gun. The approach he made to Germany's continental neighbours—where the principle of self-determination was always accepted with at least one qualification—was different. They were told that the attitude of the past century, which tried to persuade people that they 'could make Germans out of Poles and Frenchmen, is completely foreign to us. . . .' Hitler was the liar speaking the truth. He was right in telling the Poles that he was not a Hohenzollern, the Czechs and Serbs that he was not a Habsburg; he had repudiated *legitimacy*, and Europe had only an inkling of what the future had in store.

[1] See E. H. Carr, *The Twenty Years Crisis* (Macmillan, 1940), pp. 67–8.
[2] Of these early speeches by Hitler on foreign policy, all of which are included in Baynes, *Hitler's Speeches*, Vol. II, the most significant is that of 17 May 1933, given on pp. 104–58.

CHAPTER 2

Hitler's Policy in the East and in Austria

After Hitler had seized power there could be little doubt about his ultimate warlike intentions. At a Cabinet meeting held at the Reich Chancellery on 8 February he again stressed that for the next four to five years the main principle must be: 'everything for the armed forces'. Germany's position in the world was decisively conditioned by the Armed Forces: the German economy was also dependent on that factor.[1] Hitler however had not yet won absolute power; he headed a coalition and was facing an election campaign. The struggle for power inside Germany was still the governing consideration: rearmament, for technical reasons alone, had to wait until the nation was aroused to a new sense of its 'historic mission'. Hitler also told his Ministers a few days before that a 'united front, extending from the trade unions to the Communist Party of Germany, was forming against the present Government and that the Reich President had declared himself willing to dissolve the Reichstag. The slogan 'Attack Against Marxism' was to be adopted by the government.[2] On 28 February, the day after the Reichstag fire, the campaign against the Marxists was ruthlessly intensified; Communist and Socialist deputies were subsequently either jailed or expelled, and the Jews subjected to systematic slander and a savage boycott. Hitler was to win the majority he desired at the election of 5 March. It was followed by the Enabling Act of the 21st. Germany was soon to be a single party state and the regime consolidated.[3]

Internal events had a disproportionately greater effect on Germany's relations with other Powers than a new departure intended in foreign policy itself. Poland, Czechoslovakia, the Soviet Union, Great Britain, Austria, Italy and above all France had all some

[1] DGFP (C), Vol. I, pp. 35–7.
[2] Ibid., p. 15.
[3] For a concise account of these events see M. Broszat, *Der Nationalsozialismus, Weltanschauung, Programme u. Wirklichkeit*, Stuttgart, 1960, and Bullock, op. cit., pp. 242–4. For the text of the Cabinet Meetings of 15 and 20 March see ND: PS-2962–3.

reason to fear the 'wild, nameless, enthusiastic thing' in their midst, and it is somewhat surprising that Hitler, in his 'revolution of nihilism', succeeded, where the genuine French and Russian revolutionaries had failed, in completely warding off foreign intervention. But the danger was real, and for the first eight months in office, while still an apprentice in foreign policy, he was constantly reacting to moves made by other Powers to anticipate him. Owing to Germany's central geographic position it is perhaps convenient to start with the East and then to switch to the South and West.

East

It was only to be expected that Germany's two Eastern neighbours and France's allies, Poland and Czechoslovakia, would be among the first to take alarm. A Polish attack had seemed imminent at the end of the previous year. General Blomberg, now Defence Minister, and General Adam, chief of the disguised General Staff (*Truppenamt*), in memoranda prepared in March 1933 were especially alive to the danger in the East. 'We cannot at the moment', wrote Adam, 'prosecute a war. We must do everything to avoid it, even at the cost of a diplomatic defeat.'[1] Early

Poland

in January 1933 the question of revision of the Eastern frontier had, perhaps prematurely, been ventilated in discussions between members of the German Foreign Ministry and French and Belgian diplomats. The *Stahlhelm*,[2] too, a para-military organization with strong nationalist affiliations, was especially outspoken on the question of revision. The Poles took alarm. On 6 March Marshal Pilsudski reinforced the Polish garrison on the Westerplatte Peninsula near Danzig.[3] Whether by this action he seriously intended to provoke a preventive war against Germany, and whether Pilsudski was incited by the French to do so, is still a matter of some considerable controversy,[4] but it does not seem to be borne out by the recent publication of German documents.

[1] The two Generals pointed out that German supplies of ammunition for a war with Poland were only sufficient for fourteen days' fighting and that successful defence against Poland, even on the Oder was, owing to the likelihood of Czech intervention, problematic. See Meinck, *Hitler und die Deutsche Aufrüstung, 1933–1937*, p. 19. Meinck quotes documents prepared for the Krupp trials (Nos. 104–5).

[2] DGFP (C) Vol. I, pp. 2–5 and pp. 111–2.

[3] According to the Polish Danzig Agreement of 1921 Poland was allowed to keep 88 men on the Westerplatte. On 6 March this force was raised to 200 men.

[4] See H. Roos, *Die Präventivkriegspläne Pilsudskis von 1933, Vierteljahreshefte für Zeitgeschichte* (October 1955), and Celovsky, *Das Münchener Abkommen*, p. 85.

At a Cabinet meeting of 25 April, Neurath admittedly referred to alarmist telegrams emanating from the German Legations in Warsaw and in Prague.[1] 'The situation', he said, 'is so tense that provocations from our side must in all circumstances be avoided.' Reports of imminent incursions by Polish armed bands had also come to the notice of the Reich-Chancellor. 'In itself such a possibility', Neurath continued, 'can be regarded without concern, since the fact of an incursion by a Polish band would be advantageous from the point of view of foreign policy.' It would provide Germany with a good cause for rearmament and keep public interest alive in a revision of her frontier with Poland.

German policy under Hitler was in fact to develop on lines very different from those predicted by Neurath at a Cabinet meeting of 7 April.[2] On 2 May Hitler told the Polish Ambassador that he was a nationalist, and a nationalist to such a degree that he would refuse to 'annex foreign nationalities by conquest and try to rob them of their language and custom'. Early in May Bülow was also successful in preventing Goebbels from delivering an inflammatory election speech on Danzig.[3] The way was thus opened for the famous German-Polish rapprochement of January 1934.

Immediate fear of Poland and the prospect of her ultimate partition were the two things capable of keeping Russia and Germany together. At first it seemed that Hitler did not intend any radical break with the Treaty of Rapallo of 1922.[4] Even before 30 January 1933, however, relations were strained.[5] On 2 March, after the Reichstag fire, Hitler made a virulent attack on the Soviet Union. A further speech of 23 March, in which he stated that the suppression of Communism in Germany need not jeopardize friendly relations with the Soviet Union, failed to lead to any practical

Russia

[1] DGFP (C) Vol. I, p. 343 and fn.

[2] Ibid., p. 259.

[3] DGFP (C) Vol. I, pp. 365–7 and pp. 372–4. For the Polish official account of negotiations with Germany that summer see *Documents Concerning Polish–German and Polish–Soviet Relations, 1933–1939,* published by the Polish Government, London, n.d.

[4] For a full account of German-Soviet Relations before 1933, see E. H. Carr, *The Bolshevik Revolution,* Vol. III, p. 376, and *German Soviet Relations before the War,* p. 64. See also G. Freund, *The Unholy Alliance,* Chatto & Windus, 1951, Chap. II.

[5] In the summer of 1932 it was feared in Moscow that Papen, then Chancellor, had sounded the French on the possibility of an alliance against Russia, DGFP (C) Vol. I, p. 91 fn. See also A. Hilger, *The Incompatible Allies,* pp. 256–7.

results.[1] Early in April *Derop*, a Soviet organization for marketing petroleum, together with the premises of other Soviet commercial interests, were raided. Dirksen, the German Ambassador in Russia, and other diplomats pressed hard for a normalization of diplomatic relations. Their efforts, strongly backed by Mussolini, were not in vain. On 5 May the extension of the German-Soviet Non-Aggression Pact of 1926 was, after a long delay, ratified.[2] Military circles too, both Russian and German, were not altogether unsuccessful in preserving something of that comradely spirit of co-operation associated with the post-Rapallo epoch. In May General von Bockelberg, representing the German Defence Ministry, visited the Soviet Union for an exchange of technical information. The visit itself was described as a success, and it was still believed both by the German and Russian sides that the principle of the Treaty of Rapallo of 1920 still held good.[3]

That summer mutual suspicion grew. In August 1933 the Russians loudly protested that Papen had disclosed to the French Ambassador in Rome facts, even to the last detail, on German-Soviet military co-operation. Later in August German military stations in Russia were closed, and Soviet officers forbidden to attend courses in Germany.[4] The German High Command were, for almost identical reasons equally suspicious of Soviet treachery and the two countries were soon to be engaged in a long distance propaganda bombardment. Following the arrest on 22 September of two Russian correspondents attending the Leipzig trial of Communists accused of starting the Reichstag fire, the Soviet Embassy in Berlin lodged an energetic protest.[5] At a Cabinet meeting of the 26th, when the Russian démarche was discussed, Bülow, the State Secretary, pointed out how the Russian Government, having hitherto shown great patience, had now withdrawn all their Press representatives from Germany. He said emphatically that they were awaiting a statement from the German Foreign Ministry which might lead to an improvement of relations. Hitler's response was something of a rebuff. 'The Russian Government', he declared, 'will never forgive Germany for our having smashed

---

[1] The full text of these speeches can be found in Baynes, op. cit., Vol. I, pp. 254–61 and Vol. II, pp. 1019 et seq.

[2] DGFP(C) Vol. I, p. 356 and fn. and especially pp. 372–4.

[3] Ibid., pp. 464–70 also p. 273 fn. See also Hilger, op. cit., p. 250.

[4] DGFP (C) Vol. I, pp. 741–3, fn. and pp. 767–8.

[5] Ibid., pp. 845–7 and fn. on p. 845.

Communism in Germany. . . .' It is evident from the meeting that while he intended no dramatic rupture with Russia he was glad to see the vast military and economic machinery associated with, but not necessarily dependent on, Rapallo fall into abeyance.[1] Rapallo had died a natural death, and while Hitler could no longer depend on Russia, the need for her support later diminished.

Early in 1933 there were issues, more burning than Danzig and the Polish Corridor, which could have provided France, above all if she were supported by other Powers, with a legitimate pretext for a preventive war. According to Articles 80 and 88 of the Treaties of Versailles and St. Germain Germany was pledged to recognize Austria's integrity, and Austria was required to give the most curious undertaking not to 'alienate' her own independence. Since nationalist disturbances in Austria had repercussions among the German minority living in the South Tyrol, Italy too was opposed to an *Anschluss*. Mussolini however did not wish to see French and Czech influence increase in Austria. He felt flattered by the triumph in Germany of a regime, which had borrowed so much from Fascist Italy, and, fondly believing that he could prevail on his less experienced brother dictator to heed his advice, his aim was to caution rather than to punish. He tried after 30 January, first to win Germany over to the idea that she should herself support the Dollfuss Government and enter into some scheme of economic co-operation with Italy in the south east; secondly, to persuade the Austrian Nationalists and clericals to form a united front against the Socialists. Dollfuss's proclamation of Austria as an 'authoritarian corporative state' on 14 March was an indication of Mussolini's partial success.[2]

It soon emerged that Hitler's Austrian policy was not to conform with Mussolini's wishes. On 18 March Hans Frank, the Bavarian Minister of Justice, warned Dollfuss over the Munich wireless station against violations of the liberties of the Austrian Nazis who were now an organized body. A protest registered by Dollfuss had the full backing of Italy. Dollfuss retaliated by

[1] DGFP (C), Vol. I, pp. 848–55. See also Dirksen, *Moscow, Tokyo, London*, pp. 117–29.
[2] DGFP (C) Vol. I, pp. 52–5. For a full discussion of internal developments in Austria, see Eichstädt, *Von Dollfuss zu Hitler, Geschichte des Anschlusses Österreichs, 1933–1938*, pp. 7–21. For more general accounts, see Shepherd, *Austrian Odyssey*, Part I, chap. II, and E. Wiskemann, *The Rome–Berlin Axis*, chap. II. Also DGFP(C) Vol. I.

demanding entry visas for German visitors to Austria.[1] Hitler was filled with a desire for vengeance and saw in economic coercion his best choice of means. On 24 May he discussed his plans with his Ministers at some considerable length. Reiterating the *Mein Kampf* theme he claimed that it was no use committing the 'blunder made before the World War in making a wrong evaluation of Austria. . . . An accommodating attitude or willingness to negotiate on our part would be exploited by the present Austrian regime merely to take the wind out of the sails of the national-minded opposition in Austria.' As a reprisal, visas for travel to Austria would be granted from the German side only on payment of 1,000 RM, which would, he thought, deprive Austria of her large tourist income and lead to the collapse of the Dollfuss Government and to new elections. This would make possible Austria's final *Gleichschaltung* and 'obviate the need for actual *Anschluss*'. Although Italy could be bought off by concessions in other areas the likelihood of an *Anschluss* in the near future was not acute as the other Powers would also have to give their consent. It is evident from the discussion which followed that while Neurath and Hugenburg were not in full sympathy with Hitler's brutal decision, they agreed to put it into operation.[2]

On 24 May Hitler had indulged in much wishful thinking. Events later in the summer were to prove that the Austrian Government could not be overthrown by economic warfare alone: there was to be no 'parallel Revolution'. On 13 June Habicht, a member of the German Reichstag and a leader of the Austrian Nazis, was, together with Cors the official leader, arrested. As a result Hitler ordered the arrest and later the expulsion of the Austrian Press Attaché. The arrests took place at a time when German terrorism[3] was beginning to have serious repercussions abroad, for Dollfuss was personally attending the World Economic Conference in London. Here he found a ready-made platform from which to voice his country's grievances. Indeed he was loudly applauded in quoting Schiller's line: 'The best man cannot live in peace if an evil neighbour will not let him'. Neurath, who was also present and who was booed by the London crowd, described in letters to Hitler and Hindenburg of 19 June his new impressions of London

---

[1] DGFP (C) Vol. I, pp. 206–7, pp. 397–8, pp. 424–5 and pp. 460–1.
[2] Ibid., pp. 486–90.
[3] Ibid. pp. 547, 556–7, 561 and 567–8.

since he was last there as Ambassador in 1932. He drew Hitler's attention to the way the French were following the Austrian conflict and trying to create an atmosphere favourable for intervention, even of a military kind, and he conveyed to Hindenburg the severe censures, delivered to him by no less a person than King George V himself, against the treatment of the Jews.[1] Soon internal political developments were to make things all the more difficult for Dollfuss.

No sooner had Neurath returned than Hugenburg, chairman of the German National People's Party and Reich Minister of Economics, resigned. His Party immediately went into ignominious voluntary dissolution. The *Zentrum* Party, representing the interests of the Roman Catholic Church, soon shared the same fate. Henceforward only the Vatican itself could secure the rights of the Church for the future. After hurried negotiations between Papen and Pacelli (later Pope Pius XII) a concordat, which Hitler never intended keeping, was concluded on 5 July.[2] Hitler had dealt two well directed blows against the conservatives in Germany, and when Papen, later in 1933, tried to mediate in favour of Dollfuss, he no longer had a well organized body of public opinion in Germany behind him.[3]

National Socialist outrages in Austria reached a new height of intensity in July; at the end of the month Dollfuss appealed to Britain, France and Italy to use their good offices in favour of a settlement.[4] Bülow and Neurath, fully alive to the dangers to which Germany was now exposed, persuaded Hitler early in August to order Habicht to discontinue terrorist acts. They were assured that a *coup de main* was out of the question. Nevertheless the economic struggle against Austria was to be continued in all its intensity and interference on the part of Italy decisively rejected.[5]

[1] ND (IMT) Neurath, 12 and 13.

[2] All the relevant documents can be found in DGFP (C) Vol. I under *Vatican*. Pacelli had no illusions about Hitler's insincerity, for in August he told Kirkpatrick, the British diplomat, that he had no alternative but to sign—a pistol was pointed at his head—DBFP (second series) Vol. V, p. 446.

[3] See Papen's Memoirs, pp. 278–82 and DGFP (C) Vol. I, pp. 707–8. In August 1934 Papen was later, as Minister to Vienna, to inaugurate a new era in German–Austrian relations, see Chap. 5.

[4] See below and DGFP (C) Vol. I, pp. 689–91 and pp. 704–6. See also DBFP (second series) Vol. V, Chap. VI.

[5] DGFP (C) Vol. I, pp. 708–12 and pp. 718–9.

The *Wilhelmstrasse* victory over the Austrian Nazis bore no fruit and Hitler can hardly have been serious in his injunctions to Habicht, who again delivered a broadcast on the 9th, attacking the Dollfuss Government for having invited foreign intervention. On the 12th Cerruti delivered a sharp protest and told Neurath that Mussolini had become 'quite unusually agitated' on receiving the report on Habicht's broadcast. The same day Neurath, when informing Hitler of the Italian démarche, found the Chancellor 'very indignant over the manner of Mussolini's intervention'. Hitler declared that he 'would not stand for that sort of tutelage' and reminded Neurath that Habicht's speech did not contravene his own orders.[1] The dispersal of the Austrian Legion, made up of some 2,000 Austrian Nazi refugees from their camp in Lechfeld near the Austrian frontier, eased the danger in September of an imminent *coup de main*, and it seemed that Dollfuss had once more consolidated his position. Nevertheless, months of coercion were already giving Mussolini reason to revise his attitude to Germany. He had had his first quarrel with Hitler. On 6 October Ulrich von Hassell, the German Ambassador in Rome, reported that because of the Austrian crisis 'the idea was growing stronger and louder in Italy' that National Socialism was not 'the legitimate sister or daughter of Fascism but is something different and Germanic'.[2]

[1] Ibid., pp. 737–41 and pp. 763–6, pp. 770–2 and p. 798.
[2] Ibid., p. 895.

CHAPTER 3

Hitler's Break with the League

Apart from the Corridor and Austria, France had two further possible pretexts for intervention affecting Western no less than Eastern and Southern Europe: German violations of the Treaties of Locarno and Versailles. According to the Treaty of Locarno of 1 December 1925 Britain and Italy guaranteed both sides of the frontiers between Germany and France, and Germany and Belgium, together with the observance by Germany of Articles 42 and 43 of the Treaty of Versailles, proscribing the mobilization of troops and the construction of fortifications on the left bank of the Rhine and 50 kilometres on the right bank. In the event of a 'flagrant' breach of the Treaty, Britain and Italy were bound to render France or Belgium immediate aid; a 'qualified' breach would bring the cumbrous machinery of the League into operation. Hitler was determined that France would not catch him out over Locarno, and it will be seen later how until 1936 Germany adhered to her obligations in the Rhineland which she had contracted voluntarily.

In the German Foreign Ministry's view a move against Germany under Part V of the Treaty of Versailles was more probable than under Locarno.[1] It applied to the whole Reich, not just to the West, and would be welcome, not merely to Belgium, but to Poland and Czechoslovakia. Part V prohibited the possession by Germany of heavy artillery, tanks, submarines, ships of over 11,000 tons and all military aircraft. The German army (*Reichswehr*) was not to exceed 100,000 men, including 4,000 officers. Under Article 213 a commission of investigation could operate on German soil if Treaty infringements were suspected. Until the summer of 1934 German rearmament did not seriously exceed these limits, and it could only have had serious consequences if Hitler refused defiantly to recognize those future limits, proposed by the British and Italians, but not necessarily by the French.

[1] A Foreign Ministry memorandum to the Defence Ministry of 23 October 1933, see Note on Sources, p. 195.

On 16 March Ramsay MacDonald submitted a draft convention to the Disarmament Conference,[1] according to which all European armies were to be transformed into militias of short term service. Five years after the proposed convention came into force, French effectives, stationed in Europe, were to be reduced to 200,000 men, and at the end of the same period the number of German effectives raised to this figure. The truce in building capital ships, binding on the signatories of the London Treaty of 1930 until the end of 1936, was to be extended to other states, with the reservation that Italy might lay down one keel not exceeding 26,500 tons as a counter balance to the French ship, the *Dunquerque*. While the plan envisaged the reduction of military aircraft belonging to all states, Germany was not conceded the right to possess them.

Needless to say German military experts—who in any case were never enthusiastic about a militia—were reluctant to accept it, and the German Naval High Command were particularly outspoken. On 24 March Admiral Raeder informed Blomberg that the construction of the *Dunquerque*, which in speed and armament was greatly superior to the existing 10,000 ton German pocket battleships, 'has fundamentally changed our strategic and tactical position'. In reply Blomberg stated that in the course of negotiations at Geneva Germany could not possibly demand the right to construct vessels of 25,000 tons. He feared that if Germany pressed her claims for a more powerful fleet, it would be less easy to gain British support against France for recognition of increased land forces. In a later interview with Raeder, Blomberg declared that the German army of 200,000 men, as envisaged by the MacDonald Plan, was insufficient and that Germany could not dispense with submarines or military aircraft.[2]

Early in May after much discussion on the MacDonald Plan, Hitler and his cabinet had to decide whether to accept it as it then stood. At a Cabinet meeting of the 12th, Neurath, who had been kept informed on the progress of negotiations by the German

---

[1] Already under Papen in September 1932 Germany had withdrawn from the Disarmament Conference. On 11 December that year Great Britain, France, Italy and the United States agreed in principle that Germany should be 'accorded *equality of rights*' in a system which would 'provide security for all nations'. Germany could thus take her place at the conference which re-opened on 2 February 1933.

[2] See Note on Sources, p. 195.

delegate to the Conference, Nadolny,[1] spoke against its acceptance
but was apprehensive because of Germany's isolation.[2] Even Italy,
he claimed, was no longer backing Germany. Hitler was decidedly
in favour of rejecting the plan. 'Unless', he declared, 'we were accorded heavy weapons any departure from the system of the
Reichswehr was unthinkable. . . .' The threat of sanctions, in the
event of Germany's leaving the Conference table, had to be faced
courageously and the fact made known that their application
would be regarded by Germany as tantamount to the tearing up of
the peace treaties. A declaration would be issued indicating that
Germany's further remaining in the League of Nations had been
made 'exceedingly doubtful by the actions of our opponents'. In
the discussion which followed Blomberg and Neurath stressed
that a German representative should be present, but not negotiate,
at Geneva. Hitler replied that he would only make his proposed
declaration after consulting with Schacht, who was attending the
preliminary meeting of the World Economic Conference in the
USA and who was most certainly in favour of accepting the Plan.[3]
Hitler's advisors however were not of one mind: whereas Blomberg insisted on non-acceptance of the British plan, Nadolny was
emphatically of the opinion that Germany had no alternative but
to accept it.[4]

The next day President Roosevelt appealed to the participants
of the Conference to exclude offensive weapons from their armament, and Hitler was requested by Neurath to quote passages from
this speech.[5] In these changed circumstances Hitler duly made a
public declaration on the 17th. But far from carrying out the bombastic threats of the 12th, the world listened to his famous 'peace
speech' (*Friedensrede*). In it he described the British plan as a
'possible solution' provided it did not entail the destruction of
Germany's existing defence forces. Germany, he said, agreed to
the transitional period of five years and was prepared to renounce

---

[1] DGFP (C) Vol. I, pp. 378–80 and pp. 437–40.

[2] Ibid., pp. 409–12.

[3] Schacht in a written report to Hitler of 15 May had described Ramsay
MacDonald's impressions of Germany's position as 'alarming': there were,
he thought, even rumours of her partition. MacDonald therefore awaited a
conciliatory gesture from Hitler: there was also, Schacht claimed, opposition
in the United States to German rearmament. Ibid., pp. 423–4.

[4] Ibid., pp. 435–6 and pp. 444–5 and Nadolny, *Mein Beitrag*.

[5] See *Foreign Relations of the USA, 1933*, Vol. I, pp. 143–5 and DGFP (C)
Vol. I, pp. 451–5.

offensive weapons, provided the heavily armed Powers destroyed theirs within a specified period. Yet at the end Hitler made a carefully veiled warning. If violence were done to Germany by means of a 'simple majority vote' she would, with a 'heavy heart', have to draw the conclusion that her continued membership of the League of Nations was incompatible with her 'national honour'. Two days later Hitler instructed Nadolny to declare Germany's acceptance, despite the sacrifices involved, of the MacDonald Plan as the basis for a Disarmament Convention.[1]

Before negotiations were resumed later in the summer Hitler had expressed himself equally willing to discuss a security plan, adumbrated by Mussolini in October the previous year. Mussolini's primary aim was to divert German ambitions from an *Anschluss* and from the annexation of the South Tyrol to the northeast of Europe. On 14 March 1933 his plans had matured; he proposed that Italy, France, Great Britain and Germany should work for the preservation of peace in the spirit of the Kellogg Pact and consider revision of the peace treaties in accordance with article 19 of the Covenant of the League. He also urged that the *equality of status*, theoretically conceded to Germany should, if the Disarmament Conference were to lead to only partial results, have effective application. Hitler, who was already quarrelling with Dollfuss and who disliked any invocation of the League, told his leading Ministers on 23 May that Germany would only negotiate on Mussolini's plan if the Disarmament Conference broke down. But after much discussion, sometimes of a heated kind, Hitler accepted an amended version[2] of the Pact which was initialled in an emasculated form on 7 June, and signed on 17 July. Since the Pact was soon to prove less acceptable to France and her allies than to Germany it was never ratified and a chance of tying Hitler down was missed.

Hitler, in expressing himself willing to accept both Italian and British mediation, however reluctantly, had accomplished two master strokes in diplomacy, and before considering the tactics he was to employ later at the Disarmament Conference it is necessary to examine the MacDonald Plan in relation to his intended programme for future German rearmament. The technical difficulties of rearmament were very great, almost commensurate with the

[1] DGFP (C) Vol. I, pp. 462–3.
[2] DGFP (C) Vol. I, p. 482, pp. 496–7 and pp. 532–6.

legal difficulties: the entire German economy had to be put on a firm footing. According to General Thomas, two Five Year Plans were adopted in 1928, the first to be completed by 1933 with the aim of supplying 16 divisions for defence against Poland, the second by 1937–1938 for 21 divisions and 300,000 men, a figure which on mobilization could be trebled and which was considered just adequate for defence against France.[1] Although, owing to shortages of raw materials, the first programme was never put into operation; a start was made after 7 April 1933 with the second; initial progress was, however, slower than expected, and a mere 10,000 to 20,000 additional men were recruited. The MacDonald Plan could therefore early in May be reviewed in a more favourable light. It would have allowed Germany 200,000 effectives, two-thirds of the number required in five years, and although Blomberg had already complained[2] that this figure was too low his objections were not over-riding: with a little hard bargaining and treaty evasion Germany might still find the extra 100,000 men. Renunciation of offensive weapons, above all of tanks and planes for tactical purposes, posed a more serious obstacle, but even these weapons could not yet be produced on a scale sufficient to make the plan completely unacceptable. Finally, since no direct supervision of the German military establishment was envisaged, the plan had at least one positive merit.

German acceptance of the MacDonald Plan, was not, however, the main issue. The French were soon to express their dissatisfaction with it and seek: first, more stringent terms for a future convention; secondly, action under article 213 of the Treaty against illegal German rearmament. Their success depended on British support. Of the two issues the second constituted the greater danger to Germany, and the generals of the Defence Ministry did all in their power to forestall it. In a minute of 26 April 1933[3] a subtle distinction was drawn between leakages of evidence on rearmament from hearsay and that which could be proved from documents.

---

[1] The facts below are taken mainly from General Thomas's *Grundlagen* (*Basic Facts*) and from lectures given by staff officers on the expansion of the German Army in the Military Academy after 1936 (see Note on Sources). See also B. Müller–Hillebrand, *Das Heer 1933–1945*, Vol. I, p. 18, and Meinck, op. cit., pp. 86–7.

[2] See p. 18.

[3] Of the Working Committee of the National Defence Council. *Reichverteidigungsrat*.

But good internal security on the custody of documents was not enough. Despite the *Manchester Guardian* disclosures of 1926, many experiments of secret weapons were still carried out on Soviet soil.[1] What if, in the changed political situation of the autumn of 1933, Russia played foul and handed over to France even some of the incriminatory documentary evidence which she unquestionably possessed?

Germany's position was distinctly unnerving. On 2 September it was learnt in the Defence Ministry from what was described as a 'reliable' source that France and Britain were sounding Russia on the possibility of divulging military information. This news had to be treated with great circumspection for French and Polish military personages were visiting Russia at that time, and the French Press was actually publishing details of what Germany was alleged to have been producing. On 18 September Schönheinz, the German Military Representative at the Disarmament Conference in Geneva, listed the allegations, and in case he were asked difficult questions inquired whether the facts contained in them were correct. He was told by the Defence Ministry on 10 October that regrettably many of them were.

The French Government were well informed on the extent of German secret rearmament,[2] and at a joint meeting of Cabinet Ministers in London on 25 September drew their British colleagues' attention to a dossier which they had prepared on the subject.[3] The British, however, when sounded, were not prepared to assume obligations on sanctions, and thus the French were all the more determined on stricter terms than the MacDonald Plan. They proposed dividing a future convention into two periods of four years' duration: in the first, the efficiency of supervision should be tested; in the second, while a measure of rearmament would be permitted to those states with restricted armaments, a start would be made with the disarmament of the more powerful. While Hitler was opposed decidedly to such a radical amendment, he told[4] Neurath

---

[1] See E. H. Carr, *German-Soviet Relations between the Wars*, pp. 93–6.

[2] See A. Castellan, *Le Réarmement clandestin du Reich 1930–1935*, pp. 195–8 and pp. 513–22.

[3] DBFP, Second Series, Vol. V, Chaps. VI, VII and VIII describe Anglo-French negotiations; for the Conference of 25 September, see Vol. V, doc. No. 406.

[4] DGFP (C) Vol. I, pp. 686–7, a conversation of 21 July 1933 between Hitler and Henderson, British Labour M.P. and President of the Disarmament Conference.

on the 30th that he was still ready to negotiate on the MacDonald Plan as it originally stood even if 'not all our wishes were fulfilled by it . . .'. It would be wrong in his opinion, 'to ask for more than we were able for technical, financial and political reasons actually to procure in the next few years'.[1] Early in October it was learnt that the British were giving way to the French, and that the French were revising their original plan, but the precise details were still unknown.[2] After a Cabinet Meeting of the 4th Hitler told Bülow that he and Blomberg were 'agreed that we must not run the risk of negotiating at all on a new draft that was in the last analysis unacceptable to us. . . . It was time therefore, in order to prevent such a development, to revert to the "original question" [Blomberg], to demand by ultimatum the disarmament of the others and to declare that we would leave the Conference as well as withdraw from the League of Nations in the event that the others rejected disarmament . . .'. Hitler also suggested delivering a major speech in order to appeal to world opinion, and the German Disarmament Delegation was instructed accordingly.[3] By 12 October it was clearly evident that both the British and American Governments had acceded in all essentials to the French amendment. On the 13th Hitler described its terms somewhat tediously to his Cabinet. Germany, he said, could not arm the reserves which would have accumulated after four years, and there was no guarantee that the heavily armed Powers would start to disarm under the second part of the Convention. 'Especially intolerable' were the provisions regarding supervision, which technically can be carried out only with respect to us. . . . It was therefore necessary for Germany to leave both the Disarmament Conference and the League. He would accordingly dissolve the Reichstag, order new elections and call upon the German people to 'identify themselves through a national plebiscite with the peace policy of the Reich Government'. Mussolini was to be the only foreign statesman to be informed in advance.[4] Hitler had already obtained Hindenburg's approval for his decision, and there seems to have been no concerted opposition to it from his fellow ministers. It was confirmed by the Cabinet the next day and duly put into force.[5]

---

[1] DGFP (C) Vol. I, p. 882. [2] Ibid., pp. 885–9 and pp. 892–3.
[3] Ibid., p. 887. [4] DGFP (C) Vol. I, pp. 922–6.
[5] For post-war statements by Papen and Neurath on their alleged opposition, see IMT Vol. XVII, p. 17 and Vol. XIX, pp. 150–1. Blomberg's Memoirs

Hitler in this the first of a succession of *faits accomplis* had won for his country greater freedom of action. German statesmen dreaded nothing more than those occasions when the British and French were closeted together in negotiations on German affairs behind their back,[1] and events were to prove that they could achieve far more in separate negotiations with other Powers than when Geneva was a general clearing house for diplomatic business.

Hitler's success at home was no less notable. However much he detested and vilified the Weimar statesmen, he now made it clear, in his appeals to the German electorate, that his policy was merely the logical fulfilment of theirs. But he possessed the confidence which they lacked. On 24 October 1931 the leaders of the *Reichswehr* trembled at the possibility of winning no concession at the conference: they were convinced that 'ninety per cent of the German people' would feel failure to be a 'hard blow'.[2] Yet Hitler, having returned completely empty-handed, won almost universal acclamation. In the plebiscite of 12 November, 95.1 per cent of the electorate concurred in his decision. He was now indisputably master of his own house, and by winning mass enthusiasm had taken the first step towards the restoration of military sovereignty.

(see Note on Sources, p. 195) describe Nadolny's dissenting attitude. See also Nadolny, *Mein Beitrag*, p. 141 and Meinck, op. cit., pp. 43–51.

[1] On 13 July 1932, four days after the declaration of Lausanne, the British and French Governments reached a separate agreement which greatly piqued German sentiment. (Wheeler-Bennett, *Disarmament Deadlock*, p. 47.)

[2] See Note on Sources, p. 195.

CHAPTER 4

Germany's Improved International Standing

(April 1934)

Possible French Counter-Action

Hitler's first essay in 'sudden diplomacy' may have evoked an outburst of applause in Germany: but how would other Powers react? Neither Germany's decision to leave the League, which could only take effect after two years, nor her withdrawal from the Disarmament Conference could, in the opinion of the *Wilhelmstrasse*, given in an unpublished memorandum of 23 October 1933, offer France grounds for proceeding against her.[1] While other countries, Brazil, the Argentine and Japan, had left the League without incurring risks, participation in the Disarmament Conference had been voluntary. Germany's armaments were defined by the Treaty of Versailles which was still valid: by leaving the Conference Germany did not release herself from any obligation to remain disarmed; on the contrary all the greater caution had to be exercised. Although the existence of para military organizations and police formations in the Rhineland had for long been recognized, France could find a pretext for intervention only if the Commission on Effectives, established by the League, decided that such formations had a military character. All military preparations within the Rhineland in the future should, it was claimed in the memoranda, take the possible activities of such a commission into account.

The Foreign Ministry's arguments in favour of observing Locarno and Versailles had a direct bearing on policy. In October the civil authorities were reminded by the Defence Ministry that Party organizations in the Rhineland must not assume a military character, and the Service chiefs were told that if necessary military preparations in the Rhineland might have to be suspended.[2]

---

[1] See Note on Sources, p. 195.

[2] ND: 140-C (IMT). It is evident that Blomberg had two types of military preparations in mind: (*a*) those with the long term aim of expanding national

Although Germany incurred no major risk after 14 October, it is evident from a directive for possible operations, signed by Blomberg on 25 October, that Germany's prospects in a defensive war had not improved to any appreciable extent since the previous March. Even if the Council of the League did not decide on concerted action France could resort to economic sanctions and induce Poland, Belgium and Czechoslovakia to follow suit. In the event of a violation of German territory 'local armed resistance' was intended 'regardless of the prospects of success'. Defensive action was only to be offered by formations coming under the orders of the High Command, and it would have to conform with the laws and usages of war as defined in the Hague Convention of 1907.[1] The military intentions of Blomberg's directive cannot be described as full blooded warfare but rather as 'resistance to arrest' in the event of a police action. Nevertheless until Germany had new forces to meet the threat from both East and West everything was to be gained by a respite.

In the autumn of 1933 Hitler declared his peaceful intentions, and did everything to prove to the French that Germany had no interest in Alsace and Lorraine.[2] He concentrated mainly however in neutralizing Germany's long and highly exposed Eastern frontier. He had evidently in October 1933 offered both Poland and Czechoslovakia non-aggression pacts, but since the latter declined to negotiate he concentrated on the former. Poland for her part had even stronger reasons for putting her relations with Germany on a new footing. Fearing that her future might be settled by a Four Power Directorate of Europe and that Germany might now act outside the framework of the League, she took the initiative. On 15 November 1933, Lipski, the Polish Minister in Berlin, asked for an assurance from the Reich that force would not be used for the solution of the Polish problem. On the 24th a draft Declaration was forwarded to Moltke, the German Minister in Warsaw, who was reminded that it did not imply a final recognition of the Eastern

defence; (*b*) immediate measures, such as road blocks, demolitions and evacuations, which would be necessary if sanctions would be imposed. The latter could not be easily concealed.

[1] This would have precluded participation by the para-military organizations. Air Force formations were to operate as component parts of the two authorized Services; the police would come under the control of the Army.

[2] Interview with Fernard de Brinon, November 1933, Baynes, *Hitler's Speeches*, Vol. II, p. 1147.

status quo. Pilsudski on 28 November approved the German draft, but warned Moltke against any mention in the text of Locarno, which had a bad name in Poland. Negotiations were soon complete and the Declaration signed on 26 January 1934.[1] Although Poland reserved the right to adhere to existing international obligations (i.e. her treaties with France) she agreed to deal directly with Germany in the future. This made it difficult for her to commit herself still further to France, and although at Stresa in April 1935 and again in March 1936 she agreed to support France, she was no longer the first party to take the initiative against Germany. Yet the Polish problem was shelved, not solved, and even when relations on the surface were satisfactory, German military staffs continued to plan against that nation whom they had always despised: there was indeed something prophetic in Gathorne-Hardy's comment that Pilsudski was merely given the promise Polyphemus gave Ulysses that he would be the last to be eaten.[2]

Politically the Treaty with Poland was bound to hasten the general dissolution of the Rapallo structure. According to instructions from Neurath to the German Embassy in Moscow of 13 November, Rapallo was to be 'appropriately and fully observed'.[3] Opinion in Russia at that time seems to have been divided. Although Russian generals, including Marshal Tukhachevsky, the Deputy Commissar for War, did all in their power to restore good relations with Germany, an alternative was now open to them. On 26 December 1933 the German Embassy in Moscow learnt that France had offered Russia a military alliance. Neither Hitler nor his Ministers were in the slightest disturbed by the news. The Russians, they thought, wanted an alliance directed against Japan rather than the Reich. Early in 1934 Nadolny, Dirksen's successor as German Ambassador in

---

[1] See Namier, *Europe in Decay*, pp. 281–5, in which Namier reproduces a personal letter from Benes of 20 April 1944. See also Namier, *Diplomatic Prelude*, pp. 11–16. Celovsky, *Das Münchener Abkommen*, p. 88, accuses Namier of not having quoted his evidence, but he does not refer to *Europe in Decay*. All the relevant documents can be found in DCFP (C) Vol. II, under *Poland and Danzig*, but they do not radically change Namier's account.

[2] *A Short History of International Affairs*, p. 369.

[3] The relevant documents on Soviet German relations can be found in DGFP (C) Vols. II and III under *Russia*. An unpublished German intelligence report of January 1934 laid great stress on the positive attitude of Generals in the Red Army to Germany.

Moscow, advocated better relations with Russia but was sharply rebuffed.[1]

After 26 January 1934 Hitler, realizing that France was not likely to proceed against Germany unless she were supported by her eastern allies or Russia, was free from any serious threat, except over Austria, and he could pursue the central object of his policy, the expansion of the armed forces. Opposition came, not merely from the French but from the more conservative of his own generals who, true to the von Seeckt tradition, were reluctant to go beyond the plan of 21 divisions and 300,000 men by 1937–1938.[2] The generals, however, insisted that they alone should, according to Hitler's explicit promises of 3 February 1933,[3] train the rising generation in the profession of arms. But 300,000 men was not a high figure. What would happen to that large part of the youth who were not destined for the field grey uniform?

The generals had a rival whom Hitler could use to goad them into accepting an accelerated programme of rearmament: Captain Ernst Röhm and the SA.[4] Keen competition was already developing behind the scenes for control over an existing organization for training units drawn from the various youth organizations in Germany, known as the *Reichkuratorium für Jugendertüchtigung*.[5] Since military training, no less than the production of weapons, had to be considered in the light of the Treaty of Versailles the *Kuratorium*

S. A.
vs.
Army

---

[1] Nadolny's mission was a complete failure. On his visit to Berlin in May 1934 when he discussed a memorandum of 30 May with Neurath and Hitler he was so outspoken that, according to Hossbach, Hitler's adjutant, op. cit., pp. 37–8, disciplinary proceedings were threatened against him. Since he was also opposed to Germany's departure from the Disarmament Conference, he was not likely to achieve success as a professional diplomat in the Third Reich. Later in the year his place was taken in Moscow by Count Werner von der Schulenburg, who, although advocate of the Eastern School of German foreign policy, was a man of a more placid temperament, given to collecting icons and carpets. See Nadolny, *Mein Beitrag*, pp. 167–8; Hilger, *The Incompatible Allies*, pp. 264–7, and Dirksen, *Moscow, Tokyo, London*, p. 186.

[2] Meinck, op. cit., p. 80 and p. 89 et seq.

[3] See p. 6.

[4] For the background of the SA movement see Waite, *Vanguard of Nazism* and H. Mau, *Die Zweite Revolution, Vierteljahrshefte fur Zeitgeschichte* 1953 (January). Mau und H. F. Krausnick, *Deutsche Geschichte der Jüngsten Vergangenheit*, pp. 50–69. The most complete account is given by H. Förtsch, *Schuld und Verhängnis*, p. 43 et seq.

[5] I am much indebted to an internal monograph of the Institut für Zeitgeschichte, Munich by Dr. Thilo Vogelsang, called *Der Chef des Ausbildungswesens* (Chef AW). Dr. Vogelsang has used many original documents in the custody of the Institute.

was at first placed under the Ministry of Interior instead of Defence, with the *Reichswehr* merely exercising an outside control. But, staffed for the greater part by elderly men, the *Kuratorium* was treated as an object of ridicule by both the SA and by Army officers. While Blomberg agreed that it should be controlled by an efficient body, he did not wish to see the power of the SA and Röhm augmented. He thus succeeded, soon after Hitler came to power, in having the *Kuratorium* transferred from the Ministry of Interior to the Ministry of Labour under Seldte, head of the *Stahlhelm* and Röhm's 'respectable' rival. But the *Stahlhelm* was rapidly losing influence and power. In these circumstances Röhm and his rival General von Reichenau, now Blomberg's Chef de Bureau, competed for control over the *Kuratorium*. On 1 July 1933 they struck a bargain whereby the *Kuratorium* was dissolved and a new organization, the AW (*Ausbildungswesen*), established with SA Gruppenführer Krüger at its head. All training outside the *Reichswehr* was now entrusted to SA officers and the AW was recognized as the only legitimate liaison staff between the SA and *Reichswehr*. On Hitler's orders it was to train 250,000 men within a year for the disposal of the Reichswehr in an emergency. Since Krüger, at the end of 1933, had accepted Army officers on his staff, he lost popularity. He was leader of that faction of the SA whose relations with the *Reichswehr* were friendly; he certainly intrigued against Röhm.[1]

But the SA was not merely dependent on the AW for its reserves of strength. At the end of 1933 it numbered in all over a million men. By a law of 1 December 1933 it was declared to be a statutory arm of the Government, with Röhm occupying a seat in the Reich Cabinet and in the National Defence Council. At the same time the senior age groups of the *Stahlhelm* were incorporated into the ranks of the SA and not into the *Landeswehr* under the Defence Minister.[2]

Rapid accretion of power to the SA however brought with it fresh difficulties. Observance of the Treaty of Versailles had hitherto tended to operate in favour of the SA, and in conversations with foreign diplomats Hitler could plead that the training given amounted to little more than cross-country runs and picnics.

[1] The AW was itself dissolved in the autumn of 1934 when Krüger fell into obscurity.

[2] Wheeler-Bennett, *The Nemesis of Power*, p. 308, fn.

After the passage of the law of 1 December 1933, the real character of the SA could no longer be camouflaged. On 5 December, François-Poncet, the French Ambassador to Berlin, told Bulow that he had received an invitation to meet Röhm, and that Paris was worried.[1]

The expansion of the SA was already having a profound effect on the bilateral negotiations, which were continued after 14 October, on Germany's future military establishment. On 24 October in a conversation with Sir Eric Phipps, the new British Ambassador, Hitler demanded a convention of eight years' duration which would allow Germany 300,000, instead of the 200,000 troops of the MacDonald Plan. He did not ask for offensive weapons and bombers. He also proposed that under the Convention the heavily armed Powers should not increase their armaments. The British in an attempt to make Hitler tone down his demands, proposed in a memorandum of 29 January 1934, that Germany should have no military aircraft for a period of two years.[2] It soon emerged that Hitler was willing only to renounce bombers. Eden, then Lord Privy Seal, having conferred with the French, visited Berlin from 21 to 22 February. Although Hitler persisted in his claims, he made one radical concession. He gave five pledges for the demilitarization and supervision of the SA and SS.[3]

It is more than probable that Hitler changed his attitude to the SA not merely because of foreign policy, but because of pressure from his generals. On 26 January General von Reichenau was appointed acting chairman of the Working Committee of the National Defence Council (*Reichverteidigungsrat*), charged with all questions concerning mobilization.[4] Reichenau was an old opponent of the SA, and a clash between him and Röhm was only to

[1] There is evidence to suggest that Röhm had tried to cover up a highly irregular move by telling Hitler some half-truth of a kind which suggested that the invitation for the talks had come from French circles. Otherwise it is difficult to see why Röhm, with the approval of the Foreign Ministry, was to make a second attempt, apparently without success, to contact François-Poncet at the end of January and on several occasions later. DGFP (C) Vol. II, pp. 174–6 and fn. and p. 422.

[2] DBFP (second series), Vol. II, doc. No. 206 and DGFP (C) Vol. II, pp. 436–7.

[3] DGFP (C) Vol. II, pp. 511–8 and pp. 520–3. The five pledges were that the SA should not be allowed: possession of arms, training with arms, field manoeuvres, concentrations in camps, use of personnel of the *Reichswehr*. The last point would have made the AW illegal.

[4] See a useful article on this body in the *Wehrwissenschaft Rundschau, 1956*.

be expected. Before Hitler met Eden, Blomberg and Reichenau had apparently won him over to their side, for on the 21st Röhm tried to contact François-Poncet with proposals of his own but without success.[1] On 28 February, when Hitler addressed a senior SA and Army officers on his plans after the reintroduction of conscription,[2] Röhm was induced to recognize the Defence Ministry as the sole authority for national defence, and to agree to accept not merely orders from the Ministry itself but from the commanders of Military Districts and frontier units.[3] Hitler, however, did not wish to turn the 'SA as a whole', as a result of this agreement, 'into enemies', and his hesitation suggests that he could still use the S.A. to put pressure on the Army.

Within a few days a fresh quarrel broke out. Early in March the commanders of SA *Obergruppen* and *Gruppen* were enrolling men for one to one and a half year's service in machine-gun detachments (*Stabswachen*). In a letter to Hitler of 5 March[4] complaining about this, Blomberg stated that 'selection and training' was to be undertaken 'with the aim of making an appearance in public', by which he most certainly meant in defiance of the Treaty of Versailles or—still worse—with a revolutionary aim. Blomberg continued that within one Military District 6–8,000 SA men were to be held permanently under arms with rifles and machine guns. He considered it 'especially objectionable' that these detachments were being established in connection with the so-called SA relief camps situated for the greater part in the large towns, even in Höchst am Main, in other words, in the Neutral Zone. 'Such action makes all the care taken within the Neutral Zone taken by the Armed Forces and the Krüger [i.e. AW] camps influenced by it, illusory.' Although Hitler's reactions to Blomberg's protest are not known, it is evident from a directive Röhm issued to his subordinates of 6 March[5] that he had again given his promise of

---

[1] DGFP (C) Vol. III, pp. 262–5. François-Poncet was quite unaware that Röhm was already out of favour. See his *Souvenirs*, p. 182 et seq.

[2] Förtsch, *Schuld und Verhängnis*, pp. 47–8 where Hitler's address is described but the exact words are not recorded.

[3] *Obergruppenführer* Juttner had also at a meeting of the working committee of the Reich Defence Council of 23 and 24 January 1934 given similar assurances. He said: 'The SA therefore is not only prepared but also under the obligation to fulfil all demands of the armed Forces . . .', ND: 404-EC.

[4] ND: 951-D.

[5] Röhm drew the leading SA commanders' attention to previous assurances that the SA should not make appearances with arms in public. He also denied

submission,[1] but unfortunately few primary sources on the subsequent deliberations between Hitler, Röhm and Blomberg have survived.[2]

Although the SA were already falling out of favour their armed detachments had most certainly alarmed the French at what was perhaps the most vital juncture in the disarmament negotiations. Early in April they were asked by the British whether they would accept as the basis for negotiations the British memorandum of 29 January. With minor German amendments, this was accepted by Hitler on 16 April. François-Poncet attempted to persuade Barthou to do so, but after some hesitation the French Cabinet took an uncompromising stand, declaring on 17 April that increased German military expenditure had destroyed the basis for further negotiations,[3] Once more Hitler, without fear of sanctions, could blame French intransigence for the failure of negotiations, and, when the Conference met for the last time between 19 May and 11 June, its results were stillborn.

Provided that the German rearmament programme did not exceed the new limits which Hitler himself recognized, real progress was possible. Hitler, having broken with the SA, did not in fact ask for more than he could get. For one thing the German War economy had not got over its initial difficulties, and it was decided to develop it not from where it had 'left off' in 1918 but

having discussed the question of the armed detachments (*Stabswachen*) with either François-Poncet or the German Embassy in Paris, ND: IMT: 951-D. According to the description of this document in IMT it was a letter to Röhm from Hitler. The internal evidence and the distribution mark make it clear that it was a directive from Röhm to his subordinates.

[1] Also on 6 March Reiner, head of the newly established SA *Ministeramt*, was quoted in the *Deutsche Zeitung* as having claimed that his office would clear up misunderstandings on the SA with heads of foreign missions in Berlin. On the 8th Reiner, in the presence of Röhm, was politely cautioned by an official of the Foreign Ministry, DGFP (C) Vol. II, p. 571.

[2] Sir John Wheeler-Bennett's contention that a pact of a far-reaching kind had been clinched by Blomberg and Hitler on board the *Deutschland* seems most improbable (*The Nemesis of Power*, pp. 311–3). It is not supported by the existing evidence, and Hitler in his meetings with Röhm may have left him with the impression that he was really on their side. This seems probable from the minutes of Hitler's Cabinet meeting of 3 July 1934, DGFP (C) Vol. III, pp. 117–22.

[3] DGFP (C) Vol. II, pp. 742–3, 747–8 and fn. p. 769, DBFP (second series) Vol. VI, docs. No. 385–95. For a concise account of differences of opinion in France see Meinck, op. cit. pp. 82–4 and François-Poncet, *Souvenirs*, p. 178. The important German memorandum of 16 April 1934 can be found in RIIA, Docs. 1933, p. 384.

from scratch. Priority was therefore given to the construction of barracks, training grounds, air fields and dockyards rather than to raising and equipping new formations which might have had consequences in international relations.

The number of men under arms after 1 April 1934 (the beginning of the new financial year) increased at the relatively small rate of 50 to 60,000 men.[1] Hitler's plans for the future were more ambitious. At the end of 1933 he was considering raising the size of the army threefold.[2] The first practical step towards this end was considered in a memorandum by General Fromm, head of the General Army Office (*Allgemeine Heeresamt*) in a memorandum prepared in the spring of 1934; 300,000 men and 21 divisions were to be called to the colours between November 1934 and April 1935 and not in 1937 and 1938 as previously intended. Fromm had evidently recommended the plan on main grounds: it would facilitate a smooth transition from an élite to a conscript army, and strengthen the army's position *vis-à-vis* the heads of the SA and SS. In a memorandum of 20 May, Beck, Chief of the *Truppenamt*, complained that the plan would no longer mean the formation of a peace-time army but mobilization: 'Until now the watchword has been that we must have no war for ten years.' Hitler's programme could not in Beck's view be carried out in secrecy, and if Hitler hoped to complete it by 1 April 1935 and then confront the world with a *fait accompli*, he was mistaken: other Powers would certainly act first. Beck also had purely military objections. The nucleus army of 100,000 men would lose cohesion if its size were trebled in such a short time, and since general military service could only be introduced at the earliest in October 1935, the 300,000 men would be inadequately trained to serve in turn as a nursing force, for the new divisions would in fact be understaffed. Beck's remonstrance had no effect: by an order of 6 June Hitler's plan was to be implemented.[3] On paper Hitler's programme did not exceed that

---

[1] See the proceedings of the 6th session of the working committee of the National Defence Council of 23–24 January 1934: ND: 404-EC., and a report of the Economic Ministry of 30 September 1934, ND: 128-EC and 286-EC.

[2] Meinck, op. cit. pp. 87–8. Meinck quotes an extract from the Liebmann documents held by the Institut für Zeitgeschichte, Munich. See also B. Müller-Hilleband, *Das Heer*, p. 21, et seq.

[3] Förster, op. cit., pp. 22–4, is wrong in stating that because of Beck's protests Hitler's plan was not put into effect.

which he proposed during the disarmament negotiations. But in order to equip his forces with the proscribed weapons more than 300,000 men were necessary. This figure were merely given for 'political reasons' and included only combatants. When auxiliaries were added the total would amount to 400,000 men.[1] Hence German military expansion, which, in 1934, only embraced a part of the male population, was to continue unabated. Moreover, the number of men between the ages of 25 and 35 who had already received military training, since conscription was prohibited in 1918, was small and dwindling. Without reserves the formation of a war-time army, capable even of shouldering the burden of defence, would be impossible. A special training organization was therefore established at the end of 1934. The introduction of one year's compulsory military service was planned for the autumn of 1935.

[1] See Note on Sources, p. 195.

CHAPTER 5

Hitler Reverses His Policy in Austria

In June 1934 German rearmament had not yet passed the blueprint stage, and for some months it was not likely to lead to international complications. Hitler however had not yet dissociated himself from the more radical of his revolutionary followers; civil war could break out in Germany and in Austria before the army was ready.

After Germany left the League, Dollfuss, not wishing to be dependent on the *Heimwehr* (a Fascist para-military organization, financed by Italy)[1] was willing to patch up his quarrel with the National Socialists. He proposed late in 1933 admitting their leaders into his Cabinet[2]; negotiations were surreptitiously opened with representatives of Habicht, leader of the Austrian Nazis in exile. From the start Hitler's attitude was clear; Dollfuss would first have to give legal recognition to the Austrian branch of the Nazi Party before serious negotiations could start.[3] Although on 1 January 1934 he permitted Habicht to go to Vienna and meet Dollfuss, acts of terrorism committed by the Nazis in Austria unexpectedly caused Dollfuss to cancel the visit on the 8th, when, with some difficulty, Hitler radioed a message through to the plane on which Habicht was travelling, ordering it to return to the Reich.[4] Although Dollfuss still wished to negotiate, conditions inside the country made it progressively more difficult for him to do so. They became so acute that on 31 January General Muff, the German Military Attaché in Vienna, gained 'the well founded conviction' that the Austrian SA leaders had received from Reschny, their *Obergruppenführer*, orders to make preparations for direct action on 15 March.[5] Although the order was to be kept

---

[1] For more detailed enquiries, see Eichstädt, *Von Dollfuss zu Hitler*, pp. 45–50 and Jedlicka, *Ein Herr im Schatten der Parteien*, Chap. V, and RIIA Survey, 1934, pp. 416–507.

[2] DGFP (C) Vol. II, pp. 33–4 and pp. 263–8.

[3] Ibid., p. 197.

[4] Ibid., p. 295 and fn. and pp. 309–12.

[5] Ibid., pp. 437–8.

secret, even from the civilian party members, it must have been known in Austrian official circles, for Muff's informant was an Austrian Army officer. There may have been substance to his report, for within a few days Rosenberg also described an SA plot to seize power.[1] Although the German Government flatly denied these rumours, Dollfuss compiled a dossier of them and submitted it to the French, British and Italian Governments. But before these Powers could agree on the attitude to be adopted, violence was to break out within Austria over an entirely separate issue. On 15 February Dollfuss, under pressure from Mussolini, suppressed with great severity a revolt by the Social Democrats.

The long term results of the revolt were correctly foreseen by the Austrian Nazi leaders; a large part of the disgruntled rank and file of the Social Democrats defected to the Nazis who had shed no blood of their 'fellow German citizens'.[2] The immediate result on the other hand was less favourable. On 17 February Italy, France and Great Britain issued a communiqué on the necessity of maintaining Austria's independence and integrity in accordance with the relevant Treaties.[3] On 17 March Italy strengthened her hand still further by economic treaties, known as the Rome Protocols, with Austria and Hungary, which it was believed in Berlin also provided for political consultation. The Rome Protocols were thus far from popular, and the correct conclusion was drawn in Berlin that continued Nazi provocation in Austria might result in an Italo-French accord and the complete isolation of Germany.[4]

In these circumstances Hitler, with promptings from the Foreign Ministry, had once more to revise his policy towards Austria. On 16 March he bluntly told Habicht that propaganda attacks on the Austrian Government must cease. He also stated 'expressly that he desired neither an *Anschluss* nor a *Gleichschaltung* of Austria'.[5]

[1] In a letter evidently to the Munich Branch of the *Völkischer Beobachter* of 3 February, Rosenberg complained that certain Austrians, when passing from Berlin to Vienna, were recently informed that Austrian SA formations stationed in Bavaria would be ordered to march over the frontier on 8 and 9 February, whereupon a military dictatorship would be established. An English informant had expressed surprise to him that the SA might act behind the Führer's back. Rosenberg concluded that the SA High Command should if necessary take appropriate counter measures, ND: 4013-PS.

[2] DGFP (C) Vol. II, pp. 498–501.

[3] See RIIA *Survey* (1934) pp. 454–5.

[4] For Bülow's interpretation of the Rome Protocols see his memorandum of 19 March and 9 April, DGFP (C), Vol. II, pp. 636–7 and pp. 728–30.

[5] Ibid., pp. 614–7.

Hitler's orders to Habicht certainly created an opportunity for a *détente* with Italy, and there were many of Hitler's advisors, including Hassell in Rome and Papen, still Vice-Chancellor, who were more than willing to take the initiative. On 29 March Papen in an unofficial visit to Rome[1] suggested to Mussolini that the two heads of Government should meet as early as possible, perhaps at the end of April: Venice was considered the most suitable meeting place.

At a conference of 10 April with Neurath, Hassell, Blomberg and Bülow, Hitler said that if the meeting was to take place, he would explain to Mussolini that 'neither Italy nor England could have an interest in letting Germany be defeated by France with the result of watching the latter exercise supremacy in Europe'. He also confirmed his disinterestedness politically and economically in Austria and was ready 'to write off Austria for some years to come and hand her over to economic fertilization by Italy'. But he would not use such precise language to Mussolini. News of the meeting was, he said, being 'celebrated in Vienna as a success by Dollfuss', and his final decision would be made after Papen's return. Neurath then spoke in favour of the meeting, and Blomberg made the characteristic comment that it was 'abnormal and unhealthy' for two leader types such as Hitler and Mussolini not to have a personal meeting.[2] Hitler, however, was not going to Canossa to capitulate to Dollfuss—the only course (in Bülow's mind) open to Germany.[3] Instead he took up the cudgels again. On 18 April he told Habicht that financial restrictions for visas to Austria were to remain in force and economic warfare to be intensified.[4] Hitler in making these threats had unquestionably given Habicht and his followers a free hand. But Dollfuss for his part was equally headstrong. He had promulgated a new Austrian constitution of the corporative type on 30 April. Thereafter clashes between the Heimwehr and the Austrian Legion became more frequent.[5] On 23 May General Muff, the German Military Attaché

---

[1] Ibid., pp. 690–1. See also Hassell's despatch of 3 April, pp. 704–7.

[2] Ibid., pp. 735–6. No record of what Papen subsequently advised Hitler has been found but this wily personage, ably supported by other members of the Cabinet, most certainly removed the Chancellor's lingering doubts.

[3] This is evident from Bülow's memorandum for Neurath of 9 April in which he suggested that the visa restrictions for entry into Austria should be lifted, DGFP (C), Vol. II, pp. 728–30.

[4] Ibid., pp. 757–8 and pp. 789–90.

[5] Ibid., p. 737 and pp. 839–41.

in Vienna, discussed the entire situation with General Fritsch, chief of the Army High Command. Muff claimed that German aspirations had, owing to Italian intervention, miscarried and that Italy's influence in Austria was very great. He did not believe that the Nazi Party, whose leadership was poor, could on its own resources bring about a *coup de main*, and the Austrian Legion in Bavaria would only be called upon after there was a swing of the pendulum in Austria itself. Muff said that in the Austrian question Germany lacked a clear policy, and that it was not known abroad whether it was formed by the Party or the Foreign Office. As a result of provocation, Austria might become the centre of all opposition to the Reich. Muff continued: 'we must come to an understanding with Italy.... Such an understanding is the only salvation of German policy in Austria.' He ominously pointed out that it was expected that Hitler would sever his ties with some of his subordinates at home and that this would be taken as a sign of strength abroad. Fritsch replied that this question should be taken up by Muff with Blomberg, but no record of any subsequent interview has survived.[1]

The alarm among the Generals over possible developments in Austria was shared by others. On the 24th Neurath in a letter to Frick, Minister of the Interior, explained how border incidents might endanger Germany's foreign policy; he therefore urged necessary counter measures.[2] Although those in ministerial responsibility in Germany, above all Röhm and one of his deputies Langer, agreed that the para-military organizations and party officials should be withdrawn from the frontier,[3] Neurath's protests met with no lasting results. At the end of May events in Austria had got so far out of control that even the Party Leaders in Austria, whose reputation can hardly be described as temperate, protested that the SA were allowed to do just 'what they please', sometimes 'the exact opposite' of the party.[4] The absence of centralized control over the Nazi movement in Austria was most certainly discussed by Habicht and Hitler early in June, but no record of the meeting has survived, and it led to no change. The Foreign

[1] DGFP (C), Vol. II, pp. 835–7.
[2] Ibid., pp. 839–41.
[3] Ibid., pp. 887–8.
[4] ND: 868-D and DGFP (C), Vol. II, p. 859 and fn, recording conversations between Baron von Wachter Habicht's Deputy and Foreign Ministry officials.

Ministry which also feared repercussions on the disarmament negotiations learnt from Rieth in Vienna on the 12th that developments were 'rapidly assuming threatening forms which might soon bring about an extremely serious situation'. Rieth wished to go to Berlin before Hitler's departure for Venice and report verbally.[1] Although he was too late to contact Hitler, Frick at the instigation of the Foreign Ministry requested the Prime Minister of Bavaria on the 14th to take speedy and effective action to halt incidents organized from Bavaria.

The letter was circulated to the heads of all ministries concerned, the SA High Command in particular being reminded that 'this intolerable state of affairs' jeopardizes 'their reputation'.[2] Yet, despite repeated reminders, no satisfactory explanation had been given to the Foreign Ministry on why outrages continued.[3] It might be asked why, in a totalitarian state in which the process of regional and departmental *Gleichschaltung* (levelling down) was allegedly complete, did Cabinet ministers exercise so little control? Personal vengeance, even at the cost of expediency, goes a long way to explaining many of Hitler's actions. He hated his former compatriot, Dollfuss, and everything he stood for, and even when confronted with the Duce wearing uniform, and speaking down to him, at Venice, Hitler remained intransigent. He was determined to bring about the fall of his enemy and answer *terror* with *terror*.[4]

The recently published documents on the Venice meeting add little to what is already known.[5] They reinforce the impression that Mussolini failed to appreciate that Hitler would carry out his

[1] Ibid.

[2] According to DGFP (C), Vol. III, p. 4, Frick also sent a copy of Neurath's letter of 24 May to the Prime Minister of Bavaria, but the editors in their footnote state that this letter was not printed. The reference number shows that it was printed by the editors themselves. Ibid., pp. 839–41 of the previous volume.

[3] Ibid., Vol. III, pp. 239–41 and fn. on p. 241.

[4] *Das Politische Tagebuch Alfred Rosenbergs*, edited by H. G. Seraphim.

[5] See Wiskemann, *The Rome-Berlin Axis*, pp. 36–7. According to Neurath's minute, Hitler made five points: first, an *Anschluss* was of no interest; second, a neutral person should be appointed to replace Dollfuss as head of the Austrian government; third, elections should be proclaimed by the new Austrian head of government; fourth, after the election, National Socialists should be included in the Austrian government; fifth, all economic questions in Austria should 'be handled by Germany and Italy in closest consultation'. According to the Italian minute point five included 'all' and not merely 'economic' questions. The proposals in general were interpreted in Rome less as an agreement than as an expression of German opinion. DGFP (C) Vol. III, pp. 10–12, 13–14, 18–19 and p. 132 fn.

threats with such celerity and thoroughness. Soon after Hitler's return, Hassell described the meeting as having made an 'unusually profound impression on the whole of Italy'. Mussolini, he claimed, in contrast with Suvich, his Deputy Foreign Minister and leader of the anti-German element in the *Palazzo Chigi*, was of the opinion that the Austrian problem would have to be solved in 'friendly negotiations between Italy and Germany'.[1] Yet Mussolini remained suspicious. Later in June, after Dollfuss again demanded that terrorism should cease in order to create favourable conditions for negotiations with Germany, he invited him to a meeting at Riccone for the end of the month.

Soon a 'cloud' was to be cast over the memory of Venice.[2] Mussolini's displeasure turned into rage. On 30 June Röhm, together with Heines, his deputy, Gregor Strasser, Generals von Schleicher and Bredow and scores of others were brutally murdered by firing squads of the SS, the ultimate beneficiaries of the purge. Papen himself miraculously escaped; his entourage did not.

Although General Beck was horrified by the murders committed in Germany and later in Austria,[3] Blomberg 'thanked the Chancellor for the resolute and courageous action by which he had saved the German people from civil war'.[4] Yet, as Muff's conversation of 23 May with Fritsch suggests, the Generals were also expecting a break with the radicals in Austria. In this they were to be sadly disappointed.

On 4 July Neurath instructed Hassell that nothing had happened in Germany (meaning the Röhm purge) to alter the view that Dollfuss 'must go' before terrorist acts should cease. And Mussolini's simple words of counsel, conveyed by Hassell that 'the Germans should now keep quiet [in Austria] for a few months', merely evoked Hitler's rejoinder, 'there was no urgency regarding the Austrian question'.[5] As a result disorder in Austria, provoked by the SA and other malcontents who had previously looked to Röhm

---

[1] DGFP (C), Vol. III, pp. 63–8.

[2] Ibid., pp. 122–3 and fn. on p. 122. See also pp. 83–5 and Hassell's despatch of 19 July, pp. 193–4.

[3] See Beck's correspondence with Bülow, Förster, op. cit., pp. 26–7.

[4] See minute of Cabinet meeting of 3 July, DGFP (C), Vol. III, pp. 117–122.

[5] Ibid., pp. 122–3 and pp. 131–2 especially fn. on p. 132.

rather than Hitler as their ultimate deliverer, grew.[1] On the 14th Dollfuss passed two new laws prescribing the death penalty for the unlawful possession of arms and acts of terrorism. Hitler refused Rieth permission[2] to contact Dollfuss in order to prevent executions being carried out under these laws. He seems to have paid no heed to any last-minute warnings of the Foreign Ministry. On the 25th the inevitable happened: Dollfuss was murdered and most of his Cabinet captured by Nazi insurgents.[3] But the Austrian army and the police stood firmly behind the new Government under Schuschnigg. Hence the Putsch, so reminiscent of that attempted by Hitler and Ludendorff in March 1923, miscarried.[4]

On learning the news, Hitler, who had been attending a Wagnerian festival in Bayreuth on the 25th, was thrown into a state of considerable excitement. He had evidently received reports about large scale 'slaughter' of National Socialists in Austria and was anxious lest third Powers (in this connection he named Great Britain) should intervene. On the other hand, Neurath, who flew to Bayreuth, saw no cause for alarm provided prompt measures were taken.[5] The immediate upshot was the dismissal of Habicht and Rieth, the latter having injudiciously witnessed in a private capacity an agreement reached at the point of the pistol affording the insurgents a free passage to the German frontier. Rieth's place was taken by Papen who, for past services, assumed the grandiose title of 'Minister on Special Mission to Vienna'.[6]

The likelihood of foreign intervention depended almost entirely on Italy. Mussolini, with whom the widow of Dollfuss was staying, was filled with indignation: he ordered troop movements of a precautionary kind and posed in the Italian Press as the champion

---

[1] See Habicht's report to the German Legation in Vienna of 18 June, Ibid., Vol. III, p. 47. Eichstädt in, *Von Dollfuss zu Hitler*, p. 46, claims that the Röhm purge may have caused a temporary lull in the Austrian dispute and that some Austrian Nazis may have been purged.

[2] DGFP(C), Vol. III, pp. 173–4 and fn. on p. 173.

[3] Ibid, pp. 235–53.

[4] Eichstädt in op. cit., pp. 51–60, gives a full and accurate account of the events of 25 July. For an explanation of why the *Putsch* failed see a report of 2 August prepared by the Volksbund für das Deutschtum im Ausland for the Foreign Ministry and submitted to Hitler DGFP (C) Vol. III, pp. 283–289.

[5] Ibid., pp. 271–2.

[6] It is of interest that the Italian government, which previously regarded Papen as *persona grata*, see p. 15, was opposed to his new appointment. Ibid., pp. 273–4 and Papen, *Memoirs*, Chap. XXI.

of Western civilization.[1] But, after the dissolution of the Nazi Party in Austria and the withdrawal of the Austrian Legion in August,[2] the immediate danger of foreign intervention soon passed. Henceforward until 1938, Hitler could no longer hope, by means of economic pressure, blackmail and terrorism, to force an *Anschluss*. Instead he could only prepare its way by the 'evolutionary process' of infiltration and by remaining on good terms with Italy.

To all intents and purposes, however, the 'Brown Revolution' with its spontaneous ruffianism had been suppressed in Austria no less than the Reich and the Generals had no further scruples about recognizing Hitler. On 3 August, two days after the death of Hindenburg, they took their fateful oath of personal allegiance to Hitler. They could now give rearmament their undivided attention.

[1] DGFP (C) Vol. III, pp. 251–3, and p. 259 and pp. 268–9.
[2] Ibid., p. 281 and pp. 293–4.

CHAPTER 6

Military Sovereignty Restored

Hitler's generals, elated now that Röhm was out of the way and that Germany was again an *Obrigkeitstaat* (an authoritarian State), could take a more optimistic view of the future. With Poland all but neutralized, and Russia still reluctant to enter the French system, they had as yet nothing to fear from Czechoslovakia. At the eighth session of the Working Committee of the National Defence Council of 19 September 1934, General Beck, in comparing Germany's position with that obtaining at the time of a previous session of 18 July 1933, declared: 'The basic military situation has radically changed. In the construction of the peacetime Forces, particularly in the Army and Air Force, considerable progress has been made.' Germany, he continued, was still dependent, except in the regular army, on untrained reserves. This greater degree of confidence was even more emphatically reflected in a new draft directive of 15 October, evidently issued by the Naval High Command. The words, 'local armed resistance', as well as those clauses restricting freedom of action of the field commanders, were explicitly to be deleted from the directive issued by Blomberg on 25 October 1933,[1] and the North Sea, instead of the Baltic, was to be the centre of operations. The same measures were to be taken with or without a declaration of war by a hostile Power, otherwise initiative would be stultified. War could, according to this draft, only have one object: 'defeat of the enemy'. Owing to the state of armament it would be mainly defensive. But this would not rule out a limited switch to the offensive, provided the expansion of forces permitted.[2]

Timorous language was now being abandoned; German staffs had made up their minds: 'a riot is still a riot even though the riot act has not been read'; their policy had passed from the stage of feverish preoccupation with frontier defence.

There can be no question about the strategic principles which were to govern German planning in the future. Nurtured in the

---

[1] See p. 26.   [2] See Note on Sources, p. 195.

teaching of Clausewitz, the Generals had always looked on the 'battle of annihilation' as the key to victory: they were convinced that it would govern operations by foreign Powers. In January 1934 the Intelligence Department of the *Truppenamt* reviewed the current theories of war held abroad from published and restricted works.[1] Their conclusions throw considerable light both on Germany's military situation at that time and on the nature of warfare after progress had been made in German armaments. According to the new school of 'total war' the aim was not only to destroy the enemy on the field but his entire resources: war would be waged by economic means and by propaganda no less than by weapons. It was pointed out that, whereas in Germany a 'strategy of annihilation' and a 'strategy of attrition' were considered of equal importance, the entire emphasis abroad was on the former. The experience of World War I had not been forgotten: only when operations were carried right into the heart of enemy territory would the outcome be conclusive. Forces would be assembled as near the frontier as possible and their distribution made to conform with the character of operations intended. The main concentrations would be on vital sectors of the front and the intervening areas would be covered, where possible, with fortifications. While in theory the assembly should be completed before the start of hostilities, it was considered more practical, particularly in France and Poland, first to gain a springboard by means of an initial thrust, and then to continue operations on a larger scale when more forces were available.

Nothing was more important than the timing of the first blow; most army staffs were convinced that enemy forces could be paralysed before they had taken up positions behind the frontier. The review drew attention to the uniformity of modern military theory. The French, it was believed, had assimilated German ideas on the offensive, and there was no suggestion that one day they would put their entire trust in an 'impregnable' barrier of fortifications. The idea was also gaining ground in France, no less than elsewhere, that armour, which was still principally regarded as an auxiliary arm of infantry, might at some future date be organized into independent units. One weakness in the French army was alluded to and some of its leaders were conscious of it: formations of seasoned troops were diluted with conscripts of one year's service.

[1] See Note on Sources, p. 195.

This defect could only be made good by extending the period of military service. Above all the French Army could take the field with the minimum of delay. The Government reserved the right to call up certain age groups in peace time, hence a state of partial mobilization could be achieved before the proclamation of general mobilization. While parts of the French Army could be ready in a matter of hours, general mobilization would require twenty-one days.

According to a later *Truppenamt's* appreciation of 30 January 1935 it was believed that work on the Maginot line between 1933 and 1935 had increased the defensive power of the French Army about three times: enormous headway was also reported to be in progress in Czech and Russian armaments.[1] That Germany still needed a respite to develop her armed forces is the conclusion to be drawn from these reviews, and no greater mistake could be made than to assume that she was the only Power who after 1933 was rearming, or that she alone set the pace in an armaments race.

The *Reichswehr* had already before 1934 made some progress in developing those weapons prohibited by the Treaty. In the autumn of 1934 it was to start equipping new formations with them. Yet if Hitler felt that it was safe to rearm, he could not simply jettison the Treaty of Versailles and still less Locarno. There was one telling reason alone why he could not do so.

Hitler had attempted but failed in the autumn of 1933 to persuade the French to accept Germany's annexation of the Saar before awaiting the inevitable results of the plebiscite due to be held in January 1935.[2] The French might occupy this valuable industrial region because of German treaty violations. Until it was securely in German hands after 1 March 1935, Hitler's policy was perforce that of the first offender waiting for his terms of probation to end before committing his next offence. For example, on 2 June 1934, he had told Raeder that the construction of submarines had to be kept secret in view of the plebiscite. But it is evident from a further conversation of 2 November that, because of the critical situation foreseen in the first quarter of 1935, six submarines were to be built.[3]

[1] In January 1935 special intelligence reports were prepared for the Defence Ministry on the progress made in the armaments of Foreign Armed Forces. The figures given in them may have been exaggerated for they were used for political negotiations.

[2] See François-Poncet, *Souvenirs*, p. 169.   [3] ND: 189-C and 190-C.

The date of the plebiscite, 10 January, was in fact to be the turning point. A few days afterwards, on the 16th, Hitler declared in instructions to the German Navy that owing to political pressure being applied by Britain and France, 'armament plans were to be put into operation more speedily, so that the actual level reached shall be as high as possible when the negotiations start'.[1] Hitler had made it clear that in future he would no longer bargain in order to increase armaments, but that he would increase armaments to be in a better position to bargain.

Meanwhile the leading European Powers were making predictions, some of a wild and extravagant nature,[2] on what Hitler could do after the plebiscite, and towards the end of 1934 several French schemes were maturing for the encirclement of Germany.

In March 1934 Hitler had rejected a Soviet proposal for Russo-Polish and Russo-German guarantees of the Baltic States. Direct Franco-Russian negotiations were subsequently opened. On 18 May it was incorrectly reported in the Press that an alliance had been concluded.[3] The news caused no alarm in the *Wilhelmstrasse*, where it was evidently believed that the new turn in Russia's policy was a *pis-aller* after her failure to revive Rapallo.[4] Later in the summer a new system of security, known as the Eastern Pact, was canvassed by the French and amended by the British. This would include the USSR, Germany, Poland, Czechoslovakia and the Baltic States. Each signatory was to agree to render to the others mutual assistance if attacked by one of the other signatories, and to consult together if attacked by a third party. According to a supplementary treaty Russia and France were to assume obligations towards each other similar to those of Locarno: Germany, on British instigation, was invited to accede to it.[5]

Bülow and General Blomberg believed that Germany should give a favourable reply as soon as possible.[6] On Hitler's insistence

---

[1] See Note on Sources, p. 195.

[2] For example the British Embassy was reported by the *Abwehr* (i.e. OKW Military Intelligence) to believe that the radical party elements would gain control. The Russians evidently feared a German move in the Baltic. See also Dodd's *Diary*, 19 August 1934 and 7 December 1935. For a full account of the Saar plebiscite see RIIA, *Survey, 1934*, pp. 578–627.

[3] RIIA, *Survey, 1934*, pp. 411–2 and *Survey*, 1935, Vol. I, pp. 58 et seq.

[4] The Russians were alleged to have declared during these negotiations that the Germans had made better proposals to them two years earlier. See Note on Sources, p. 195.

[5] DGFP (C) Vol. III, pp. 164–70.   [6] Ibid., pp. 316–7 and pp. 325–33.

the reply was amended on the 31st, so as to exclude all reference to Germany's adhering to her own disarmament proposals of 16 April 1934. In a memorandum of 8 September in which Germany's objections were published,[1] it was argued that Germany would derive no benefit from French assistance against Russia or vice versa, as envisaged in the Pact, and that Germany could not be expected to extend her commitments unless she were accorded full equality of status.

After Germany and Poland had virtually rejected the Eastern Pact, it was only to be expected that France and Russia would conclude some sort of an agreement between themselves. On 18 September 1934 Russia was admitted to the League of Nations. This new success in the French *Einkreisungspolitik* does not seem to have caused Hitler or his advisers anxiety. According to a *Truppenamt* survey on Russian policy for the period July to September 1934 the conclusion was drawn that a 'real interest in the French policy of encirclement no longer exists'. Having strengthened their own position, and recognizing that for the moment it was futile to struggle against National Socialist Germany, the Russians might be led back to 'sober *Realpolitik*'.[2]

For a time this optimistic prediction was justified. In October, a new Russian Ambassador, Jakob Suritz, took up his post in Berlin. He was evidently agreeably surprised by the cordial reception given to him by Hitler.[3]

The one constant nightmare of the Soviet statesmen was a combination of capitalist states; the French could by this means exert pressure on them. Early in December a proposed visit to Paris by Hess gave rise to rumours of a Franco-German rapprochement. Allegedly to remove this danger Russia concluded a Protocol with France on 5 December 1934, according to which the two Powers agreed not to enter negotiations which would prejudice the Eastern pact. At Litvinov's instigation Czechoslovakia was to be

[1] Ibid., pp. 377–8 and pp. 382–3. According to the editorial fn. on p. 377 Bülow's memorandum had not been found. There can be no doubt that it was the basis of the memorandum of 8 September, ibid., pp. 396–402.

[2] See Note on Sources, p. 195.

[3] This information evidently reached the Defence Ministry through an informant. See also DGFP (C) Vol. III, pp. 532–3 and pp. 682–5. According to Dodd, Suritz was very protocol in manner, and Hitler at the end of 1934 was secretly negotiating with the Russians. *Diary*, 30 October, and 1 November. See also RIIA, *Survey*, 1934, p. 387.

included in future Franco-Russian agreements; she acceded to the Franco-Russian Protocol on 11 December. It will be seen later how the Franco-Russian-Czech alliance was to cause a radical new departure in German military policy as early as March 1935.[1]

In the meantime French negotiations with Italy and Britain were Hitler's major anxiety. Late in 1934 he was accused of trespassing on an Italian sphere of influence. He had in fact been presented with an opportunity, too good to be missed, for taking advantage of the existing tension and rivalry in the Balkans occasioned by the murder of King Alexander of Yugoslavia on 9 October 1934. The Italians and French, hitherto on different sides in Balkan alignments,[2] were now coming to terms and Laval was in the difficult predicament of having to make his new pro-Italian policy acceptable to the Yugoslavs.

There were, however, obstacles in the way of a Franco-Italian rapprochement. According to Hassell, the French were not ready to make generous concessions in the colonial field, and as late as the middle of November 1934 the prospects for an agreement seemed poor. In the first week of December, Mussolini was reported to have come round, the reason being, according to Hassell, that if he failed to do so the French might, on the occasion of a visit by Hess to Paris, do a deal with the Reich. This, and not Italian designs on Abyssinia, was regarded in Berlin as the final impetus behind the negotiations.[3]

In the course of these Franco-Italian talks the Germans were reported by the Italian Embassy to be behaving more 'correctly' towards Austria,[4] and on 23 November Mussolini, not wishing to be too dependent on the French, made a simultaneous secret approach to the Reich through General Fischer, the German Military Attaché in Rome.[5] Mussolini placed the *Reichswehr*, *vis-à-vis* the party, very prominently in the forefront. He was lavish in his praise. The Attaché for his part tried to convince the Duce that

[1] See Chaps. 7 and 9.

[2] See H. Seton-Watson, *Eastern Europe Between the Wars*, p. 364 and pp. 389–92.

[3] Hassell's despatches of 26 October and a German Foreign Ministry Minute of 31 October, quoting Hassell's despatches of 15 and 23 November, and especially 13 December 1934, described German reactions to the Franco-Italian negotiations. See Note on Sources, p. 195.

[4] An *Abwehr* report of 17 November 1934 on views of the Italian Embassy in Berlin. See Note on Sources, p. 195.

[5] DGFP (C) Vol. III, pp. 669–72, author's translation.

arbitrary acts would not recur, a point deliberately excluded from his official report of the same date, so as not to exasperate relations between the two dictators. He concluded: 'Perhaps we soldiers can still contribute something towards a relaxation of . . . tension.'[1] Mussolini may have been prompted to make his approach because of a very faulty interpretation of internal developments in Germany then current in Italy.[2] At all events, cordial relations between staff officers of the two countries were cultivated, and in December intelligence material was exchanged. Since, moreover, the Franco-Italian negotiations had proceeded none too smoothly, the Rome Agreements of 7 January, concluded between Laval and Mussolini can hardly have seemed menacing.

Not only did the Agreements remove causes of colonial friction but they laid the basis for Franco-Italian co-operation in Europe. A non-intervention convention was proposed between Austria and the remaining Danube States; in the event of a threat to Austrian independence, before this convention was concluded, France and Italy would consult on joint action, and if necessary invite other Powers to join them. The two Governments re-affirmed the Declaration of 11 December 1932 according Germany equality of status, but put on record recognition of the principle that no country was entitled to modify its armament obligations by unilateral action. If Germany took such action, France and Italy would concert together on the attitude to be taken. It is far from certain whether Mussolini and Laval came to a dramatic and secret deal over Abyssinia, as suggested by Dr. Arnold Toynbee,[3] but they were later to urge the British to accede to the major provisions of the Rome Agreements and then, with united voice, to demand Germany's adhesion to a new Disarmament Convention.

It has been seen how on 22 February 1934 Britain had played

---

[1] Ibid.

[2] According to Fischer, the German Military Attaché in Rome, Cerruti, the Italian Ambassador in Berlin, together with Suvich, the Under Secretary for Foreign Affairs, were constantly reporting to Rome that since 30 June Germany was no longer a power factor of such importance. That Hitler reversed his policy in Austria, after a demonstration of Italian military strength on 25 July, may have confirmed this view although no mention was made of it. Fischer drew the conclusion that Mussolini was exploiting German weakness in order to strengthen his hold on the Danube area and that with this object in mind he had opened negotiations with the French. See Note on Sources, p. 195.

[3] RIIA, *Survey*, 1935, Vol. II, p. 29.

the 'honest broker' between Germany and France. The main issue had then been German armaments on land and para-military organizations. France was thus the country most deeply affected. By the autumn of 1934 it was clear that Germany would in future be an air power and therefore a threat to Britain as well as France. The murders of Röhm and Dollfuss, together with the persecution of Church leaders, had also shaken British confidence in Germany. Later a succession of psychological misunderstandings, wrong appointments and ill timing of moves was to lead to the fatal course of appeasement and war.

Von Ribbentrop, Neurath's hated rival, was already, in the summer of 1934, Hitler's regular mentor on all questions concerning Britain. This aspirant to high office had joined the Nazi Party comparatively late. He had first gained prominence early in 1933 as an intermediary between Hitler and Papen, and having established his own *bureau* on foreign affairs in April 1933, sought some dazzling success in diplomacy, a field in which he had virtually no experience. Cold shouldered by the professional diplomats, he was at first only allowed *ad hoc* missions. But he knew how to wait his turn and was a past master in the art of 'hanging around'.[1] Whenever Hitler let drop a chance phrase on some future line of policy Ribbentrop was swift to light upon it, and cling to it tenaciously, with none of Hitler's reservations. Indeed, Ciano was not far off the mark in thinking of Ribbentrop as an 'exaggerated echo' of Hitler himself.[2] No doubt Ribbentrop had often heard Hitler expatiate on one of his favourite themes, an alliance with Britain. Ribbentrop took Hitler's words literally and soon his anglophilia turned into anglomania, only to be disillusioned in later years. On 24 April 1934 he was appointed Commissioner for Disarmament Questions, a post which afforded great possibilities for secret diplomacy of a new style. He visited Britain in May of that year, but straight away fell into a trap.

Before Ribbentrop's arrival the British Government were considering opening Anglo-Belgian staff talks, but since *inter alia* they could have had little practical significance without parallel talks with the French, which would commit Britain too far, they were not taken up. The British also realized that their obligations to

[1] See *Ribbentrop Memoirs*, Seabury, *The Wilhelmstrasse*, and G. and G. F. Craig, *The Diplomats, 1919–1939*, Chap. XIII.
[2] See especially his entry for 14 May 1941.

Belgium under Locarno would lose their *raison d'être* if Germany herself agreed to put her relations with that country on a satisfactory footing. In May they had won Ribbentrop over to this idea, but Bülow made light of his naïvety for adopting it, and it was turned down.[1] British concern over Belgium is not difficult to understand, above all now that Germany was an air power.[2]

Already, in the summer of 1934, squadrons of the later Luftwaffe were, under Göring's command, allowed, much to the irritation of the Defence and Foreign Ministry officials, to parade the skies in open violation of the Treaty. Bülow was particularly anxious, in view of the resentment occasioned by the Röhm purge, that the manufacture of bombers should be suspended and that Germany should adhere to her proposals of 22 February and 16 April, to which the French had not replied.[3] Hitler had no such qualms and he told an Air Force officer early in August: 'When one had written a letter six months ago to which no reply had been given, one could not be expected still to be bound to it.'[4] Yet while Hitler was determined that Germany should possess bombers, he and Blomberg agreed that Germany should still adhere to her own proposals renouncing offensive weapons for the Army.[5]

In the maritime sphere they were even more willing to make concessions. Although Raeder had told Hitler in June 1934 that the Fleet must 'later be developed against England' and that she needed ships equal to those of the King George V Class,[6] German naval armaments were so far behind that there was no point in embarking on an arms race. Perhaps with promptings from Ribbentrop, Hitler therefore told Raeder at some date before 5 November that, while Germany was not prepared to participate in the coming Naval Conference, he would at an appropriate moment

---

[1] See Ribbentrop's memorandum of 10 May. DGFP (C), Vol. II, pp. 805–9. See also ibid., Vol. III, pp. 104–7 and pp. 129–30 and ibid., pp. 148–50.

[2] In the debate on the air estimates of 19 July 1934 Baldwin made his famous declaration: 'Let us never forget this: since the day of the air the old frontiers are gone. When you think of the white cliffs of Dover you think of the Rhine . . .' Quoted from Viscount Templewood, *Nine Troubled Years*, p. 129.

[3] A letter to Neurath of 21 July, DGFP (C), Vol. III, pp. 208–9 and Neurath's reply of 27 July, pp. 257–9.

[4] A conference between German Air Force Officers and a senior Foreign Ministry Official of 10 August, ibid., pp. 306–9.

[5] For Blomberg's statements on German land forces see the Foreign Ministry Memorandum of 14 August, ibid., pp. 316–7.

[6] ND: 189-C.

approach the British on a bilateral Naval Agreement.[1] Hitler may have intended to use Ribbentrop to prepare the ground, for on 12 and 13 November Ribbentrop held discussions of a general kind with Eden and Sir John Simon. Eden claimed that Britain would be prepared for definite negotiations in February or March after the Saar Plebiscite.[2] There can be no doubt that the limitation of naval armaments was to be on the agenda.

In the meantime Anglo-German relations were to suffer a severe shock. On 27 November, the day before the Parliamentary debate on defence, Phipps, the British Ambassador, handed Neurath a note in which his Government expressed concern on intelligence, which was correct, of the new German programme for land forces. The same day Phipps met Hitler. The interview was heated, and it can only be supposed that Hitler's offer for a naval agreement failed to fall on fertile ground.[3] Hoesch, on learning from Simon of the British *démarche*, formed the impression that it was not inspired by 'evil motives' but that it should be given serious thought as the ticklish subject of the new programme had been raised for the first time.[4] On the 28th the parliamentary debate, ably described elsewhere,[5] took place, and the sharp opposition to Baldwin seemed to prove that British opinion was divided on the issue of German rearmament. Baldwin's mild reprimand issued during the debate, turned out to be as useful as vexatious. On 5 December Hoesch reported, that in the opinion of a Conservative Member of Parliament, failure to represent German rearmament as a treaty violation amounted, within certain limits, to recognition of German rearmament itself. Baldwin, Hoesch continued, complained not so much of the fact of German rearmament as of its secrecy, and was disturbed by Germany's refusal to co-operate within the framework of the League. The British Foreign Office, for its part, was aware of a tendency in certain quarters to draw the conclusion from the debate that Britain no longer considered the clauses of Part V of the Treaty of Versailles to be binding. On 17 December Phipps re-

---

[1] A memorandum by Bülow DGFP (C), Vol. III, p. 573.

[2] Ibid., pp. 638–41.

[3] Ibid., pp. 676–8. According to Phipps, Hitler 'jumped up, ran about the room, waved his arms . . .', Dodd, *Diary*, 30 November.

[4] DGFP (C), pp. 680–2.

[5] Churchill, *The Gathering Storm*, pp. 93–4, describes his altercation with Baldwin during the debate. Templewood, op. cit., pp. 129–30, incorrectly gives 18 instead of 28 November as the date of the debate.

minded Neurath that this was, of course, not the case. The British were thus irritated by illegal German rearmament but so far had not pledged themselves to Laval.[1]

Meanwhile the date of the Saar Plebiscite was drawing near. Towards the end of 1934 Britain had been invited by both Germany and France to send a contingent of troops to supervise the Plebiscite. She acted as arbiter, not as an ally. Hence the illusion was maintained that the Treaty of Locarno was a reality.

The results of the Saar Plebiscite,[2] overwhelmingly in favour of Germany, were announced on 15 January, and the French were particularly active immediately afterwards in putting diplomatic pressure on Germany to accept new disarmament obligations. On the 16th the Germans were invited to define their attitude to the proposed Danubian Pact, as provided for by the Rome Agreements. The French delivered their reply to the German memorandum of 10 September, declining to negotiate on the Eastern Pact. Neurath, in instructions of the 17th to the leading German missions abroad, asserted that there was a desire on all sides 'to entangle Germany in disarmament negotiations', and that the final aims of the other great Powers was 'to inveigle Germany back into the League of Nations'. There could thus be no revival of either the British and Italian proposals of 1934, or of the proposals for the limitation of armaments, which the German Government itself had recommended to Eden early in 1934. Neurath finally strongly insisted that there should be no disclosure of the actual level of German armaments.[3]

Hitler could not refuse to negotiate on French plans, which had at least some Italian and British backing. Better to prove, above all to the British, that realism required them to accept the naked fact of a resurgent Germany and tempt them by a positive proposal of his own. Soon after the Saar plebiscite a welcome opportunity presented itself to discuss Germany's case with two distinguished visitors. Surprisingly the visits were not the fruit of Ribbentrop's recent negotiations in London of the previous November but of feelers put out by *Wilhelmstrasse*. In a letter to Meissner, Hitler's state secretary, of 10 January Bülow made a strong plea that a request of Lord Allen of Hurtwood to meet Hitler should be granted.

[1] See Note on Sources, p. 195.
[2] RIIA, *Survey*, 1935, Vol. I, pp. 618–9.
[3] DGFP (C), Vol. III, pp. 838–42.

There were strong political reasons in favour of it. Allen was a National Labour peer and a friend of MacDonald and, since the Labour Party as a whole was hostile to Germany, and might win the next general election, the chance of meeting a 'loyal and unprejudiced man' from their ranks should be taken.[1] The second visitor, the Marquess of Lothian, had served on Lloyd George's private staff during the Paris Peace Conference, but his views towards the Treaty and Germany had since undergone a fairly drastic change. He was described by Hoesch, in a despatch of the 17th, as a 'left wing Liberal' and 'very influential—without doubt . . . the most important non-official Englishman who hitherto has requested an audience with the Reich Chancellor' and Hoesch 'urgently' recommended that he should be received personally by Hitler.[2]

Hitler met Lord Allen in a strictly confidential manner on the 25th. Allen explained how he had come to Germany in order to convey, in a purely unofficial capacity, a message of goodwill from the Prime Minister.[3] Allen described a 'strong change of opinion in England, favourable to Germany'. The recent attempts, by which he could only have meant the Rome Agreements, to encircle Germany 'give rise to anxiety. An understanding between England and Germany was therefore particularly important.' With feigned innocence Hitler in reply spoke of Germany's need for 40 to 50 years' peace. He described how Germany's security had been jeopardized by the Franco-Russian alliance. Russia was, he said, now by far the greatest power factor in the whole of Europe. 'Germany is ready at any time to conclude an armaments agreement with England. In the maritime sphere she has no ambition to enter into competition. . . .' She was therefore prepared to limit her naval armaments to 35 per cent of the British. He proposed negotiations whereby an armaments agreement between Britain and Germany should first be reached, for the limitation of weapons and the prevention of a general arms race. He thought that Italy, and later France, would accede to it. Lord Allen replied that the British Government 'would react advantageously' if the Reich Chancellor made a declaration in which he stated how

---

[1] DGFP (C), Vol. III, pp. 798–9. The contact with Lord Allen had been nursed since January 1934. (He was in fact expelled from the Labour Party in 1931 and raised to the peerage in 1932.)

[2] DGFP (C), Vol. III, pp. 798–9 and pp. 837–8 (author's translation).

[3] Ibid., pp. 873–6 (author's translation).

Germany would behave after she were assured equality of status. This was not to Hitler's liking. He replied that Part V of the Treaty of Versailles must first be abrogated, and that Germany would never agree to a substitute for it, imposing new conditions. But if he were convinced that this was not the aim he was prepared to give the desired undertaking. On 29 January Hitler conferred with Lord Lothian, and probably covered much the same ground.[1]

How far Hitler's subsequent attitude was influenced by his talks with Lords Allen and Lothian cannot be determined. He relished diplomacy conducted outside officially recognized channels. His meetings with private citizens are for this reason alone more important than they seem. Allen's statements were certainly not in accord with the official attitude of the Foreign Office. Indeed the British were negotiating behind the backs of the French on a naval agreement months before Simon's visit to Berlin. The Anglo-French communiqué issued on 2 February must have seemed empty of meaning.

According to the communiqué, Britain associated herself with the general aim of the Rome Agreements. She expressed her readiness to consult with other Powers if Austria's independence were threatened. Germany was to be encouraged to participate in reciprocal agreements for assistance in the event of air attacks. This extension of Locarno, originated by the French, was commended by Simon in a broadcast of 3 February: it would not merely require Britain to act as guarantor but would also provide her with the benefit of a guarantee.[2] The German Government accepted with alacrity that part of the communiqué relating to the air pact, but tried to sever it from the rest of the proposals. But the subjects for discussion had to be accepted as an 'integral and indivisible whole'. Hitler was in an awkward dilemma: to refuse to negotiate would make him appear to be in the wrong; to take part in negotiations, the aim of which was to tie him down, was dangerous. Nevertheless on 22 February he agreed to accept the conditions and to meet Simon on 8 and 9 March. But he was soon to catch a 'diplomatic cold'. On 4 March a British White Paper on

---

[1] The next day Lothian met Hess, Blomberg, Ribbentrop and Dr. Albrecht Haushofer and won von Hess's approval for a visit by Sir John Simon to Berlin. Ribbentrop re-echoing Hitler to Allen stated that an agreement should be concluded between the Germans and British, the two sane races in Europe (a phrase not used by Hitler), ibid, fn. on p. 338 and pp. 885–7. See also RIIA, *Survey*, 1935, Vol. I, p. 129. [2] RIIA, *Survey*, 1935, Vol. I, pp. 122–4.

Defence, emphasizing the possible dangers of German armaments, was published. Extension of military service from one year to two came up for discussion at about the same time in France.[1] Hitler reacted swiftly. On 5 March he postponed the date of the visit of Simon and Eden, and on the 9th the German Air Force was declared officially to be in existence. A greater surprise was to follow. Hossbach, Hitler's *Wehrmacht* Adjutant, was summoned to Munich on 13 March where he was informed the next day of Hitler's decision to re-introduce conscription and to declare it publicly just after the law had been passed for extending military service in France. It had not been planned to reintroduce conscription before October 1935 and the figure of 36 divisions for the future strength of the German Army was, according to Hossbach, decided by Hitler on the spur of the moment, subject to the approval of Blomberg and Fritsch. Hitler's decision was discussed at a Cabinet Meeting of the 15th where all present, with the exception of Blomberg, who felt nervous because of reactions abroad, expressed their approval. Blomberg's apprehensions were not shared by Neurath and were soon overcome. The next day the decision was made public.[2]

Hossbach's evidence leaves the impression that Hitler's staff were opposed neither to the timing of the move nor to the scope of the future military programme, and it seems to contradict a view put forward by General von Manstein after the war that the General Staff would have preferred to carry on with the programme of 21 divisions.[3]

There was some justification for the reintroduction of conscription. Although extension of service in the French Army could not, owing to the decline of the birth rate during the war, have added appreciably to its numbers, it could (a fact omitted by Churchill)[4] have improved its quality. Hitler's reasons were also political. It has been seen how, after the Saar Plebiscite,[5] it was no longer his aim to conceal, but to exaggerate, German military strength. This

[1] RIIA, *Survey*, 1935, Vol. 1, pp. 132–4 and p. 137. For further material see also DGFP (C), Vol. III, under Great Britain.

[2] Hossbach, pp. 94–6 and Meinck, op. cit., pp. 97–8.

[3] IMT, Vol. XX, p. 603. Manstein stated that since he was not Deputy Chief of General Staff in March 1935 he was not in a good position to know facts on rearmament. Manstein was, however, correct in stating, in general terms, that the General Staff were opposed to too rapid military expansion.

[4] *The Second World War*, Vol. I., 'The Gathering Storm', pp. 113–4.

[5] See p. 46.

is confirmed by an order to the Armed Forces of 18 March, in which Blomberg stated that the government's policy was 'to produce in our neighbours the impression of a strong armed force which, even in difficult circumstances, is thoroughly equal to the defence of the Reich. . . .' Hence military authorities were allowed to make the rather dubious claim that there were already more than 21 divisions.[1]

At the end of March Hitler scored a further noteworthy success in creating the impression that Germany was stronger than she really was. The reintroduction of conscription did not deter Simon and Eden from making their promised visit. In an interview with Hitler on 25–26 March they were 'electrified' by the new revelation, which was certainly untrue, that Germany had attained air parity with Britain.[2] Hitler was not put out by the fact that Eden and Simon were shortly to visit other European capitals, and to confer with their French and Italian colleagues at Stresa, and the shocks which he administered are vividly portrayed in Neurath's instructions of 4 April. 'Simon's and Eden's faces became perceptibly longer', Neurath claimed, 'when we gave them figures of our peacetime army, and openly informed them that our Air Force had already achieved parity with theirs.' Yet his impression was that they had 'not only been extraordinarily and agreeably surprised by the personality of the Führer—and this goes particularly for Simon who was in Berlin for the first time—but have taken home with them at least some understanding of the German problem'. It had also been agreed at the meeting that Hitler should despatch a Mission to London for a Naval Agreement.[3] Hitler had virtually torn up the Treaty of Versailles but was on good terms with at least one of its signatories.

---

[1] DGFP (C), Vol. III, pp. 1043–80. On 2 May 1935 Göring told foreign journalists that the German Army already comprised twenty-seven divisions. Telford Taylor, *Sword and Swastika*, p. 107.

[2] See also RIIA, *Survey*, 1935, Vol. I, pp. 147–9 and *A History of the RAF*, Vol. I, pp. 12–3, HMSO, 1953.

[3] For a further account of the meeting see also Schmidt, *Hitler's Interpreter*. The interview left a lasting impression on Hitler. In November 1936 he told Dr. Schmidt, the Austrian State Secretary, 'The British mentality is a sober one and can be influenced by force only. I experienced this myself when I conferred with Sir Simon [*sic*] here in Berlin. Only when I assured him that the German Air Force had reached the strength of that of the English were we able to express ourselves with mutual respect: thus our Naval Agreement came into being. . . .' Hitler evidently believed, in common with certain German statesmen before 1914, that Britain could only be bludgeoned into co-operation. DGFP (D), Vol. I, p. 342.

CHAPTER 7

A Diplomatic Revolution

(March–December 1935)

After Hitler had dealt his well-aimed blow against Versailles, what would happen to Locarno? Was it to share the same fate, or was it now an anachronism which could privily be laid aside and forgotten? Freed from the encumbrances of Versailles, Locarno, instead of affording Germany a measure of protection could, if it were to prove effective at all, be used only to hold her in check, and Hitler looked forward to the triumphant day when, to the sound of trumpet and drums, he could order German troops across the Rhine. In February 1936 he told Hassell that he had previously considered 1937 as the most favourable date to put his decision into effect.[1] But Hitler never allowed himself to be tied down by dates—better to take advantage of a momentary division among Germany's prospective opponents than to wait and risk being forestalled. Yet precisely because Hitler himself, and others, knew that the re-occupation of the Rhineland was the next logical step it was the most dangerous thing he could attempt, and for some months after 16 March 1935 Locarno had to be observed more, not less, strictly. As late as 26 June Jodl reminded members of the Working Committee of the National Defence Council that in the Rhineland, as distinct from the rest of the Reich, 'concealment matters more than results [*Deckung geht vor Wirkung*]'.[2]

---

[1] See p. 71.

[2] See Note on Sources, p. 195. Jodl alluded to Hitler's speech of 21 May (see p. 62) and to the German reply to a French *aide memoire* of 17 June 1935, in which it was claimed that the authorities of the Reich were not responsible for raising, equipping and arming formations in the Rhineland. Since international complications were at all costs to be avoided, Jodl stated that only absolutely essential military preparations were to be undertaken in the Demilitarized Zone. They were not to be too visible to the naked eye, for Jodl stressed that the intention to put them into force was to be kept secret in the Rhineland as well as in the rest of the Reich. See also IMT, Vol. IX, pp. 507–11 and Keitel's statement on the danger of German infiltration into the Rhineland to the National Defence Council on 6 December 1936 (ND: 406-EC).

However, the legal complications of repudiating one treaty, while observing the other, were considerable, for if conscription were forbidden by the Treaty of Versailles in all provinces of the Reich, how could it be additionally illegal in other provinces? Since Article 173 of Part V applied to the whole Reich, the authors of the Treaty of Versailles did not need to reincorporate its terms into those clauses (42 and 43), exclusively concerned with the Rhineland, which were later inscribed into the Treaty of Locarno. It is evident from two unpublished Defence Ministry Directives of 14 and 18 March that the prohibition of 'material preparations for mobilization in the Rhineland' included the ban under Article 173 on conscription, an infringement of which could provide the French with 'a welcome pretext' for intervention.

The German General Staff had real cause for anxiety. Towards the end of March the French were reported to have started concentrating troops near their eastern frontier; these concentrations were complete in May. But while Hitler had a plan for making ready ten divisions to advance into the Rhineland should the French attack,[1] French preponderance was assured. Hitler therefore had no alternative but to submit to *force majeure* and wait.

The danger was not only acute in the West. Locarno may at one time have been of additional value to Germany in that it left open the possibility of revision of her eastern frontiers which Britain had refused to guarantee. What would happen, German international lawyers were later to argue, if another Power stepped in and agreed, where Britain had defaulted, to uphold some of these frontiers? It is more than a coincidence that towards the end of March 1935 Russia should have agreed to enter fully into the French system of alliances. It has been seen how at the end of 1934, the Defence Ministry showed little concern over the new pro-French line adopted in Moscow, and even after the signature of the Franco-Russian Protocol of 4 December 1934 it was thought that Litvinov was promoting the rapprochement for his own personal ends. A speech by Molotov of 28 January 1935 directed against the Western Powers was interpreted as a setback to Litvinov.[2] After the visits of Simon and Eden to the Continent, however, the Russian Government showed concern lest the project for an Eastern Pact should not be given due prominence. At this

---

[1] See Note on Sources, p. 195.
[2] See also Hilger, *The Incompatible Allies*, pp. 268–9.

stage while Russia was anxious to speed up negotiations, France was reluctant to commit herself for fear of being embroiled in war outside Europe. On 9 April, it was announced that the two Governments had agreed in principle to a convention, and that an agreement between Russia and Czechoslovakia should also be negotiated.[1] The Franco-Russian Treaty was signed on 2 May. It was followed by a supplementary Russo-Czech Treaty on the 16th, which was ratified on 9 June.[2]

France had now a new security system which more than compensated her for the loss of Poland; French distrust of Russia became evident only before ratification at a later date. The Treaty had immediate repercussions in Germany. A possible preventive war against Czechoslovakia came up for serious discussion at the end of March and early in May 1935 and will be discussed later.[3] At an internal conference of Foreign Ministry officials on 4 May Gaus, the legal expert, inveighed against the Franco-Russian alliance; he quoted a recent statement by Sir John Simon in the Commons, that in the event of a conflict arising from it, Britain would not consider herself obliged to support Germany under Locarno.[4]

In the spring of 1935 the success of French encirclement of Germany depended mainly on Britain. Whereas Ramsay MacDonald was not prepared to give specific pledges on the question of the Rhineland and Austria he recognized that a united front had, at least outwardly, to be shown. On 11 April he, together with Sir John Simon, Laval, Flandin and Mussolini, met at Stresa where they conferred on Germany's recent treaty violations and on their own future policy. When the Conference opened it was already known that France would conclude a treaty of alliance with Russia. But Hitler could not yet afford to react to it in a defiant manner. His offers, he declared on the 11th, of non-aggression pacts with Germany's neighbours still stood, despite the Franco-Russian alliance.

[1] RIIA, *Survey, 1935*, Vol. I, pp. 76–9, and also Beloff, op. cit., vol. I, Chap. XII.

[2] RIIA, *Docs, 1935*, Vol. I, pp. 138–40. This meant that Russia would only be obliged to go to the aid of Czechoslovakia if France first fulfilled her obligations under the treaty of 1925, and that Czechoslovakia must render aid to Russia if France did so first under the treaty of 2 May 1935 which was not yet ratified.

[3] See Chap. 9.

[4] See Note on Sources, p. 195. Gaus also said that Germany should do all in her power to cultivate good relations with Poland.

Hitler's *beau geste* was no doubt intended to strengthen British objections to assuming new commitments. It was successful. During the discussions MacDonald showed himself even less willing than Mussolini to fall in with French wishes. At his instigation, a French draft resolution for the League on measures to be put into force against Germany was considerably whittled down. In the final communiqué, all three Powers were agreed on the French resolution reprimanding Germany, the desirability of an Eastern pact, the maintenance of the independence of Austria, further negotiations for an air pact. They put on record that the German method of unilateral treaty repudiation 'had undermined public confidence in the security of a peaceful order'. Anglo-Italian obligations under Locarno were reaffirmed and the two Governments declared that they would faithfully fulfil them. At an extraordinary session of the Council of the League on 15–17 April, the French resolution, agreed on at Stresa, was carried by 13 votes out of a possible 15, with Germany unrepresented and Denmark abstaining.

In Germany the weakness of these Stresa resolutions were appreciated but in general underestimated. In a Defence Ministry survey for the end of April, it was correctly realized that the most important problems were left over for future negotiations. The fact that sanctions were not agreed to, but were to be dealt with by the Council of the League, was regarded with particular satisfaction. It was claimed that owing to Britain's efforts at mediation the ring round Germany was not completely closed.[1]

Towards the end of May, as a result both of the extension of Soviet commitments and of Stresa, Hitler had to redefine his attitude to Locarno. To insist too vehemently on its incompatibility with the Franco-Russian Pact was to warn the world that Germany would soon consider herself free from her obligations in the Rhineland. A markedly obdurate attitude might also perpetuate Germany's isolation and arrest those forces of paralysis which were to destroy the unity of her opponents. On the other hand, if Germany were to promise to observe the Treaty of Locarno unconditionally in spite of the Franco-Russian Treaty, no legitimate pretext could be found for a future attempt to remilitarize the Rhineland. Hitler had to promise to behave correctly and yet leave open a loop-hole

[1] See Note on Sources, p. 195.

for the future. He manoeuvred cunningly. In his speech of 21 May[1]
he appeased Italian sentiment by declaring that Germany neither
intended nor wished to interfere in the internal affairs of Austria
nor to effect an *Anschluss*. Germany's eastern neighbours, with
the exception of Lithuania, were given similar assurances. But also
on the 21st Hitler made what looked like an innocuous reservation.
Germany would continue to observe the Treaty of Locarno, provided that other Powers were prepared to do so. In this connection
he believed that an 'element of legal insecurity' had crept into
Locarno because of the Franco-Russian alliance.

Hitler's objections to the Franco-Russian Pact were given in
greater detail in a memorandum forwarded to the other Locarno
powers on 25 May.[2] In it no mention was made of the Russian
guarantee of Czechoslovakia,[3] the key to an understanding of
Hitler's real objections.

Even more important than Hitler's attacks on the Franco-
Russian Treaty were his attempts to divide the Stresa Powers from
each other. The Stresa front had all the weakness of a purely defensive position. Each link had to be guarded with vigilance and
without interruption: careful exploitation of even momentary
disunity might endanger the whole delicate structure. Yet the collapse of Stresa was due to extraneous events no less than to inherent
weakness. After Hitler's speech of 21 May it received two shocks
from which it never recovered: the Anglo-German Naval Agreement of 18 June and the crisis over Abyssinia. In June Ribbentrop
arrived in London, and on the 18th the German and British
Governments exchanged notes on naval construction. Germany
was permitted to possess a fleet equal to 35 per cent of the British.
While not exceeding the ratio of this total, she was allowed to
possess a submarine tonnage equal to that of the British Commonwealth. As a counter-concession she agreed not to exceed 45 per
cent of the Commonwealth strength in submarines without giving
the United Kingdom previous notice.[4]

---

[1] Baynes, *Hitler's Speeches*, Vol. II, pp. 1218–47.

[2] For the text, see RIIA, 1935, *Docs.* Vol. I, pp. 264–7. For a convenient
account of the legal arguments see Beloff, op. cit., Vol. I, pp. 158–9.

[3] See a conversation between Bülow and Dodd, the American Ambassador,
of 16 April (Dodd's *Diary*). Bülow raised strong objections to a possible
Russo-Czech Treaty. For a general discussion on Locarno and the Rhineland see
Baubach, *Der Einmarsch deutscher Truppen in die entmilitarisierte Zone am Rhine.*

[4] Sir Samuel Hoare (Viscount Templewood), then Foreign Secretary, has
attempted to justify the Agreement, *Ten Troubled Years*, Chap. X. Eden's

The Naval Agreement was resented in Italy and violently attacked in France. It had the effect of making Laval, who was informed that negotiations were in progress, but who had not given them official sanction, all the more dependent on Italy. Mussolini therefore reaffirmed his adhesion to the Stresa resolutions on 15 June 1935.[1]

The Abyssinian crisis, which was coming to a head that summer, need not be discussed in any detail here. Germany's attitude was one of watchful but benevolent neutrality. On 2 October, the day before the invasion, Mussolini spoke to Hassell.[2] He expressed his determination to accomplish his venture at all costs and he was convinced that the aim of British policy was to vanquish his country. In the course of the conversation Hassell made a significant comment. The Führer was vehemently anxious that Fascism should survive, but he stressed the fact that 'the time for the struggle between the *static* and the dynamic nations was by a long way premature'. Even at this stage Hitler evidently had a vision of the two regimes locked in a common destiny. But the dominant note in Hitler's advice to Mussolini was still one of caution. This is to be explained, not only by the comparatively little progress in German rearmament, but by Hitler's assessment of Italy's military prospects.

Before the campaign German Military Intelligence estimated that fighting would last three years. Despite the change in command there was no reason for several months to reverse this unfavourable estimate, particularly since Italy was under strong pressure from Britain. While Italy's economic weaknesses were also fully recognized, her essential needs could be covered from alternative markets, even if Britain and the USA both cut exports

claim to Léger, the French Under-Secretary for Foreign Affairs, made shortly afterwards, that the Treaty circumscribed Germany's naval power, ibid., pp. 144–5, is at complete variance with Admiral Raeder's contemporary evidence. In his view, given in an address to his subordinates on 2 August 1935, naval construction for a decade could now be carried out within a 'substantially larger framework'. The agreement 'will give us the possibility to create a modern fleet developed according to a plan and adjusted to Germany's maritime needs'. Germany's Fleet had still to measure up against that of France with whom she was expected to attain parity in 1942. See Note on Sources, p.195. See also ND: Raeder 12 and Raeder 13. Raeder describes the Agreement also in *Mein Leben*, Vol. II, Chaps. I and II.

[1] RIIA, *Survey*, 1935, Vol. I, pp. 189–91. See also A. J. P. Taylor, *The Origins of the Second World War*, Chap. V.

[2] See Note on Sources, p. 195. See also RIIA, *Survey*, 1935, Vol. II, p. 183.

to her. Since economic sanctions were not likely to deter Mussolini, it was questionable whether they would be applied. The imposition of military sanctions seemed even less likely, and it was correctly predicted in Berlin that the League would 'content itself with a formal protest'.[1]

Although an open conflict seemed unlikely, Britain was concentrating her forces in September for the defence of her vital interests in the eastern Mediterranean.[2] She could not therefore in the immediate future combine with France over European issues. It was believed that she was merely using the League for the promotion of her own ends, and the part played by public opinion in forcing the Government to raise its standard at Geneva and rally the smaller Powers around it was not sufficiently recognized. The alternating course of British policy during the early stages of the war in adopting at one moment a firm line against Italy, at the next in associating herself with France in schemes for a compromise, continued. The net result was the imposition of 'soft' sanctions on 18 November but failure to make them effective by including oil. It will be seen how later the question of extending sanctions to oil was to be intermittently raised and postponed.

A novel situation affecting Germany had, however, come about in that British statesmen had to ask the French, and their allies, for assistance against a potential aggressor. The French, on whom the British were so dependent for support, could thus indulge in some hard bargaining. Anglo-French negotiations opened in September, and the French asked, but were given no satisfactory answer, whether they could rely on British support in the event of an attack by Germany, or if the Franco-Russian Pact came into operation. The negotiations thus provided Hitler with further evidence that the Treaty of Locarno was being tilted against Germany, and at the turn of the year they were even more vehemently attacked in the German Press than the Franco-Russian Treaty itself.[3]

[1] See Note on Sources, p. 195.
[2] RIIA, *Survey*, 1935, Vol. II, pp. 212–39 and pp. 252–4. In September Britain was promised support by Greece, Yugoslavia and Turkey. These Powers had consulted with Roumania and Czechoslovakia, RIIA, *Survey*, *1935*, Vol. II., pp. 267–8.
[3] RIIA, *Survey*, *1935*, Vol. II, pp. 257–67. Anglo-French discussions were surveyed in a German War Ministry report of 25 November and in a report submitted by Stülpnagel to Fritsch of 15 November 1935. See Note on Sources p. 195. For the attitude of the German Press see RIIA, *Survey*, *1936*, p. 522.

This Treaty, though still a matter of some concern,[1] had lost much of its sting. It had not yet been ratified, and if it were to prove effective, permission had first to be obtained from Poland and Roumania, for the transit of Russian forces to Czechoslovakia. In this the French were not successful, and for a time the Russians sought a rapprochement with Berlin.[2] The French in failing to put teeth into their alliance with Russia before ratification were soon to play into Hitler's hands. On 21 November François-Poncet informed Hitler that the Treaty would soon be debated in the French Parliament. On the 26th he repeated a previous warning to his own Government that Hitler might use ratification as a pretext for re-militarizing the Rhineland, and that steps should be taken to forestall him. Laval refused to heed his Ambassador's advice.[3] In order to ward off the danger he made a new and abortive effort to reconcile Britain with Italy and so restore the Stresa front.

On 7–8 December in negotiations with Sir Samuel Hoare, one of many plans for the partition of Abyssinia was accepted. After premature publication, the plan, amid public uproar, was disowned on the 18th, and Hoare forced to resign.[4] The momentous consequences of the miscarriage of the plan were not foreseen in Germany. Even after 18 December the German Foreign Ministry persisted in its belief that Britain would in future co-operate more closely with France against Germany. No predictions were made of a change in Mussolini's attitude to Germany which, combined with irresolution on the part of Britain, was to afford her within a few months a chance of repudiating Locarno.

---

[1] According to Neurath under cross-examination at the Nuremberg trials, German intelligence staffs learnt early in 1936 that an invasion of Germany was planned under the Franco-Russian Czech Treaty, Meinck, op. cit. p. 149.

[2] War Ministry Surveys of 25 and 29 November 1935. See Note on Sources, p. 195.

[3] *Souvenirs*, p. 248.

[4] Templewood, op. cit. Chap. XI.

CHAPTER 8

The Remilitarization of the Rhineland

(March 1936)

On 19 December, when Mussolini was hard pressed both militarily and politically, it was reported from Rome that the leading Italian newspapers were again concerned with Italy's relations with Germany and Germany's position in Europe. This news was deemed important enough to be brought to the Führer's attention.[1] Early in the following month there were fresh indications that Mussolini was seeking a rapprochement, and Attolico, the Italian Ambassador, was reported to be using his influence in this direction. On 6 January Mussolini conferred with Hassell, who had evidently been instructed to report to Berlin. Mussolini considered the Hoare-Laval Plan to be dead and stated that Italy's relations with Britain had so radically worsened that they could improve only after a considerable lapse of time. He went on to say that, instead of drawing closer to the Little Entente, Austria should have a foreign policy parallel to that of Germany. Italy would have no objection if Austria were to become a 'German satellite'. On being asked to do so by Hassell, Mussolini confirmed this important statement. The Duce also remarked that greater Anglo-French solidarity could be expected in the future; that Franco-Italian talks on air co-operation would yield nothing unless there was a political agreement; and that Stresa was 'dead'. He believed that a Five Power Directorate of Europe, which should include Poland, was possible.

On 17 January Hassell visited Germany and held two important

---

[1] The text of many of the documents used in this chapter has been published, together with a commentary by E. M. Robertson in *Vierteljahrshefte für Zeitgeschichte* (April 1962). Besides Hassell's official memoranda he had kept purely private notes, which are indispensable for an understanding of the internal intrigues in Berlin. His family have kindly placed these notes at the disposal of the Institut für Zeitgeschichte and they have appeared in the publication described above. Many of the official documents for this chapter are now to be found in DGFP (C), Vol. IV.

discussions, the first with Attolico, the second with Hitler. Hassell did not conceal his mistrust from Attolico to whom he observed that Germany had three fears: that (a) Italy would return to Stresa; (b) she would encourage Vienna to pursue an anti-German policy; (c) Italy's military prospects seemed far from promising. Attolico hotly refuted these charges and claimed that not only France, but also Britain, desired Italy's return to Stresa. To prove this he showed Hassell a report from Grandi according to which the aims of British policy were: the conclusion of a permanent, not an *ad hoc*, treaty with France[1]; the restoration of Stresa, and a rapid conclusion of the Abyssinian War. Finally, Attolico declared that Badoglio would attack at the end of March. Attolico evidently tried to create the impression that Italy was in no way dependent on German good will and that it was open to her to come to terms with Britain. If she ignored Italy, Germany might thus be completely isolated. Yet he expressed one apprehension. Should Italy be compelled to leave the League of Nations she would find it extremely awkward if Germany simultaneously offered to rejoin it.

Hassell drew his own conclusions both from this interview and from his earlier one with Mussolini. He did not believe that Mussolini's recent statement on Austria was a subtle Machiavellian stratagem designed to embroil Germany in a dispute over Austria, for Attolico emphatically reminded him that Austria's integrity must be respected. Hassell then described the interview to the Führer. Having summoned Neurath Hitler stated that Germany was to all intents and purposes isolated. She had no trustworthy friends: Poland was unreliable, and Italy in a difficult predicament. This isolation would become all the more serious and take on a moral complexion if Fascism collapsed. Since Italy must not be weakened, the quarrel of 1934 should be patched up. German benevolent neutrality was thus to be continued. Hassell was instructed to inform Mussolini that the Führer was interested in his statement on Austria. During the interview Hitler also told Hassell that Germany had no intention of re-entering the League.

Hitler's reply to Mussolini's proposal of 6 January was a cautious request for reconciliation, and it certainly does not seem that he already foresaw how Italy's growing quarrel with Britain would

---

[1] Attolico also showed Neurath a despatch from Grandi to this effect early in February.

provide him with an opportunity to repudiate Locarno. Hassell too recognized that Mussolini's overtures should be treated with reserve. On his return to Rome, he found the Duce less outspoken on the anti-Italian tendency of British policy than at the previous interview.[1] Hassell later contended that since Italy was losing ground in Austria it might be supposed that she was making Germany a present of something which she no longer possessed. But with great realism he recalled how Mussolini was fully aware that it was difficult to get anything from Germany. He recommended that Germany should indeed take advantage of Mussolini's more favourable attitude but beware lest Italy use the threat of a rapprochement with Germany to bring pressure to bear on France. Failure of a German-Austrian agreement might also be used by Italy as a pretext for linking Austria to the Little Entente. Hassell expressed his conviction that there should be no illusions: that if she were not careful Germany might find herself a pawn in Mussolini's game.[2] Hassell's warnings are understandable. Schuschnigg had visited Prague on 16–17 January and was seeking the friendship of both the Little Entente and Italy.[3] Mussolini could not dispose as he pleased of Austria, Italy's protégé. It was open to him to encourage good relations between her and Germany's opponents.

It is not surprising that after Mussolini's meeting with Hassell the *Wilhelmstrasse* followed with keen interest the activities of two competing groups at the Duce's court. On the one hand it was feared that Suvich, the Under Secretary for Foreign Affairs, and the old guard of the *Palazzo Chigi* still thought in terms of a pro-French policy.[4] In this respect Cerruti, the Italian Ambassador in Paris, was the *bête noire*. He had previously been accredited to Berlin and now did not conceal his dislike of that capital. In opposition were the *novi genti*, among whom Ciano was the most notable. In Hassell's opinion Ciano, who was already coveting Suvich's post, was a strong advocate of a forward policy. Attolico,

---

[1] On 31 January 1936 Hassell referred to an earlier despatch of 22 January in which he may have described the second interview in greater detail.

[2] This despatch of 6 February was brought to the attention of the Führer.

[3] Allegedly his object was not merely to improve economic relations between the Danubian States but to draw them closer to the League and Franco-Russian system of alliances. See also RIIA, *Survey, 1935*, pp. 409–11.

[4] The two tendencies in Italian policy were described to Hassell by Attolico on 19 February. Neurath was very suspicious of Suvich.

Ciano's protégé, formerly Ambassador in Moscow, had, in September, taken over Cerruti's post in Berlin.[1] No fundamental purge of the Italian Foreign Office was expected until after the Abyssinian war: Mussolini's intentions were hence even more unpredictable than usual, and further approaches to him were hazardous. But if Mussolini were successful in Abyssinia, and defied the extension of sanctions, Hitler could reply to ratification of the Franco-Russian Treaty in an equally defiant manner and march into the Rhineland. The possibility was open to Britain and France therefore to anticipate any 'parallel action'.

Late in December and early in January the German Press attacked Anglo-French staff talks.[2] On 1 January François-Poncet, suspecting that these attacks were intended to prepare the way for the reoccupation of the Rhineland, complained to Hitler but was assured that the question of Locarno would not be raised. On the 10th he reproached Bülow sharply and warned him that the occupation of the Rhineland would have serious consequences.[3] In the middle of the month, when there was considerable speculation over this possibility, Laval announced that the Treaty with Russia would come up for discussion in the French Parliament. This gave new impetus to the campaign against the Treaty in the German Press, which meant that Britain's interpretation of her obligations under Locarno was now of fundamental importance.

It has been seen how a distinction had been drawn in the Treaty between a *flagrant* and a *qualified* violation.[4] The latter would bring into play the cumbrous machinery of the League of Nations. It was nevertheless open to the guarantors to define their obligations in any given situation in advance. Britain could either reinforce her ties with France and her allies, or concentrate on extending those provisions which were intended to safeguard the interests of all parties equally. The service staffs, including the Air Force, were consulted early in February on the importance of the demilitarization of the Rhineland and, with some reservations from the Army, did not consider it a 'vital British interest'. The British Government therefore were not prepared to give the French any additional assurance, but instead persisted in the idea of supplementing Locarno with an Air Pact. Their proposal was discussed

(Wolfers)

---

[1] See also Dodd's references to Attolico, *Diary*, 12 September 1934 and 19 September 1935.　　[2] RIIA, *Survey*, *1936*, p. 252.
[3] *Souvenirs*, p. 249.　　[4] See p. 25 and p. 58.

by Phipps and Hitler on 13 December and by Neurath and Eden in London later in January but yielded no results.[1]

Britain, therefore, despite rumours of a rapprochement with Russia,[2] remained unwilling to define either her attitude to Locarno or to the French system of alliances. On 12 February, the day after the Franco-Russian Pact was submitted to the French Chamber of Deputies, Eden was asked in the Commons to define Britain's obligations. He replied that they were specified in the Treaty of Locarno itself. This purely legalistic approach certainly created the impression in Hitler's mind that Britain was temporizing momentarily, and that once the Abyssinian question was cleared up she would 'set in motion the machinery of the League against Germany'.[3] Hence everything depended on Mussolini's resolve and capacity to resist. How would he react to an extension of sanctions? How would an extension of sanctions affect his attitude to Locarno?

The two questions were connected. Already on 25 January Mussolini published an article in the *Popolo d'Italia*, in which he claimed that Anglo-French staff talks upset the equilibrium of Locarno and might have fatal consequences for that system. This however was merely one symptom among others for Stresa still found its advocates in Italy.[4] Much depended on the course of the war in Abyssinia.

The German War Ministry estimated that oil sanctions could prove effective only after several months. It was believed that in view of Italy's improved military prospects, which were already apparent by the middle of February, those parties in favour of sanctions, under the leadership of Eden, were pressing to have them imposed. A decision would have to be reached soon, and throughout February the committee of experts appointed by the League studied the technical aspect of the entire question and

[1] RIIA, *Survey, 1935*, Vol. I, pp. 200–2. Neurath visited London on the occasion of George V's funeral.

[2] Early in January Potemkin, the Russian Ambassador in Paris, told some of his colleagues in the diplomatic corps that Britain was using her influence to hurry forward ratification. In the view of the German Embassy in Paris the Russians were deliberately highlighting Anglo-Soviet solidarity so as to concentrate on the Far East.

[3] This was the view which Prince Starhemberg, Vice-Chancellor of Austria, expressed to Papen after a visit to London. Papen's despatch of the 12th recording it was later quoted by Hitler.

[4] On 19 February Attolico described the various currents in Italian policy.

presented their report on the 12th.[1] The threat of sanctions was therefore impressive, and Mussolini could only discount it if he could get Hitler into difficulties with the western Powers. On 12 February Baron Aloisi, the Italian representative at Geneva, approached Hassell and, without being invited to do so, asked him what Germany would do concerning the Treaty of Locarno if the Franco-Russian pact were ratified. Hassell replied that nothing had been decided and posed the counter-question whether Italy contemplated repudiating the Treaty. No decision, according to Aloisi, was imminent, but it could be taken if sanctions were extended. Hassell assured Aloisi that if Germany reached a decision the Duce would be informed.

On or about the 11th Hassell was summoned to Munich. His account of a long conversation with the Führer which was held *à deux* on the 14th confirms in all essentials, and even details, Hossbach's record of the events which immediately preceded it. According to Hossbach Hitler made his decision to reoccupy the Rhineland before 12 February, the day on which he first discussed it with Fritsch who evidently agreed but stated that it must not lead to war.

Hitler told Hassell on the 14th 'that he was at present preoccupied with an extraordinarily far-reaching question', which until now he had only discussed with Neurath, Ribbentrop, Göring, Blomberg and Fritsch.[2] According to Hassell's private notes of 15 February Hitler needed to bolster up the régime at home by a spectacular victory in foreign policy. The evidence strongly suggests that after 14 February, Hitler was determined on action, with little regard to its consequences. But he had to persuade his advisers that the moment was opportune. He therefore asked Hassell whether he thought it expedient to use the ratification of the Franco-Russian Treaty by the Chamber of Deputies or Senate as a pretext for repudiating Locarno and re-garrisoning the Demilitarized Zone with troops.[3] Hitherto he had regarded the spring of 1937 as the target date. He intended hinting to Mussolini that they should use the distortion of the Locarno Treaty by the inclusion

[1] RIIA, *Survey*, 1935, Vol. II, pp. 329–34. A firm attempt to impose oil sanctions was made on 20 January.

[2] *Vierteljahrshefte für Zeitgeschichte*, April 1962.

[3] For the military reasons in favour of the reoccupation of the Rhineland see Bülow's minute of his conversation with Beck of 1 December 1934, DGFP (C), Vol. III, pp. 698–9.

of Russia as a pretext for the repudiation of Locarno by Italy, whereupon Germany would follow suit. Blomberg had recently suggested that Göring should carry out this delicate mission to Mussolini. But Hitler did not see how it could be kept secret. It was thus entrusted to Hassell. In the course of his reply Hassell said that Hitler's proposed move was 'in the air'. He pointed out how the Japanese Ambassador in Rome recently reminded him on two occasions that other Powers 'were waiting impatiently for some kind of German action in order to be able to start something themselves'. It seems that Hassell did not wish to give Hitler encouragement for he continued: 'But the Führer himself has recognized how difficult the decision concerned is.' Italy, he claimed, was fully conscious of the terrible predicament into which she had fallen, and there was strong opposition, led by Grandi, against burning the bridges that remained.[1] One point, Hassell insisted, would have to be cleared up, 'namely, whether in the event of Mussolini's refusal, we yet wish to carry through our decision, or whether we would only do so in conjunction with him'. After a short pause for reflection the Führer replied that as things stood 'it seemed to him right and proper to say to Mussolini that in all circumstances we would carry through our move but that we would urge him to make his repudiation (of Locarno) first in order to avoid ours bringing him also into an extremely difficult position *vis-à-vis* Germany. If he repudiated, and we followed, he would win the great advantage that English and French policy from now on would be principally directed against Germany.' Hassell reluctantly agreed to act on these lines and said he would return to Berlin for further instructions after a brief visit to Rome.

When Hitler met Hassell on the 14th he believed that he could talk Mussolini into denouncing Locarno and that Mussolini's action would be the signal for remilitarizing the Rhineland. Before Hassell returned on the 19th Hitler had received proposals, this time from London. In a highly confidential conversation on 12 February Bismarck, Counsellor of the Embassy in London, was

[1] At this point Hassell was interrupted by the Führer who exclaimed: 'But Starhemberg has told Papen that he has the impression that England wishes to defeat Mussolini.' Hassell replied that everything he said applied primarily to the Foreign Minister (i.e. Suvich). 'Mussolini himself and Ciano think somewhat differently. . . .'

informed by Ralph Wigram, an official of the Foreign Office,[1] that his government was drafting a *Working Agreement* between Britain, Germany and France. Because negotiations might be jeopardized by a leakage to the Press, the French were not to be informed until after the German and British Governments had agreed on the terms.[2] The *Working Agreement* was to include an air pact, but not, Wigram hinted, 'certain things' to be found in the Treaty of Locarno, by which he might have meant the clauses governing the Rhineland. Moreover Germany would not be required to return to the League, but would merely assume the obligation not to change the *status quo* by force. He expressed concern over the possibility that at a suitable opportunity Germany would reoccupy the Rhineland; and he claimed that his Government did not regard the Franco-Russian Treaty as their concern.

Bismarck observed that there was some danger that the British were offering the *Working Agreement* in the knowledge that it would be rejected, and that this would provide them with a suitable pretext for acceding to the Franco-Russian Pact. Such suspicions may have been borne out by a conversation between Bismarck and a Polish diplomat on 14 February and by a report from an informant on the 15th.[3] Yet the British démarche yielded positive results. Wigram promised to invite the Press to play down attacks on Germany. He was apparently successful. On the 15th negotiations were continued on a more official level by Lord Cranborne, the Parliamentary Under-Secretary of State for Foreign Affairs.

It is not clear what lay behind the proposals. Since the French were not to be consulted, the British Government might have been prepared to concede to Hitler the right to remilitarize the Rhineland in stages. This would also explain why the proposals did not,

---

[1] Wigram's tragic disillusionment and his untimely death in December 1936 are referred to by Sir Winston Churchill in *The Second World War*, Vol. I, p. 155. DGFP (C), Vol. IV, pp. 1135–9.

[2] According to the German News Agency on 15 February a reporter of the French newspaper *L'Oeuvre* learnt that three days earlier Bismarck held a conversation in the Foreign Office on an air pact.

[3] Bismarck reported on 14 February that he lunched with a foreign diplomat who described common Anglo-Russian interests in the Middle East. The despatch was evidently shown to the Führer. Bismarck was asked to name his source on 2 March and he replied on the 5th. It was the Polish Counsellor of Embassy.

according to Hassell's private notes, fall in line with Hitler's ideas.[1]

Neurath had already studied the *Working Agreement* before Hassell returned from Rome and was much impressed. He did not conceal from Hassell his strong misgivings about Hitler's action, but according to Hassell's private notes he was not so outspoken in Hitler's presence.[2] It was not enough merely to think of the present, Neurath told Hassell, but to remember that the immediate result would be a 'general combination against us'. The British feeler had at all costs to be taken up with care, for the form a German reaction to ratification would take was being openly discussed: things could thus go awry (*und es sich also um ein Querschiessen handeln könnte*). Later that day Hassell noted that Neurath was coming more and more to this point of view.

At 12.15 the two diplomatists were summoned to the Reich Chancellery where they found Hitler and Ribbentrop. In the course of the conversation Hassell again expressed his reservations and described the high state of excitement in Italy on account of the military victories expected. He also spoke of a 'slight British lack of interest' in the war. With Neurath's approval, Hassell stressed that there was no great hurry: other opportunities would arise for getting rid of the Demilitarized Zone. In his reply Hitler stated that there was a danger 'that the Demilitarized Zone would gradually acquire a kind of inviolable status' rendering the problem increasingly more difficult to tackle. He believed that Italian successes would 'goad the English into greater intransigence rather than vice versa' and that for psychological reasons 'it would be wrong to believe that a man like Mussolini would be more inclined to compromise after achieving success. On this occasion attack was the better strategy (lively agreement from Ribbentrop, *sic*.).' In order to reduce the danger Hitler declared that the entry would be accompanied by the following proposals to the other Locarno Powers: (*a*) the continuation of the Demilitarized Zone on both sides, (*b*) a Three Power pact guaranteeing the inviolability of Belgium[3] and Holland, (*c*) an air pact, (*d*) a long-term non-aggression pact with France, (*e*) the revival of the conception of the Four

[1] *Vierteljahrshefte für Zeitgeschichte*, April 1962.

[2] Ibid.

[3] Neurath reminded Hitler that the retention of the former German districts of Eupen and Malmédy, lost to Belgium after the war, must be assured to Belgium.

Power Pact of 1933, restricted in scope to questions immediately concerning the West.[1] In the further course of the conversation Neurath again broached the subject of British feelers—but this 'aroused no interest in the Führer'.

At a later interview on the 19th Hitler 'spoke excitedly' about a report, just received from Paris, according to which Cerruti assured Flandin that Italy would stand fast by Locarno and Stresa. In the opinion of Hitler and Ribbentrop greater caution was now needed. But Hassell dismissed the danger. Neurath, moreover, raised no further objections but seemed reconciled to the decision. Later in the evening the Führer said that Germany should strike immediately after the Franco-Russian Pact had passed the Chamber of Deputies. Neurath and Hassell, however, felt that it was absolutely imperative to make sure of the far less certain Senate.

Hassell returned to Rome where he carried out his mission both promptly and skilfully. He was received by Mussolini on the 22nd.[2] Mussolini told him that if sanctions were extended Italy would leave the League of Nations and *ipso facto* no longer consider herself bound by Locarno. He would immediately deliver an ultimatum to this effect to the French Ambassador. Hassell then steered the conversation round to the delicate theme of the Franco-Russian Pact. He believed that it would pass the Chamber of Deputies, but perhaps not the Senate. Mussolini, on the other hand, believed that after some delay it would be passed by both bodies. Hassell remarked that 'such a decision would place us before very serious decisions for we could not let this violation of Locarno go by without some sort of reaction. The Führer has reached no kind of decision. He is accustomed, moreover, to make his decisions all alone within thirty-six hours.' In response to this caveat Mussolini stated that while Italy disapproved of the Franco-Russian Pact she did not consider that it directly concerned her: she would thus take no action if it were ratified. Hassell then asked whether this meant that if Germany reacted to ratification Italy would not support Britain and France against Germany. Mussolini confirmed that this was so.

[1] Here Hassell noted in the text that Poland should be included. This was also Mussolini's wish.

[2] Hassell's second visit was evidently not kept secret, at least for long; RIIA, *Survey, 1936*, p. 577. The Survey gives 24 February for the date of his interview with Mussolini. The interview actually took place on the 22nd.

Mussolini's reply to Hitler's feeler certainly gave cause for satisfaction. But what if his ultimatum to the French, which he mentioned to Hassell, were to succeed and if the French agreed to wreak sanctions? Mussolini evidently carried out his threat. On the 23rd Flandin, who was reported by Hassell to have been taken aback when Cerruti informed him of the Duce's attitude, agreed that France would do all in her power to remove Mussolini's anxieties over sanctions. There were further ugly signs of a change. On 26 February Hassell met Suvich who gave him a minute of the meeting with Mussolini on the 22nd. Mussolini was reported to have said that Italy would not join the other Locarno Powers if Germany's response to ratification were 'within legal limits'. Hassell replied that the wording of the minute was quite incorrect and he asked that the necessary alterations should be made. In Hassell's opinion Mussolini had been persuaded by his advisers that he had previously been too outspoken. Mussolini's wavering may have made Hitler feel anxious, and on 26th two American journalists found him 'very much troubled about something'.[1]

Meanwhile British feelers for a *Working Agreement* were followed up. On 25 February Neurath instructed von Hoesch to sound Eden on whether his Government was prepared to consider concrete proposals. Eden told Hoesch on the 27th that Britain could only do so after his meeting with Flandin at Geneva in the near future. Hoesch hinted that Eden should use his influence with Flandin to delay ratification of the Franco-Russian Pact through the Senate and formed the impression that Eden desired Anglo-German-French co-operation, and would only be too glad if the Pact were not ratified. Hoesch's report was not believed. A marginal note opposite the passage describing Eden's good intentions reads: 'Attolico has reported to the State Secretary [i.e. Bülow] that there is news from Paris to the opposite effect.' Attolico had in fact told Bülow on 2 March that according to a report from the Italian Embassy in Paris, the British were using their influence with the French to get the treaty ratified speedily by the Senate.

It has been seen that Hitler wished to make his move coincide with the passage of the Franco-Russian Pact through the Chamber of Deputies. Nothing would have been more disadvantageous, according to Hassell's private notes,[2] if for some reason or other

---

[1] Dodd's *Diary*, 26 February, and François-Poncet, *Souvenirs*, p. 250.
[2] *Vierteljahrshefte für Zeitgeschichte*, April 1962.

that body refused or delayed to sanction it. The debate took place
to the accompaniment of a 'running fire' of hostile German comment, which weakened opposition against ratification. Hence
François-Poncet's contention that Hitler tried but failed to dis-
suade French parliamentarians from voting for ratification must
be dismissed.[1] But the question remains why on 21 February, when
the pact was still being debated, Hitler showed such a 'conciliatory
disposition' in an interview with Bertrand de Jouvenel.[2] This in-
direct approach to the French Government may have been intended to soften the blow which was coming. It seems more likely
however that Hitler was thinking of the German public. Even on
19 February, two days before the interview, he was preparing the
speech which he intended to deliver to the Reichstag on the day
his troops marched. He always made it a matter of principle to
justify every act both as reasonable and as inescapably necessary.
On 7 March, when he delivered his speech, he specifically referred
to the interview by means of which he claimed '. . . I tried once
more to approach the French people with the request for an understanding.'[3] On the 28th, the day after the Treaty was ratified by a
large majority, the interview was published in France. On the 2nd
Bülow learnt from Attolico that the French wished to hurry the
pact through the Senate. Hitler was now ready to act for it was
also on the 2nd that Blomberg issued the deployment order. No
date however had been fixed for the advance.[4]

Whether even at this stage Hitler thought that he could rely on
Mussolini is uncertain. Everything was to be gained if sanctions
were extended by the League on 2 March. Despite the clamouring
of British parliamentarians, who again called for the application
of oil sanctions on the 24th, Mussolini was soon freed from all
anxiety. On 2–3 March Eden conferred with Flandin. Smarting
from the effect of Mussolini's ultimatum, Flandin persuaded his
British colleague that sanctions should again be postponed. Although the Italian Press chanted a 'paean of triumph' on the 3rd,

[1] RIIA, *Survey, 1936*, p. 256. The tone of the German Press was most
bitter when Tukhachevsky visited Paris in the second week of February.
Hodza, the Czechoslovak President, also visited Paris at about that time.

[2] Baynes, op. cit., Vol. II, pp. 1266–71.

[3] For the text of the speech, see Baynes, op. cit., Vol. II, pp. 1271–93, and
François-Poncet, *Souvenirs*, p. 250.

[4] According to Blomberg's instructions marching orders were to be given
as late as possible so as to reduce the time between the start of preparations
and the advance. ND: C-159 and Meinck, op. cit., pp. 151–2.

Mussolini was not deflected from the course of action, outlined to Hassell on 22 February. On 3 March Suvich handed Hassell a revised minute of the conversation of the 22nd which this time reproduced Mussolini's words correctly. 'Had attempts been made', Hassell concluded, 'to water down Mussolini's statements they must be considered to have failed.' Hitler was now assured that Mussolini would not stand by his obligations under Locarno. Flandin was no more successful in other respects. He asked Eden for an assurance that Britain would honour her obligations even if Italy repudiated Locarno. The British Cabinet, however, had decided that the Rhineland was not a 'vital British interest', and Flandin was given no such assurance.[1] Eden's negative reply may have persuaded the French to hurry through the ratification of the Pact. On 4 March the Foreign Affairs Committee of the French Senate agreed to it in principle.[2] Hitler evidently reacted to this step. On 5 March Blomberg issued a further directive ordering the advance to take place on the 7th. Also on the 5th the German missions accredited to the other Locarno Powers received their instructions. At the time Hitler was to address the Reichstag on the 7th they were to deliver a memorandum giving the reasons for the action and proposals for the future.[3]

Hitler certainly reached his final decision with some difficulty. Personal contacts between British and French were always looked at askance in Germany and there is no reason to believe that Eden's meeting with Flandin was an exception. According to Hossbach 5 March was a day charged with tension. 'An erroneous appreciation of events, or reports which were off the mark, made a démarche from England and France appear possible.' Hossbach found Hitler in an 'excited' conversation with Ribbentrop. Having explained the situation Hitler asked him whether the movement of troops could still be halted and when at the latest a decision had to be taken.[4] The causes of Hitler's anxiety were evidently ill founded; they are not reflected in the sober appreciation of the *Wilhelm-*

[1] RIIA, *Survey*, *1935*, Vol. II, p. 339 and *1936*, pp. 260–1.

[2] The codeword for the operation was *Winterübung* (Winter Exercise) for the Army, *Sonderübung* (Special Exercise) for the Air Force. See also ND: 196-C instructions for the Navy from which it is evident that the Russians were not likely to move because of ice in the Baltic.

[3] The decision was confirmed by the Reich Cabinet on the 6th.

[4] Hossbach replied that the movement of troops could still be stopped, but that the latest time for reaching a decision could not be determined without clarification, *Zwischen Wehrmacht und Hitler*, pp. 97–8.

strasse given in instructions to the German missions accredited to the other Locarno Powers on the 5th. Even according to the French view the occupation would not constitute a *flagrant* but merely a *qualified* breach of the Treaty of Locarno, in as much as the peaceful entry of a limited number of troops would not, according to Article 2, constitute an act of 'unprovoked aggression'.[1]

Germany's chances in the event of a full scale French attack were hopeless and the real question facing Hitler was political rather than military. It was not whether France 'could', but whether she 'would', march. A year or two earlier her choice would have been immeasurably easier. She could then have overwhelmed Germany with her regular army without proclaiming general mobilization. In 1936, her military preponderance remained but, because German power was growing, mobilization would, in the opinion of her military experts, have been essential. Neither the government nor people were prepared for such a drastic step.[2]

Hitler knew that France was not likely to act alone, and he had to concentrate on dissuading her allies. In this connection the German memorandum, drafted on the 5th and delivered to the other Locarno Powers on the 7th is of considerable interest. It has been seen that on 19 February Hitler was contemplating reviving Mussolini's idea of a Four Power Pact in a modified form. He did not intend wounding Mussolini by a German offer to rejoin the League at the precise moment Italy was secretly threatening to leave it. At some point before 5 March Hitler came round to the idea that Germany should promise to rejoin the League, with the only provision that the new situation should be recognized. He also even offered to include Lithuania in the 'Pax Germanica'.[3]

It seems that Hitler at first attributed far too much importance to Mussolini, and this may explain why he originally set out to appease Italian rather than British sentiment. Certainly Mussolini's

---

[1] The memorandum was evidently altered on minor points on the 6th.

[2] See Gamelin, *Servir, Le Prologue du Drame, 1930–Aout 1939*, Libraire Plon, Paris, 1946, pp. 206 et seq. See also *The Rhineland Crisis of March 1936*, by W. F. Knapp, St. Antony's Papers No. 5, Chatto and Windus, London, 1957.

[3] For the text of Hitler's declaration of 7 March, see RIIA, *Survey, 1936*, pp. 263–5. According to the instructions issued by the *Wilhelmstrasse* on the 5th, even the return of colonies was not to be taken as a condition *sine qua non* for Germany's return to the League. Hitler gave no guarantee to Lithuania on 21 May 1935. See p. 62.

thundering language, which was to prove so infectious, appealed more to him than the rather tepid requests for a 'Working Agreement'. But what was Italian support really worth? Despite the extreme alternative, apparently open to Italy, of either slamming the door on the League or of standing by Stresa, she could hardly, with her armed forces bottled up in Abyssinia, influence the military situation on the Rhine by a mere *coup de théâtre*. Her moral support might prove positively detrimental to whichever party sought it. Britain's possible reactions counted for much more. Admittedly, her refusal to assist France could not have been regarded as a serious military loss, for French preponderance over Germany was overwhelming. On the other hand, Britain's moral stock still stood high, and little sacrifice would have been called for if she had put her signature to a French ultimatum. How far these factors weighed with Hitler is not known. From the start he had certainly refused to commit himself over the Four Power Pact, and the question was not raised by Hassell in his talk with Mussolini on 22 February. The way was thus open for offers to Britain.

Hitler, according to Hassell's private notes, may have been persuaded to declare Germany's readiness to re-enter the League by either Bülow or Ribbentrop.[1] In this connection Neurath made some revealing comments to Dodd, the American Ambassador. On 29 February Dodd found Neurath, who never had a reputation for truthfulness, to be 'more frank' than on any previous occasion. He was surprised to hear him say: 'We are contemplating a return to the League' on certain conditions. He insisted that the Führer showed signs of compromise, especially about returning to Geneva. Whereupon Dodd observed: 'This surprised me a little'.[2]

The events which followed 7 March showed that in fact more was gained by an apple of discord thrown into the ranks of the Stresa trio than by a promise of safe conduct from one party alone. All three had reason to condemn Germany's action, but since their policy was in varying degrees at cross-purposes concerted action was stultified. Whereas the British were prepared to negotiate on Hitler's spurious offers concerning the League, which was more than they themselves had asked of Hitler, the French were not.[3] Mussolini for his part welcomed Hitler's *fait accompli*, which he

---

[1] *Vierteljahrshefte für Zeitgeschichte*, April 1962.
[2] Dodd's *Diary*, 29 February.
[3] See RIIA, *Survey, 1936*, pp. 274–6.

had deliberately encouraged, but deeply resented the offers which accompanied it. On 7 March, when he told Hassell that Germany 'went too far', he confined this censure to the question of the League, not to Hitler's failure on 5 March to confirm his guarantee to Austria. Hassell even gained the impression that the Italians believed that 'our move was made in concert with the English, and that we thus had preferred to work in unison with London instead of with Rome'. He later noted that Italy was again courting France.

The Stresa front had been turned on both its flanks, and Hitler survived the most serious international crisis since 1933. His success is often thought of as a turning point in the history of the inter-war years, and to this day it is argued that if Hitler could have been stopped he should have been stopped in March 1936. While a more detailed study of the German evidence, far from undermining, lends added support to this view, it remains difficult on principle to draw a clear line across any given point of time and to claim that the errors of human judgement lie on one side and not the other.[1] The loose phraseology of the Treaty of Locarno was intentional, a fact which can only too easily be overlooked, and those responsible for it have to carry their share of blame no less than their successors. But even if Britain's commitments had been made unequivocally clear the simple objection that the Rhineland was not worth defending might have frustrated all actions on its behalf. The German documents moreover lead their readers a stage further. However Hitler and Mussolini mistrusted each other no formal contract was needed if they chose to act together in a 'confederacy of violence'. Mussolini was the first to try his hand, the case against him was clear, and the means sufficient to prevent his conquest of Abyssinia. Hitler was genuinely afraid that collective security might be converted from an idea into an organization. This alone would have proved to him that international relations were not just a simple extension of the Darwinian 'struggle for existence'.

[1] French policy is ably discussed by W. F. Knapp, St. Antony's Papers, No. 5, Chatto and Windus, London, 1959.

CHAPTER 9

Rearmament and Operational Plans

(June 1937)

By March 1936 Hitler had completed the last stage in the re-establishment of German military sovereignty over the whole Reich. Henceforward, no act on German soil could provoke a French attack.[1] But Hitler, unlike the more conservative of his generals, did not wish to use the armed forces in order to bargain for the restoration of Germany's pre-1914 frontiers, but to conquer *Lebensraum.* At some juncture therefore there had to be a switch over from a defensive to an offensive strategy, and between March 1936 and the end of 1937, Hitler devoted his full attention to the war economy and to the future military establishment.

Full military sovereignty could only provide Germany with the possibility of becoming a great power, and, although conscription after March 1936 could be extended to the whole country, it was not such an advantage as it seemed, for only a part of German reserves in manpower could be absorbed into the Armed Forces. Hitler could of course construct a great fortified barrier against a possible French invasion running from the Swiss frontier to Luxemburg. But fortifications are costly and many years were to lapse before the work bore fruit. As late as 14 May 1937 Jodl found if necessary to warn his colleagues on the Working Committee of the *Reichverteidigungsrat* that in view of the 'present political constellation the German Armed Forces are far from ready for war'[2]. Almost exactly a year later Hitler for the same reason had to postpone an immediate invasion of Czechoslovakia until the end of September 1938.[3]

---

[1] The favourable change in Germany's entire position as a great Power was discussed at the 12th meeting of the National Defence Committee, on 14 May 1936. See Note on Sources, p. 195. A draft speech prepared for the meeting, which is to be found in the same file, was probably prepared by Bülow who spoke at the meeting. For Beck's views, see his memorandum of January 1937, Förster, op. cit. pp. 44–7.

[2] See Note on Sources, p. 195.   [3] See p. 125.

Although Germany was still a long way behind in her armaments, the progress already made before March 1936 was considerable. After the premature reintroduction of conscription in March 1935 the *Reichswehr* was to consist by the autumn of 1939 of 12 corps and 36 divisions, amounting to 580,000 combat troops as well as 115,000 auxiliaries. How far there was an immediate increase cannot be established, for police formations outside the Rhineland, which were now incorporated into the Army, were military in all but name.[1] Twenty-one divisions were already raised by April 1935, and it was decided on 13 May to increase this figure to twenty-four and to establish three embryo armoured divisions by the end of March 1936. There were two important changes in organization. On 21 May 1935 the Defence Minister became War Minister and Commander-in-Chief of the Armed Forces (*Wehrmacht*), while the heads of the respective branches of the Services also took the new titles of Commander-in-Chief. Also on 21 May the Reich Defence Law was passed, giving the government very great powers in the event of mobilization and defining the duties of the Working Committee of the *Reichsverteidigungsrat*. At a meeting of the Working Committee on 26 June 1935 Reichenau breezily declared how good it was to see soldiers on the street again. He had previously estimated that only 60 per cent of the German youth were physically fit, and he was astounded to learn that 80 per cent was the correct figure. There was however a temporary obstacle. The 1915 age group consisted of 470,000 men from which the armed services could call up 266,000. Only a limited number of the 205,000 men who remained could be absorbed into the labour service, and Reichenau, perhaps anxious because of the rival attraction of Party organizations, was worried by the fact that 130,000 German youths would not receive a 'strictly disciplined education from the State'. Rapid expansion was to remove his anxiety. During the second mobilization year (i.e. October 1935–6) it was intended to raise four further infantry divisions and to disband two cavalry divisions. The General Staff, who were in favour of increasing the infantry strength, at first intended to suspend development of the motorized and armoured divisions. In the autumn of 1935 the three prospective armoured divisions were still included in the total of thirty-six divisions. In January 1936 this

[1] A directive of the *Chef der Heeresleitung* of 16 April 1935. See Note on Sources, p. 195.

ruling no longer applied. German planning had now exceeded the limits of the programme announced on 16 March 1935.

Early in January 1937 the first proposals, with the specific aim of converting three police brigades, stationed in the Rhineland, into the military forces, and for re-garrisoning the area, were worked out. The Reich in future would be divided into twelve instead of ten Military Districts. This took effect immediately after 7 March, thus making possible further increase of military strength. It is evident from a directive signed by Fritsch on 1 April 1936 that 36 instead of 32 (and earlier 28) divisions were to be raised in the third mobilization year (October 1936–November 1937).[1] This increase was certainly very considerable on paper, but it must be remembered that the framework of the peacetime army was to be formed as quickly as possible so as to avoid splitting up divisions in the future. The needs of the other services were not neglected. By 1 April 1937 all formations of the Luftwaffe were to be raised. Aircraft factories for the production of new models were to be built in 1936 and run at mobilization capacity after January 1937. In addition the armament industry had to provide fortifications in the Rhineland and Heligoland.[2]

The vast increase in expenditure roused strong criticism. In August General Fromm, head of the Organization Department of the Army High Command, stated his objections in an official memorandum.[3] The new estimates drawn up on military expenditure until 1945 were far greater than those made on 18 July 1935. The wartime army would be mainly equipped with material by 1 October 1939. After 1939 minimum production for all demands would have to be maintained in order to achieve maximum production after mobilization. Total yearly expenditure therefore would not fall but would rise from 7,570 million RM in 1940 to 8,070 million in 1944. 'This situation is unbearable for any length of time', wrote Fromm. He later asked: 'Is there, or is there not, a fixed intention to send the armed forces into action at a definite point of time?'

Shortly after the appearance of the Fromm study a decision was taken of particular importance, and it may have had the effect of

[1] See Note on Sources, p. 195.

[2] ND: 3474-PS, memorandum of 2 December 1936. See also a conference of 31 August 1936, ND: 1301-PS.

[3] See Note on Sources, p. 195.

reducing the strain on the war economy. Hitherto, owing to the lack of instructors for training, one year's military service had been in force. This would clearly have provided the army with a greater number of reserves—at least in the initial stages of expansion—than two years' service, as only certain age groups could be called up at a time. While Fritsch and Beck fully recognized that reserves were insufficient they adhered strictly to the Seeckt policy of concentrating on quality rather than on numbers. On 24 August 1936, Hitler, apparently after some hestitation, agreed to their proposal that military service should be extended by a year. As a result the proportion of regular or first-wave formations increased at the expense of reserves. A defect in the cycle of mobilization was also removed: Germany was least prepared for war between October, when recruits were released, and March, when new intakes were sufficiently trained. With two years' conscription the state of readiness was standardized.[1]

After 24 August Hitler had again to justify an unpopular measure. Previously he could find in the galling provisions of Part V of the Treaty of Versailles the slogans for rearmament. By March 1936 the non-territorial provisions of the Treaty were dead, and only an urgent sense of some new mortal peril from outside could inspire the German people to fresh sacrifices. Earlier in August Soviet Russia had extended the period of military service: she had completed two five year plans and her achievements imbued both Hitler and his generals with that strange feeling of fear and admiration which was so often to unbalance their judgement. Until the execution of the most outstanding Soviet generals in the early summer of 1937, Russia, instead of France, the Comintern, instead of the Treaty of Versailles, were the main targets of German propaganda, and the anti-Soviet theme reached its peak at the Annual Party Rally in September 1936.[2]

Before the Rally Hitler's economic experts, as well as General Fromm, had been vocal in expressing their criticism over the cost of armaments. The two officials most intimately concerned were Hjalmar Schacht, Commissioner for the War Economy since 21 May 1935, and General Thomas, head of the Armaments Department of the Armed Forces. In December 1935 Schacht, through

---

[1] See Hossbach, *Zwischen Wehrmacht und Hitler*, pp. 181–2 and Förster, op. cit., pp. 23–4.

[2] See Meinck, op. cit., pp. 157 et seq.

Blomberg, repeated a warning to Hitler made the previous May, that any radical extension of the existing armaments programme would jeopardize the entire economy.[1] After the reoccupation of the Rhineland the strain on Germany's war economy was still greater: her reserves in all essentials, including food, fuel and rubber, had dropped. Schacht accordingly told Göring on 12 May that he was under the impression that the programme would not be extended. Göring in rebuking him observed that to his knowledge no limit had been fixed.[2] At a further conference of 26 May 1936, dealing with raw materials, Schacht pointed out that in order to procure currency capable of meeting Germany's shortages, exports would have to be raised by 25 and not 10 per cent as anticipated. The necessary increase in exports could only be obtained at the expense of armaments. Göring insisted that in spite of vested interests the rate of rearmament must not be reduced. His policy prevailed.[3] On 27 April 1936, Hitler had already appointed him as the final authority both over party and state for all questions concerning raw materials and currency.

Hitler was incensed by Schacht's criticism, and in a secret memorandum of August 1936, gave full expression to his own views on the organization of the German war economy. The memorandum is one of the few documents written by Hitler himself between 1933 and 1939. It belongs to a period for which there are singularly few documents that throw light on the inner counsels of his government. It has all the appearance of a directive or official manifesto hurriedly dictated, and it shows signs neither of careful preparation nor of thought.[4] Hitler let himself go, and hurled abuse at his victims, who on this occasion were those respectable financiers and industrialists who contributed so much to his rise to power a few years before. He made it clear that if they failed in their job the State might follow the example set by the

[1] ND: 1668-PS and 293-EC. General Thomas's *Basic Facts* contains additional material.

[2] ND: 1301-PS. See also ND: 286, 497, 493-EC and Schacht, *Account Settled*, pp. 98–100, where Schacht's later quarrels with Göring are described.

[3] ND: No. 1–580, published in the *Vierteljahrshefte für Zeitgeschichte* (April 1955), together with an admirable commentary by Professor Wilhelm Treue.

[4] ND, Military Tribunals, 4955–N.1. In 1944 Hitler handed one of the three existing copies of the memorandum to Albert Speer, Minister for Armaments and Munitions, with the observation that opposition to far-reaching plans from officials and industrialists had led him to draw it up.

Soviet Union—which had completed a 'gigantic' plan.[1] He claimed also that 28 million people now enjoyed a higher standard of living and on an average could spend 100–120 RM per month. All human resources had to be harnessed to the process of production. Whereas industrial output could be raised considerably, that of agriculture would soon reach its 'natural limit', and hence after a transitional period there would have to be 'a final solution'. 'This', Hitler emphatically declared, 'lies in the extension of our living space for food and raw material. . . . It is the task of the political leaders at some time to solve this problem.'

Having expressed his discontent with the economic progress already made, he ominously declared: 'The German army must be ready for action in four years' and 'the German economy must be on a war footing in four years.'

Late in August, or early in September 1936, Hitler first read his memorandum to Schacht who, greatly disconcerted, informed Blomberg of Hitler's proposals for the war economy. Schacht was convinced that they would 'certainly win great applause from the masses at Nuremberg', but that they would 'ruin Germany's entire foreign trade' and be considered as a threat abroad. The only remedy was increased exports. Schacht maintained that if Hitler persisted in forcing his plan through, Germany's food situation would be made worse. Blomberg, who on account of his almost panic-stricken attitude during the Rhineland crisis a few months earlier, had less influence with Hitler than Schacht assumed, allegedly replied: 'I entirely agree that you are right, but do you know that I am entirely convinced that the Führer will certainly find a way out of all difficulties.'[2] Göring, not Schacht, was to be entrusted with the task of implementing the plan. He brushed aside all opposition and read Hitler's memorandum to his economic staff on 4 September.[3] He commented that Hitler's memorandum was based on the assumption that a conflict with the USSR was 'inevitable' and that all measures were to be taken as if the threat of war had been officially stated to be imminent. Göring also claimed that Germany's achievement in economic

---

[1] This is the opposite of what Hitler had declared at the Nuremberg Party Rally on 12 September: 'The Soviets', he said, 'had done nothing with their resources.' Discussed in Beloff, *The Foreign Policy of the Soviet Union*, Vol. II, p. 58.

[2] ND: 1301-PS.

[3] Meeting of a ministerial conference, ND: 416-EC.

reorganization could match those of Russia. Hitler inaugurated the Four Year Plan on 9 September. Göring was made responsible for all matters pertaining to it on 18 October. At a conference with his air staff on 2 December Göring again declared: 'Russia wishes war: England is arming vigorously. Peace is desired until 1941 but we do not know if complications will set in beforehand. We are already at war but there is no shooting.' There was to be the 'highest state of readiness' regardless of financial difficulties.[1]

While Göring was superseding Schacht, General Keitel, Reichenau's successor to Blomberg as *chef de bureau* of the *Wehrmachtsamt*, was in December 1935 appointed acting chairman of the Working Committee of the *Reichsverteidigungsrat* (National Defence Council), a body whose competence was already encroaching on that of the more conservative General Staff. At one of its meetings, on 19 November 1936,[2] Keitel spoke in terms no less emphatic than Göring on the inevitability of war. His staff were responsible for the formation of plans, the aim of which was to harness the entire national resources, human and physical for the purpose of war. Certain conclusions can also be drawn on the kind of war OKW officers expected in the future. They estimated that in most European countries mobilization of the regular army required four days.[3] They now asked whether this period could be reduced and a lead thus secured in the concentration of their own forces. The aim of mobilization, when complete, was to strike an opponent before he was ready to parry the blow. The alternative of using it as a means of exerting political pressure was open only to a Power with a pronounced military preponderance. The French practice, for instance, of intensifying the rate of mobilization in accordance with the political temperature, should not be followed in Germany, for the repercussions on other countries of 'partial' mobilization would be little different from that of 'full' mobilization. As far as possible legal declarations of all kinds were to be avoided. Accord-

---

[1] ND: 3474-PS. Also at the meeting Weizsäcker, head of the Political Department of the German Foreign Office, described the danger of war as 'not acute'.

[2] See Note on Sources, p. 195.

[3] Brief summaries of OKW's plans for mobilization can be found in addresses to the War Academy by Captains Scherff and Bader. Both these officers belonged to the Organization Department of the General Staff. See Note on Sources, p. 195.

ing to Jodl: 'Whoever pronounces the ominous word "mobiliza-tion" has lost the war for political reasons. . . . The *proclamation* of mobilization is now at the end, no longer at the beginning, of mobilization.'[1] German staff officers were influenced by the events which preceded the outbreak of war in 1914 and recalled how at that time a 'superb mobilization technique' had been squandered because of political bungling. The aged Ludendorff lent the im-mense weight of his authority to this school of thought. 'It is mistaken', he wrote in 1936, 'if it is assumed that a war must begin with a declaration of war.'[2] By declaring war on Russia and France in 1914 Germany's offensive aim could easily be perceived. While the enemies' will to resist was strengthened, the German people, aware that they were embarked on a war of conquest, forgot that their survival was at stake and allowed their energies to flag.

Certain conclusions of a more general kind can be drawn from the theory of war held in OKW. The old dictum, quoted so often in the Kaiser's day, 'mobilization means war', still stood but it had assumed an even more ugly aspect. Mobilization was no longer to serve a political object, and the heads of the armed forces were merely to be provided with pretexts for putting it into effect. In this way Clausewitz's principle that war 'was an instrument of policy' was inverted: war, conceived of in its totality, became an end in itself.

OKW were not merely thinking in abstract terms. As early as 30 March 1935, when real headway was being made towards a Franco-Russian-Czech alliance, Reichenau produced a memoran-dum of the highest importance in which a new course of action was advanced.[3] It was expected that in the event of war Czecho-slovakia would mobilize against Germany. Should she allow her-self to be used as a base for hostilities against Germany a surprise attack might be made against her. No rash move, however, such as the invasion of Belgium in 1914, was contemplated. Staff dis-cussions were to be held in April[4] and complete secrecy maintained. On 2 May, the day on which the Franco-Russian treaty was signed,

[1] ND: 406-EC. A meeting of the National Defence Committee held on 6 December 1935.

[2] *Der Totale Krieg* by General Ludendorff, Ludendorff's Verlag G.m.f.H., München, 1936, pp. 87–106. See also the first chapter of that work.

[3] DGFP (C), Vol. III, pp. 1109–10.

[4] Discussed in Meinck, op. cit. p. 137 and p. 149.

Blomberg issued a directive called _Schulung_ (Training), the code name for some unspecified operation. It is now certain that _Schulung_ was intended as a surprise attack on Czechoslovakia.[1] Protests were immediately registered by General Beck, chief of the Army General Staff, who viewed with suspicion the activities of OKW. He declared in a memorandum submitted to General Blomberg on 3 May that if it were intended to put _Schulung_ into effect he would resign.[2] The French, he declared, maintained eleven infantry divisions, one cavalry and one mechanized division for immediate deployment against Germany. To act against such odds the German army would find an unpraiseworthy end in a 'non-German land'.

Although _Schulung_ was a plan, not an order, of action it was to feature regularly on Hitler's military programme. In May 1936 Blomberg issued an order stating that during tours of inspection carried out by the Führer and the General Staff the problem of an attack on Czechoslovakia would certainly be discussed, but that absolute secrecy was imperative.[3] On 26 June 1936 a general directive was issued by Blomberg to all three services on their tasks in the event of a possible war. Unfortunately this directive was withdrawn a year later and is no longer extant. It was superseded by a new directive on 24 June 1937 with the same title except for the significant omission of the word 'possible' before 'war'.[4] It was taken for granted in the Directive that there was no danger of an attack on Germany for the following reasons: lack of will for war among the Western Powers and the inadequate state of readiness of a number of States, particularly Russia. Germany therefore had freedom of action and must be prepared to exploit the fluid political situation abroad and to mobilize before her armaments were complete. Plans were made for a war on two fronts: (_a_) Concentra-

---

[1] ND: 139-C. The Prosecution at Nuremberg claimed that the directive was intended for the reoccupation of the Rhineland, IMT, Vol. II, pp. 342-3 and Vol. XV, p. 445. Jodl ingeniously claimed that it would only come into force if the French applied sanctions; that the strip of 50 kilometres, included in the Demilitarized Zone on the right bank of the river, would be occupied, while the left bank was to be evacuated. IMT, Vol. XXV, pp. 247-8. Beck's memorandum of 3 May (see below), the wording of the directive itself, and Reichenau's appreciation of 30 March make it inescapably clear that _Schulung_ (Training) was intended for Czechoslovakia.

[2] Förster, pp. 31-3. Namier has wrongly given 3 May 1937 as the date of the memorandum, _In the Nazi Era_, p. 26.

[3] See Note on Sources, p. 195.   [4] ND: 175-C.

tion Red, with the centre of emphasis on the West where it was assumed that France would attack; (*b*) Concentration Green, with the centre of emphasis on the South-East where a German attack was envisaged against Czechoslovakia.

Of the two plans Red was given priority. It assumed that if Belgium were neutral French forces would violate Luxembourg. Russia and Czechoslovakia were expected to be hostile, Austria, Italy, Hungary and Yugoslavia to be benevolent neutrals. It was believed that Poland and Lithuania would stand aloof. A major French air and land attack against Germany would be resisted as near the frontier as possible. Provided that Belgium were neutral, the occupation of the Eifel would provide flanking cover and a favourable basis of operations against the French northern wing. Germany's eastern and south-eastern frontiers would be manned by defensive formations. Concentration Green was to deprive Russia of air bases by means of a lightning operation against Czechoslovakia. Political and moral pretexts would be created beforehand. German forces would occupy Bohemia and Moravia and crush the Czechs before they were properly mobilized and prepared.[1]

The directive also showed how Operation Green could in certain undesirable circumstances lead to a conflict with Britain, who was expected to apply all her economic and military strength against Germany. At first Britain would support France from the air and at sea. Later she would attempt to win bases in Belgium and Holland. The neutrality of Britain was regarded as an 'inescapably necessary condition' for Operation Green, and the Government was asked to make every effort to ensure it. A possible war with Britain was already discussed in a naval study for operations in 1937–1938. That British intervention would bring Japan into the war was cold comfort as American neutrality was considered unlikely. The Chief of the Naval Staff considered it dangerous to discuss the possibility of war with Britain. It is also evident from a memorandum written by Fritsch in August that war with Britain could not be intended; the reasons being the Naval Treaty of 1935 and inadequate strength at sea.[2]

---

[1] Connected with Green was *Special Operation Otto* (an invasion of Austria), the aim of which was to compel the Austrian Government to renounce any attempt to restore the Monarchy.

[2] See Notes on Sources, p. 195.

Although Blomberg's directive laid greater emphasis on counter-measures against an enemy coalition than on German initiative, and although it was a study of innumerable hypothetical contingencies[1] than a plan of action, an aggressive purpose can be detected. If Russia was not prepared for war, there could be no real object in smashing Czechoslovakia as a Soviet base: if there was no will for war among the Western Powers, Concentration Red would seem superfluous. Belgium, too, had been released from her obligations under the Treaty of Locarno and there was scarcely any danger of a *Schlieffen* operation taking the wrong direction. While Blomberg could calculate with more equanimity on Germany's military prospects than in the period preceding the remilitarization of the Rhineland, he made it abundantly clear that Germany must not risk a war so long as British intervention could not be discounted. Provided Hitler observed this reservation there might be friction but no major rift between him and his professional advisers. The rift was to come with a change in Hitler's foreign policy at the end of 1937.

---

[1] Importance was also attached to Polish neutrality, as this would enable troops to be transferred from East Prussia. Nevertheless Blomberg took the possibility of Polish participation into account and showed how Lithuania might co-operate either with Poland or Russia in the Baltic. From the end of 1936 almost every possible contingency for war in this area had been discussed in correspondence between Beck and Raeder. See Note on Sources, p. 195.

CHAPTER 10

Hitler's Hostility Turns Against Britain

(October 1937)

After the reoccupation of the Rhineland the French system of alliances acquired a new, less menacing, character: instead of the prevention of a resurgent Germany, its aim was now solely protective. In Eastern Europe there had been little change. During the Rhineland crisis Czechoslovakia and Poland regarded their treaty obligations as binding; the former subsequently pushed forward her armament plans.[1] Ratifications of the Franco-Russian Pact were also exchanged on 27 March, and the Russo-Czech Treaty automatically came into force. France's standing after March 1936 in Western Europe, on the other hand, deteriorated. While negotiations for a new Locarno dragged on tediously Britain still considered herself obliged to assist both France and Belgium if either country were subjected to a German attack. Yet Anglo-French staff conferences were not authorized, for it was believed in London that Germany might make good her promises and re-enter the League. Belgium's position within what remained of the Locarno structure, unlike that of Britain, had changed. On 14 October 1936 King Leopold declared that the reoccupation of the Rhineland had placed Belgium almost in the same international position as before the 1914 War. By an agreement of 24 April 1937 Britain and France released Belgium from her obligations under Locarno, in return for which she agreed to fortify her own frontier with Germany. Thereafter the French could no longer hope to enter the Ruhr by the shortest route.

The most serious blow of all to the French system was the defection of Italy and the emergence of the Rome-Berlin Axis.

It has been seen that before the re-occupation of the Rhineland Hitler feared that in return for support against sanctions Mussolini might agree to co-operate with France in Europe.[2] In May 1936

---

[1] See RIIA, *Survey, 1936*, pp. 271–2. [2] See p. 76.

May, 1936 Mussolini won resounding victories in Abyssinia. After Italy annexed the country on the 9th sanctions could no longer prove effective, and any French offers of help could be unceremoniously declined. But the French for their part, after the election of Blum and the Popular Front, were unwilling to have any further truck with Italy. Mussolini could now display his misgivings more openly, and the new anti-French turn in his policy was reflected, soon after the Abyssinian war, in changes in the *Palazzo Chigi* where Ciano took the place of Suvich as Foreign Minister. The *Wilhelmstrasse* had been expecting these changes some months before and reacted promptly. On 18 June Hassell, who had just returned from Germany, told Ciano that both Party and Reichswehr circles were in favour of collaboration with Italy. There was however a widespread suspicion that Italy might be working to facilitate a Habsburg restoration.[1] Italy and Germany would have to adjust their policy towards Austria before real progress in improving their relations could be made.

After the outbreak of the Abyssinian War, Italian influence in Austria, which was almost exclusively economic, declined, and on 6 January Mussolini declared he would have no objection if Austria were to become a German satellite.[2] Mussolini's declaration did not bear fruit immediately, for at that time Schuschnigg was pursuing the opposite course of trying to associate his country with the Little Entente and the French system of alliances. His efforts towards this end were resisted not only by Germany but by Hungary; they were defeated and he had to content himself with the more doubtful blessings of an extension of the Rome Protocols. On 23 March 1936 Austria, Italy and Hungary agreed to consult together on issues affecting the Danube area. The first tangible indications of the waning of Italian influence could be perceived almost immediately afterwards. In May Stahremberg, the Vice-Chancellor and Mussolini's protégé, was excluded from the Austrian Cabinet.[3] Provided that Schuschnigg, who now held undisputed power, could be dissuaded from resorting to a Habsburg restoration, there was no further obstacle in the way of a temporary German-Austrian *modus vivendi*. In these circumstances limited control over the Austrian Government could be used as the

[1] Ciano's *Papers.*
[2] See p. 66.
[3] RIIA, *Survey 1936*, pp. 428–9 and Wiskemann, chap. IV.

next step towards achieving an Anschluss by the gradual process of disintegration. By 'The Gentlemen's Agreement' of 11 July Germany recognized the independence of Austria, while Austria for her part declared herself to be a 'German state'. The Treaty was in no way intended to affect Austria's relations with Italy as established by the Rome Protocols, and Mussolini, believing the danger of an *Anschluss* to be less imminent, did not conceal his gratification. On 11 July he told Hassell that Austria would no longer be 'a football of foreign interests' and that the 'last and only mortgage on German-Italian relations was finally removed'. He also expressed his misgivings over Czechoslovakia because of her friendship with Russia.[1]

Within a week Italy's dependence on Germany was to become even more galling. A serious crisis, which had been gathering momentum for some time, came to a head in Spain.[2] It did not end in a few days with an old style *pronunciamiento* but in a long and bitter civil war. The consequence was serious, for it placed Germany in an incomparably good position for bargaining. Whereas Mussolini, having once embarked on the Spanish adventure, had thrown away his last opportunity for reaching an agreement with France, which was the only card he could play against Germany, it was still open to Hitler to come to some sort of understanding with Britain. On 30 July Hassell told Ciano that Germany intended to answer a British invitation to a conference for a new Locarno within a couple of days. Hitler's ten point plan of 30 March would be used as a basis for discussions. Ciano immediately objected and saw no reason why, as stipulated in the plan, Britain should have the honour of presiding over the proceedings. Hassell also informed him that Germany's aim was to attract Britain into a group of anti-communist States.[3] This was probably Hitler's real intention at that time; otherwise, it is difficult to explain why—despite the protests of Neurath—he decided in July to appoint Ribbentrop, who was at that time still anglophil, as Ambassador to London.

With the prospect of an Anglo-German rapprochement being Mussolini's one haunting fear both he and Ciano did all in their power to prevent either Ribbentrop, who took up his post in

[1] DGFP (D), Vol. I, pp. 281–5.
[2] See DGFP (D), Vol. III, pp. 1–2 (editor's note).
[3] Germany did not reply to a British questionnaire of 7 May dealing with German proposals of 31 March. RIIA, *Survey, 1936*, pp. 335–41.

October[1], or any other highly placed German, from achieving success in London. Already by the autumn of 1936 Mussolini had a 'secret weapon'. On 3 September Grandi, his Ambassador in London, sent him a dossier of thirty-two official documents, written between 26 April 1933 and January 1936, and collected by Eden for the private information of members of the Cabinet.[1] They were an authentic selection of the most significant despatches from Sir Eric Phipps, the British Ambassador in Berlin, in which the activities of the Third Reich were sharply criticized: they were entitled 'The German Peril'. In an introduction contributed by the British Foreign Secretary, Hitler's foreign policy was described as being directed towards the destruction of the *status quo* established after the war and the emergence of Germany as the predominant Power in Europe. In Eden's view it was therefore vital for Britain to finish rearming as soon as possible. Meanwhile she should seek a *modus vivendi* with Nazi Germany.

Mussolini set out to play the role of Iago with the handkerchief. On 23 September he met Frank, who was then German Minister without Portfolio and the Party's expert on legal matters. Mussolini mentioned the existence of the dossier but he did not reveal its contents. It was also arranged at the meeting that the Duce should visit the Reich. On 20 October Ciano, not Mussolini, arrived in Berlin. He met Neurath on the 21st, whom he found to be in an anti-British mood and pleased to learn of the dossier which was to be given to the Führer. In Ciano's presence on the 24th Hitler read Eden's introduction and a telegram from Phipps, in which the rulers of the Third Reich were described as 'dangerous adventurers'. It produced 'a profound impression'. Hitler exclaimed: 'According to the English there are two countries in the world today which are led by adventurers: Germany and Italy. But England, too, was led by adventurers when she built the Empire. Today it is merely governed by incompetents.'[2] The Führer insisted

---

[1] See ND: Neurath: 16, a letter from Neurath to Hitler of 27 July and Mussolini's conversation with Frank, discussed below, in which Mussolini stated that he was certain that Ribbentrop's mission would fail, Ciano's *Papers*. Grandi in a letter to Ciano of 6 November 1936 advocated German-Italian unity to prevent attempts at splitting the Axis. See Note on Sources, p. 195. Mussolini was particularly apprehensive about Anglo-German relations at a time when a visit by Neurath to London was under discussion, DGFP (D), Vol. III, pp. 327–9, and Neurath's despatch of 14 June 1937. Ibid., pp. 338–9.

[2] Ciano's *Papers*, pp. 46–52.

that many countries which were suspicious of Germany and Italy could be won over if communism were vigorously attacked. In his opinion there could be no doubt that 'England will attack Italy, or Germany, or both, if she feels she can do so with impunity or with ease . . .'. But if she saw the gradual formation of a group of Powers 'which are willing to make common front with Germany and Italy under the banner of anti-Bolshevism . . . not only will she refrain from fighting against us, but she will seek means of agreement and common ground with the new political system'. If in spite of this England were to continue to form 'offensive plans and merely sought to gain time to rearm, we could defeat her on her own ground, since German and Italian rearmament is proceeding much more rapidly than rearmament can in Great Britain, where it is not only a question of producing ships, guns and aeroplanes, but also of psychological rearmament. In three years Germany will be ready, in four years more than ready . . .'. Ciano, however, believed that Hitler was still uncertain. He was told by Neurath that this was due to Ribbentrop 'who every so often attempts to inject Anglophil optimism' into his Chief. Ciano believed that any success Ribbentrop might achieve in his English mission would spell ruin for Neurath.

Whether the intelligence fed to Hitler on this and later occasions caused him to revise his attitude towards Britain is not known. It may have confirmed or completed an impression which was already being formed. In Hitler's mind—as far as one can understand its workings at all—the British were fundamentally realists and only understood force. It will be seen later how he himself, and more especially Ribbentrop, came to believe that appeasement was a means to gain time for armaments.[1] It is difficult to dissociate suspicions of this kind from the thesis Eden propounded.

While Ciano was in Berlin a secret German-Italian Protocol was concluded. Although neither party was obliged to support the *Axis* other in the event of a European war, each agreed to follow a common policy in Spain and South-East Europe. Germany in effect had declared the Mediterranean to be Italy's *mare nostrum* and this was to be the cornerstone of the partnership. On 1 November, after Ciano's return, Mussolini solemnly pronounced the existence of the Axis. Italy was already more than fulfilling her side of the bargain. Her strength, which might otherwise have been available

[1] See p. 108 and pp. 134–5.

for mounting guard on the Brenner, was now being drained in the new Peninsular War.[1] From Hitler's point of view <u>the longer this imbroglio lasted the better,</u> for he saw in it the seeds of a possible conflict between Italy and the Western Powers and a chance for Germany to grab what she could in central Europe.[2]

Meanwhile Hitler was turning to the third member of the Axis. The value of <u>Japan</u> as an ally in 1936 was dependent on two factors: the policy of <u>Russia and Britain</u> towards Germany; whether Japan would oppose Russia or concentrate on expansion in <u>China</u>. <u>Britain</u> was not formally committed to France's allies in central Europe, and so Hitler made every effort not to antagonize her unduly. <u>Russia</u> on the other hand had, by her treaties with France and Czechoslovakia, already joined the camp of Germany's potential enemies. Since the leading Russian generals had not yet been liquidated, Soviet military power was thought to be considerable. Consequently Japan was of value in <u>diverting Soviet strength from Europe.</u> On the other hand if Japan sought aggrandisement in China she might jeopardize German economic interests. At a ministerial council on 27 May 1936 Blomberg emphasized the need for raw materials from China. There should be 'no brusque dealings' with that country, and caution was necessary in improving relations with Japan; recognition of Manchukuo, for instance, would ruin the prospects of successful business transactions. Blomberg also thought Japan was 'questionable as a power factor'. Göring expressed similar views and advocated a common front of China and Japan against Russia. He also thought that Japanese policy oscillated. Germany too had a mission of military advisers in China under General von Falkenhausen, who, like von Seeckt, regarded China as a new field for the promotion of the Eastern school of German policy.

On 25 <u>November 1936 Germany and Japan</u> concluded the <u>Anti-Comintern Pact.</u>[3] The main body of this treaty, to which other

---

[1] Ciano's *Papers*, pp. 51–2 and pp. 60–1. See also DGFP (D), Vol. III, pp. 170–3, a comprehensive despatch of 18 December 1936 on the significance of the Spanish Civil War from Hassell in Rome.

[2] This was the opinion Hitler gave to his immediate advisers on 5 November 1937 (p. 106). The German Navy on the other hand was not in favour of supporting France, see DGFP (D), Vol. III, pp. 50–2, a memorandum of August 1936.

[3] ND: 1301-PS. According to Dirksen, the German Ambassador in Tokyo, contacts began with the formation of a German company for the exploitation of Manchuria in 1935, Beloff, op. cit., Vol. II, p. 169. For the text of the Anti-

Powers were permitted to accede, merely provided for <u>internal</u> <u>defence against the Communist International</u>. An additional secret agreement (Article 11) reads: 'should one of the High Contracting States become the object of an unprovoked attack or threat of an attack' by Soviet Russia the other party was obliged to 'take no measures which would tend to ease the situation' of the Soviet Union. The two parties also agreed to consult together should the Soviet Union use its armies for the promotion of the International. The <u>Anti-Comintern Pact was signed with reservations on both sides</u>. Germany could still adhere to her treaties with Russia, in so far as they had 'not become null and void' at the time the Pact came into force, and she was not obliged to sacrifice friendship with China.[1]

In the <u>summer of 1937</u> the circumstances in which the Anti-Comintern Pact was signed changed. The <u>military purges in Russia</u> had just been carried through,[2] and consequently the German High Command's estimate of Russia as a power factor was completely revised. Russia was taken much less seriously into account in all subsequent planning, and her forces merely provided an excuse for refusing to negotiate on arms limitation.[3] At the same time the <u>Sino-Japanese conflict</u>, which broke out in <u>July</u>, raised new and serious problems. It confronted Germany with the alternative of either maintaining her economic and military ties with China or of drawing still closer to Japan in opposition to the West rather than to Russia. At the end of August Albrecht <u>Haushofer</u>, an authority on German minority questions, described the changed

Comintern Pact see DGFP (D), Vol. 1, p. 734 fn. See also Dirksen, *Moscow, Tokyo, London*, pp. 182–3.

[1] For a full account, see an article by Gerhard L. Weinberg, *Vierteljahrshefte für Zeitgeschichte*, April 1954. In it a number of documents consisting of an exchange of notes between Ribbentrop and Mushakoji, the Japanese Ambassador to Berlin, are reproduced. These documents were used in War Trials in the Far East and have been published in English. The instructions to the German Embassy in Nanking of 30 November 1936 also show German reservations to the Anti-Comintern Pact (see Note on Sources, p. 195).

[2] The first major series of state trials took place in August 1936; the second, after the conclusion of the Anti-Comintern Pact in January 1937. In June 1937 Marshal Tukhachevsky and four generals were executed. See Carr, *German-Soviet Relations Between the Wars*, pp. 118–22, also Beloff, op. cit., Vol. II, pp. 5–8.

[3] Beloff, op. cit., Vol. II, pp. 83–4 and p. 169, describes how the second Anglo-German Naval Agreement of 17 July 1937 was delayed until Britain signed a similar treaty with Russia. Hitler also used Russian air armaments as an excuse for not disarming. See DGFP (D), Vol. I, p. 245.

situation in the Far East and drew conclusions on its probable effect on German policy. He pointed out how the moderates, who were in control of Japan before the conflict, tried to reach a settlement with Britain, even if this were to jeopardize their relations with Germany. Subsequently tension in the Mediterranean and purges in Russia provided Japan with an opportunity to attack China and foil Chiang Kai-Shek's programme of internal consolidation. Originally the Japanese believed that a limited offensive in the north would suffice: China would thus be separated from Russia and a buffer state could be established. This plan miscarried and instead Japanese forces drove down the east coast of China and in so doing antagonized the Western Powers. Haushofer also stated that if the Chinese adopted the Russian tactics of 1812 Japan would be exhausted and German interests in China menaced by chaos and communism.[1] The report was widely read and appreciated, and can be corroborated by despatches from the German Embassy in Tokyo. Japanese action was deplored by the *Wilhelmstrasse*. By spreading chaos it stimulated Communism and was considered to be contrary to the spirit of the Anti-Comintern Pact. Germany therefore was at first strictly neutral and refused to withdraw her military mission from China.[2]

Although Italy ostensibly endorsed the German view that peace in the Far East was desirable, Dirksen, the German Ambassador in Tokyo, hinted that her real attitude was essentially pro-Japanese. He believed that she was 'currying' Japanese favour at Germany's expense. Later Hirota, the Japanese Foreign Minister, informed Dirksen that the Italians desired not only a pact of benevolent neutrality with Japan but one providing for mutual consultation. Italy wished to embroil Japan with Britain, who would then be compelled to withdraw naval forces from the Mediterranean.[3] Italy's accession to the existing Anti-Comintern Pact would thus have far-reaching consequences; it would alienate Germany from Britain still further and compel her to sacrifice her interests in

[1] ND: 3817-PS. See also Ribbentrop's verbal evidence, IMT, Vol. X, p. 424. Originally Hess, Ribbentrop and Dirksen acquired copies of Haushofer's report. Later the Führer and many leading Nazis, as well as the Foreign and War Ministries and Navy, were given it.

[2] DGFP, Vol. I, despatches from Tokyo, 3 August, p. 748, and 23 August, p. 754. See also instructions of 20 July, p. 733 and pp. 742–4. See also Hitler's memorandum of 17 August, p. 750.

[3] Dirksen's despatch of 8 September, op. cit. pp. 757–8.

China. Counsels in Germany were divided. Previously in Ciano's opinion Neurath was pro-Italian whereas Ribbentrop was the fiend who kept alive Hitler's hopes of an Anglo-German understanding. In the autumn of 1937 there was a reshuffle of opinion. Ribbentrop admitted that his feelings for Britain had changed, and Ciano compared them with those of a 'woman for a faithless lover'.[1] For a time there was no certainty whether Neurath or Ribbentrop would prevail. On 22 September Neurath indignantly told the Japanese Ambassador that Germany would not recall Trautmann, her Ambassador in Nanking, who had distinct sympathies with China, and that Germany did not desire a Tripartite Pact.[2]

Meanwhile Ribbentrop, whose *Dienststelle* or Personal Bureau was busily encouraging other States to join the Anti-Comintern Pact, conferred with General Oshima, the Japanese Military Attaché in Berlin and a member of the military party. In a memorandum for the Führer of 19 September Ribbentrop stated that he was convinced that Japan would win a decisive victory. She had 'passed brilliantly the test of strength', and had successfully flouted Britain and the USA over the Shanghai incident. Ribbentrop also attempted to sever German trade with China.[3]

There can be little doubt that when Mussolini and Ciano[4] visited Germany at the end of September they exacerbated Hitler's feelings towards Britain. Despite warnings from General Geyr von Schweppenburg, the German Military Attaché in London,[5] Hitler —after some hesitation—drew closer to a noisy and bellicose Italy. On 19 October Weizsäcker in instructions to von Hassell pointed

[1] See Ciano's *Papers*, 3 May 1937 and 22 October 1937 and *Diaries*, 24 October 1937.

[2] DGFP (D), Vol. I, p. 760.

[3] Ibid., pp. 750–2 and p. 758. On 18 October following an order from Hitler, conveyed by Raumer, export of further military supplies to China was prohibited. Later Göring virtually quashed the order; memoranda of 19 and 22 October, ibid., p. 768 and p. 772. For a brief account of Oshima's activities see Namier, *Europe in Decay*, pp. 129–30.

[4] Ciano however already showed some reservations about co-operating with Germany, *Diaries*, 29 September 1937. He and the Duce no doubt still wished to keep open the door for an agreement with Britain. See also Circular to Diplomatic Missions of 30 September, DGFP (D), Vol. I, p. 1 and a memorandum of 2 October, p. 2 cf. Ciano's *Diaries*, 3 September 1937. For other outbursts of Mussolini against Britain, see Ciano's *Diaries*, 14 September 1937 and 29–30 September 1938.

[5] See *The Critical Years* by Geyr, Chaps. V and X.

out that Germany could not reject a proposal for a bilateral Italo-Japanese agreement and would prefer it to a Tripartite Pact. The next day, however, Raumer arrived in Rome, and in the presence of von Hassell presented Ciano with the contrary proposal for a Tripartite Pact. Ciano was puzzled by the change and, despite certain reservations, appeared to be gratified.[1] On the 22nd Ribbentrop, who arrived in Rome to continue negotiations, preached 'a military alliance between Italy, Germany and Japan in anticipation of the inevitable conflict with the Western Powers'. On the 25th Hitler agreed that the Pact should be signed in Rome. Changes in appointments were also considered. Ciano told Hess on the 27th that the Italian Foreign Office was the most Fascist body in Italy. He demanded Hassell's 'scalp', whereupon Hess railed against Neurath and all the old school of diplomats. On the 30th Ciano was pleased to learn that the Führer, although annoyed with Ribbentrop for not having kept Neurath informed about the Pact, had agreed that he should have his way.[2] On 1 November the Japanese agreed to the Pact which was duly signed on the 6th. Although no spectacular change followed, and although Germany hesitated about recognizing Manchukuo, the Pact was evidently regarded as a prelude to a military instrument against the West. Hitler was in an anti-British frame of mind at that time, and Ciano described it as 'anti-Communist in theory but unmistakably anti-British'.[3]

While Hitler may have hoped to extend the Anti-Comintern Pact into an alliance for an eventual encounter with Britain, he could also profit from it in the immediate future. Britain was unlikely to support France and assume commitments in central Europe so long as her vital interests were threatened by Italy and Japan. Russia moreover could hardly take an active part in a European war now that her best military leaders had been shot.

[1] DGFP (D), Vol. I, pp. 15–16, a despatch from Hassell; see also Ciano's *Papers* and *Diaries*, 20 October.

[2] *Diaries*. The English translation of this passage is faulty.

[3] *Diaries*, 5 November 1937. See also entries for 6, 21 and 24 November. See Hassell's despatch of 10 November, DGFP (D), Vol. I, pp. 27–8 and the despatches for 20, 22 and 27 November, pp. 784–6.

CHAPTER 11

The Parting of the Ways

(February 1938)

Hitler's decision that Germany should herself sign a tripartite Pact with Italy and Japan, though of trivial significance in itself, had been made in the teeth of opposition from his professional advisers, and was to prove a turning point of the highest significance above all in South-East Europe.

Mussolini's visit to Germany in September 1937 caused consternation in Vienna, where the German Embassy reported that Schuschnigg's government was trying to improve relations with Hungary and Czechoslovakia: allegedly Schuschnigg saw his 'crowning achievement' in the restoration of the Habsburgs.[1] But it will be seen that Hitler had not yet decided to change his policy towards Austria, and it is doubtful whether he genuinely believed that the Austrians were becoming *Kaisertreu*. It was more urgent for him to forestall the danger that their neighbours, the Sudeten Germans, might be torn from their teutonic allegiance and, by absorption into a multi-national state, share the supposed ignominious fate of the German Swiss.[2] Everything represented by the Czech 'idea' was abhorrent to Hitler. It was the most successful product of the settlement of Europe in 1920 and stood for a reconciliation of the conflicting hopes and interests emanating from Moscow and Geneva. An armed Czechoslovakia, too, barred the way to eastward expansion. Only her removal would assure Germany of military preponderance over central Europe.

Since 1935 the Sudeten German Party had been subsidized by

---

[1] DGFP (D), Vol. I, despatches of 7 October and 14 October, pp. 467 and 472 and 5 November, p. 478. See also Göring's conversation with Bullitt of 23 November (ND: 151-L), and Ciano's *Diaries*, 16 November 1937.

[2] Henlein constantly referred to what he called *Czechoslovakization* on 'the Swiss model', e.g., his memorandum for Hitler of 19 November 1937, DGFP (D), Vol. II, p. 51. For a more general account of the policy of Benes, see Namier, *In the Nazi Era, Curtain Raiser to the Czech Crisis of 1938.*

the Reich.[1] It was to play a role similar to that of the National Socialists in Austria and disrupt the State from within. There were, however, important differences in the tactics to be followed. Austria was an all-German State from which no party was safe from infiltration. Since an *Anschluss* might, at least in theory, be achieved be allowing the process of disintegration to take its own course, armed force was only to be used in support of a *coup de main* or in an emergency. The predominant national group in Czechoslovakia, on the other hand, was opposed by tradition to the spread of German influence in any shape or form, and although the Sudeten Germans were conveniently situated in the fortified frontier areas, they were only a minority with no decisive influence. By their own efforts they could not hope to bring about the dissolution of that alien political structure, the Czech State, where they were living 'in subjection': at most they were mere auxiliaries who could assist in the process of its fragmentation.[2]

It was dangerous for the Sudetenlanders to advocate union with Germany openly: their demands had to appear moderate, and they may have been allowed some freedom by Berlin in the formulation of policy. Like the Irish, they had been schooled for years in skilful manipulation of democratic formulae; and Konrad Henlein, their leader, knew almost instinctively how to employ tactics, which were well calculated to embarrass the Government of Prague, even more effectively in London. For this reason alone Henlein was well qualified to perform useful missions. He visited Britain in May 1936 and according to Chamberlain he created a 'favourable impression'.[3] He was again in that country in the spring of 1937, but unfortunately little is known about the outcome of these early visits.[4]

Henlein, who was to come into almost daily contact with Englishmen during the Czech crisis, may at times have influenced Hitler's attitude towards Britain almost as decisively as Ribbentrop. But unlike Ribbentrop he displayed none of the traditional

[1] See, ND: 3059-PS.
[2] There is no reference to the role of the Sudeten Germans in any military directive on Czechoslovakia. *Schulung* and later operational plans were purely military. Blomberg's directives of 24 June and 7 December 1937 both mention support from party formations in Austria. See Chap. 9.
[3] Feiling, *Life of Neville Chamberlain*, p. 281.
[4] Even Celovsky's masterly survey, *Das Münchener Abkommen*, suffers from an unbalanced documentary foundation, above all for the period before November 1937.

characteristics of the 'teutonic elephant tripping it amongst the crockery'.[1] He was tactful and his simplicity of manner—in truth his ludicrous naïvety—won him extensive sympathy. He was able to deceive even those British officials who otherwise were suspicious of anything remotely affiliated to Hitler's Germany. According to Ashton-Gwatkin, Henlein appeared to be 'genuine in his protestations' and a 'man of Peace . . . I did not dislike Henlein. He was a good-looking chap, hail-fellow-well-met, athletic.'[2] A visit by Henlein to London from 10 to 15 October 1937 was particularly successful. He told Vansittart that the aim of his party was autonomy within Czechoslovakia. He asked that any 'good advice' Britain and France could give Benes 'should be given soon', for he could no longer control his followers, ninety per cent of whom wanted absorption into Germany. Vansittart, who also thought Henlein a 'decent, honest, and moderate, or anyhow relatively moderate, man', found him embittered by the lack of progress already made with the Prague Government. Other Foreign Office officials thought he was deliberately painting an alarming picture so as to get the British and French to stir up Benes. But they thought he was right in the main and they therefore agreed to urge Benes to be more conciliatory. Unfortunately no record has been found of what Henlein told Hitler on his return, but fragments of the proceedings of a conference with the Führer of 17–18 October were reported in a despatch of 22 October from Eisenlohr, the German Minister in Prague. Eisenlohr, who evidently learnt of what took place through some confidential channel, stated that Henlein formed the opinion, from a talk with Vansittart, that 'no serious intervention in favour of the Czechs was to be feared, either from Great Britain or France'.[3] Eisenlohr was in all likelihood quoting Henlein correctly, and Hitler later paid tribute to the success his emissary had scored in London.[4]

Henlein's October visit is of additional importance in that it

[1] Grandi's description of Ribbentrop's gaffes, when he arrived in London in October 1936, are to be found in an Italian Embassy despatch of 6 November 1936; see Note on Sources, p. 195.

[2] Ashton-Gwatkin was a member of the Runciman Mission to Czechoslovakia which functioned from 4 August to 14 September. The above passage is quoted from Namier, *In the Nazi Era*, p. 143.

[3] DGFP (D), Vol. II, pp. 20–3. Eisenlohr does not state how the news of the talk between Hitler and Henlein leaked out but merely that it was learnt 'in strict confidence by the Legation and unfortunately not only by them'.

[4] Ibid., pp. 197–9.

coincided with an incident inside Czechoslovakia. On 17 October members of the Sudeten German Party alleged that they had been attacked with truncheons by the police at Teplitz-Schönau. Although incidents of this kind were not unusual, both Eisenlohr. and Henlein attached particular importance to it because of public feeling in the Sudetenland. Eisenlohr reported that the Czechs were convinced that the incident was staged, and that the Sudeten leaders were themselves under the impression that it 'might afford the occasion to bring the Sudeten-German question to a head with the help of the Reich'. Eisenlohr added that Henlein used a similar language in his conversation with Hitler on 17 and 18 October.[1] Eisenlohr's general impressions are confirmed in a memorandum for the Führer of 19 November in which Henlein showed how the broad masses of his followers no longer believed in a 'compromise with the Czech people within the Czech state'. His party desired 'nothing more ardently' than the incorporation of 'the whole of the Bohemian, Moravian and Silesian areas' in the Reich.[2] Perhaps Hitler's subsequent decisions would not have been arrived at so soon and the will to enforce them have been so brutal, had it not been for the clamouring of those who had once been citizens of the land of his birth.

On 5 November, a few weeks after his talk with Henlein, Hitler addressed his principal advisers and announced that the time had come to put an end to Czechoslovakia. Blomberg, Fritsch, Raeder, Göring and Neurath were present as well as Colonel Hossbach, Hitler's adjutant, who recorded the proceedings five days later. According to Jodl no official report of the conference was made and the versions in the possession of the War Ministry and the Air Ministry were not in complete agreement.[3] He opened on the *Mein Kampf* theme that the aim of German policy was to safeguard, preserve, and enlarge the racial community (*Volksmasse*). The question for Germany was: where could she achieve the greatest gain at the lowest cost? She had to reckon with 'two hate inspired antagonists', Britain and France. Both were opposed to any strengthening of Germany's position either in Europe or overseas. Because of opposition from the Dominions, and loss of

---

[1] DGFP (D), Vol. II, pp. 20–3.

[2] Ibid., pp. 49–62.

[3] ND: 386-PS. See also Hossbach, op. cit., pp. 217–20. According to Jodl's *Diary* for 21 January Hitler addressed the Generals on history, politics, national unity, religion and the future of the German people.

British prestige after the Abyssinian war, the return of colonies was not to be expected. At most Germany might expect Portuguese Angola. Serious discussion on colonies would have to wait until 'Britain was in difficulties' and the Reich 'armed and strong'. He 'did not share the view that the British Empire was unshakeable'. The threat from Japan in the Far East and from Italy in the Mediterranean were further reasons for Britain's precarious position. He then elaborated three possible opportunities for German action. In the first it was assumed that Germany would strike when she had attained maximum power, before 1943–5. The second and third set of circumstances would arise if France were either torn by civil war or involved in a conflict with Italy. Of the two, the second seemed more likely. The threat to Germany's flanks in a war with the West would be removed by overthrowing Austria and Czechoslovakia simultaneously. Although Czechoslovakia might not declare war on Germany on the day of the outbreak of a Franco-German war, she might do so later at a more convenient time. After the defeat of Czechoslovakia, when Germany had a common frontier with Hungary, threat of force would assure Poland's neutrality in the event of a war with the West. The Führer believed that Britain and France had tacitly written off Czechoslovakia and that the French would shrink from either attacking the West Wall or from invading the Low Countries without British support.[1] Germany for her part would not violate these countries for fear of precipitating British action. During the attack in the South-East, operations in the West would be defensive. Hitler spoke highly of Austrian and Czech armed strength and here the main effort would have to be made.

He then dilated on Germany's gains after conquering her first two victims. Provided the expulsion of two million Czechs and one million 'undesirable' Austrians could be carried out successfully, there would be additional food for five to six million German citizens. Germany would have strategic frontiers and troops could be freed for other tasks. On the assumption that one division could be raised from one million inhabitants, the Army could be increased by about twelve divisions. While Italy would not object to the

---

[1] He seems either to have ignored or not to have obtained the views of his Minister in Prague concerning the possible extension of French obligations to Czechoslovakia. See DGFP, Vol. II, pp. 30–1, a memorandum of 6 November; also Wheeler-Bennett, *Munich*, p. 30.

elimination of the Czechs, her attitude to Austria depended on whether the Duce was still alive.[1] The Führer believed that intervention by Russia could be countered by swift operations: because of Japan, it might even be completely discounted. Poland would not act for fear of Russia. The possibility of a Franco-Italian conflict was drawing nearer and he was resolved to take advantage of it, even in 1938. An early victory by France was not to be welcomed—on the ground that Britain and France might gain the support of a united Spain for ejecting the Italians from the Balearic Islands. In a war with France, Italy, fearing neither a British landing nor a French invasion across the Alps, could concentrate on attacking French possessions in North Africa. If Germany took advantage of such a conflict Britain, herself at war with Italy, would not intervene. The timing for the invasion of Czechoslovakia and Austria need not coincide with military operations in the Mediterranean and an alliance with Italy was considered unnecessary. Germany would merely exploit Italy's independent warlike actions.

Hitler took his audience completely by surprise. They learnt, with consternation, that he might act earlier than they had previously expected.[2] Remonstrances were spontaneous. Blomberg and Fritsch insisted that Britain and France should be given no cause for intervention. The Führer repeated his conviction that this danger could be discounted. Fritsch pointed out that even if twenty French divisions were tied down by Italy on the Alpine frontier, the French would still have a preponderance of forces over Germany for an invasion of the Rhineland. They had moreover a definite lead in the rapidity of mobilization. It was also pointed out that German fortifications were inadequate and that the four motorized divisions intended for the West were still hardly capable of movement. Blomberg drew attention to the strength of Czech fortifications which now resembled the Maginot line, and Fritsch replied that the problem of storming them would be studied in the winter. Fritsch also proposed cancelling his leave, but unwisely accepted the Führer's assurance that a conflict was

[1] Mussolini gave Ribbentrop his assurance on the following day (Ciano's *Papers*, 6 November).

[2] The conference also gave rise to a serious but apparently short lived scare. Blomberg learnt from what was described as a reliable source that François-Poncet had obtained a report of the proceedings on the following day, see Note on Sources, p. 195.

not imminent. Neurath doubted whether an immediate Franco-Italian conflict was so likely as the Führer assumed, but Hitler replied that the summer of 1938 seemed possible. Finally Göring's proposal that military support for Franco should be cancelled was adopted. Hitler had cause to be gratified. His audience consisted of a select few, and there was thus less likelihood of concerted opposition. According to Schacht, Hitler excluded many likely opponents, such as himself, by not calling a full cabinet meeting. Immediately afterwards Neurath had a heart attack and offered his resignation: according to Raeder, Hitler had intended to break the old man's nerves. Also during the conference there had been altercations—presaging things to come—between Göring and the two Generals Blomberg and Fritsch.[1]

Hitler was serious in the pronouncements of 5 November. The Directive of 24 June 1937 was amended in a supplement of 7 December in which operation Green (a German attack against Czechoslovakia) was to take precedence over operation Red (a German defensive in the West).[2] The new suppositions underlying Green were: 'When Germany has attained full preparedness for war in all spheres the military conditions for an offensive war against Czechoslovakia will have been established and with it the problem of Germany's living space can be solved victoriously even if one or other Great Power should intervene against us. Among many other considerations the defensive capacity of our western fortifications is of primary importance. This makes it possible to hold the Western frontier of the Reich for a long time with weak forces against an opponent many times as strong as ourselves. But even then the Government will do everything possible to obviate the risk of a war on two fronts and will try to avoid any situation to which Germany, as far as anyone can judge, is neither militarily nor economically equal . . .'. It was also laid down that if it were later necessary to use military force against Austria, army reserves as well as armed formations of the SS were to be held in readiness. Sustained resistance by the Austrian Army was considered unlikely. The supplement indicates that from the purely military

---

[1] See Schacht, *Account Settled*, pp. 126–7 and Hossbach, *Zwischen Wehrmacht und Hitler*, p. 219. See also ND: Neurath 3 and IMT, Vol. XIV, p. 36.

[2] There were two supplements. The first can be found in ND: 175-C, the second is now published in DGFP (D), Vol. VI, appendix III, K. The author's translation is used below.

point of view there were still reasons in favour of entering Czechoslovakia before Austria, and it is possible to detect in it certain of Blomberg's reservations to Hitler's pronouncements of 5 November. Although the supplement was sanctioned by Hitler on 13 December Blomberg cannot have been over anxious to see it put into effect, for that day he reported adversely on the supply of war material.[1]

Already the rift between Hitler and his generals, ably described elsewhere,[2] was widening. Its strategic implications can be stated simply. Hitler later summarized his attitude in the words: 'We are facing the alternative to strike or to be destroyed.'[3] For Hitler, the war that was not fought was lost; for his staff it might have to be postponed, even indefinitely. If Hitler announced: 'we must act before we fail', the generals replied: 'we should only act when we are certain to succeed'. But differences between them were a matter of mental perspective, not as is so often supposed, merely one of timing and method. While Beck was fully prepared to examine means by which Germany could maintain and improve her position by the use of force, he yet foresaw the social and, by implication, the moral consequences involved in the conquest and eviction of the inhabitants of neighbouring States. On 12 November, commenting on Hitler's conference on the 5th, he writes, 'the fact should not be overlooked . . . that the distribution of population (*Bevölkerungslage*) in Europe as such has so stabilized itself for a thousand years and more that far-reaching changes scarcely seem attainable without the heaviest and lasting disruption, the effects of which cannot be foreseen . . .'. Beck further argued that the importance of Czechoslovakia and Austria should not be exaggerated as surplus food areas.[4]

Fritsch and Beck however only attempted to deter Hitler when he took practical steps to implement his policy; neither foresaw the dangers inherent in examining the theoretical possibility of invading other States. In this connection their attitude to an attack on Czechoslovakia, before the crisis of 1938, is illuminating. In

---

[1] Jodl's *Diary*.

[2] Förtsch, *Die Fritsch Affäre*, and Wheeler-Bennett, *Nemesis of Power*, Chap. II.

[3] The Staff Conference of 22 August 1939, ND: 79-PS.

[4] A memorandum probably submitted to Blomberg, Förster, op. cit., pp. 61–5. Beck also criticized the value of Czechoslovakia as an area for expansion on 29 May, ibid., p. 90.

December 1935, Beck had pointed out that the army would have to shoulder the main burden in a defensive war with France and Czechoslovakia.[1] In a memorandum by Fritsch of August 1937 the emphasis completely changed; only land forces could *conquer* Czechoslovakia and win *Lebensraum* in the East. The tone of a later memorandum of 7 March 1938 by Brauchitsch is even sharper; here the word *crush* is added to *conquer*.[2]

The increasing emphasis on conquest can be attributed to non-strategic and internal considerations. The Army High Command saw their position rivalled by that of the Air Force; they also resented the encroachments of Blomberg's staff, through which Hitler exercised his control over all three services. Their dilemma was genuine. In order to preserve the traditional status of the *Reichswehr*, Fritsch had to prove that it alone was the one irreplaceable instrument of destruction; its leaders should thus have at least a controlling voice over war policy. But the means defeated the ends; they were in effect saying 'in order to stop Hitler's war we must sharpen the sword to fight it'. The reorganization of the entire structure of command and early plans for conquest were both under discussion in the same period, and the army leaders, in stressing their claims, and with it the 'total' character of modern war, may have jeopardized their own conscientious attempts, made later, to call a halt to adventure. They suffered from an additional disadvantage in not being united. Hitler could thus break resistance by new appointments and push forward his plans all the more relentlessly.

Early in the New Year he either jettisoned, or withdrew his favour from, those military and political leaders who might in the future exercise a moderating influence. Blomberg, as we have seen, despite his belief in Hitler's miraculous powers, was unwilling to give unqualified support to the policy outlined on 5 November.[3] On 15 December, two days after presenting a pessimistic report on military supplies, he was stated by Jodl to be 'highly excited'

[1] Ibid., p. 34. Beck also discussed early in 1937 the Army's political role in an age of total war, pp. 45–7.

[2] See Note on Sources, p. 195. The memorandum was written for Blomberg and was decidedly opposed to the influence of the *Wehrmachtsamt* (Armed Forces Office) under Keitel: it was evidently locked up in a vault, unread, Jodl's Diary, 6 March 1938. Brauchitsch's memorandum had an identical aim and contained many of the main ideas put forward by Fritsch. It was answered by Keitel on 19 April. See alo Jodl's *Diary*, 18 January.

[3] See p. 106.

111

apparently over a 'personal matter'. Blomberg, who in any case was disliked by his brother officers for his dabbling in theosophy, was subsequently forced to give up his post as the result of a mésalliance with an ex-prostitute.[1] Fritsch, who enjoyed far greater popularity in the army and who was more likely to inspire and lead opposition against Hitler, was also removed through the sordid machinations of Himmler and Göring on a trumped-up charge of homosexuality. Hitler took advantage of the bitter personal jealousies of those competing for the vacant posts. On 4 February 1938 he became his own War Minister; he was already Supreme Commander of the Armed Forces (*Wehrmacht*) with Keitel as his *Chef de Bureau*. The General Staff prevented Reichenau from taking the place of Fritsch, and on the recommendation of both Generals von Rundstedt and Keitel, von Brauchitsch was appointed the C-in-C of the Army. Although Brauchitsch could now approach Hitler directly without an unpopular intermediary, he was not of the same calibre as Fritsch, and on his appointment he agreed to certain changes in organization.[2] With a weaker Commander-in-Chief, Beck's position as Chief of Staff became almost entirely advisory, and he was subsequently to exercise no effective control over military decisions. The authority of the General Staff was further impaired by the appointment of Schmundt as Hitler's *Wehrmacht* adjutant. He, unlike his predecessor Hossbach, was out of sympathy with Fritsch and Beck and was given to hero-worship.[3]

Many other important changes were made in the civilian departments. Schacht was replaced by Funk as Reich Minister of Economics; Hassell was removed from Rome and his place taken after an interval by von Mackensen, formerly the State Secretary; General Ott, the Military Attaché in China, who at one time had been adjutant of Schleicher and therefore not wanted at home, was appointed Ambassador in Tokyo while Dirksen was transferred from Tokyo to London instead of Ribbentrop. By far the most important of these changes was the dismissal of Neurath as Foreign Minister and the appointment of Ribbentrop. Henceforward the *Wilhelmstrasse*, which apart from the High Command, was the one

---

[1] Jodl's *Diary*. See also Rundstedt's evidence, IMT, Vol. XXI, p. 50.

[2] Jodl's *Dairp*, 28 January and 3 February. Keitel does not appear to have been such a sycophant at that time as he later became. See also IMT, Vol. XXI, p. 23.

[3] See Förster, op. cit., pp. 19–20 and Hossbach, op. cit., Chap I.

government department in Germany with some say in the formulation of policy, could only bring pressure to bear on Hitler through a reckless and unscrupulous intermediary. Despite Göring's sporadic sorties into questions of foreign policy, Ribbentrop was Hitler's mentor, above all in those things pertaining to Britain.

The Conference of 5 November and the changes in appointments which followed mark a real turning point in Hitler's pre-war policy. Whereas in August 1936 he described a conflict with Russia as inevitable[1] he now, and in later addresses to his staff, made it abundantly clear that he would turn on the West after he had eliminated Czechoslovakia, a fact overlooked in most histories of the period where the *Mein Kampf* anti-Soviet theme is stressed. After the resignation of Vansittart and Eden,[2] Chamberlain persisted more obstinately than ever on his policy of appeasement, and the return of Colonies was given priority. On 3 March Henderson discussed with Hitler Chamberlain's proposals. A plan for the limitation of armaments was curtly brushed aside on the highly spurious pretext that Soviet military power constituted a threat to the Reich. Hitler dismissed Chamberlain's offer for the redistribution of African territory with the comment that opinion in Britain and France was not 'ripe' to give it consideration. From Hitler's words it can paradoxically be inferred that he was speaking on behalf of the Western democracies themselves, and this ought not to have evaded Henderson's notice.[3]

Already when Henderson met Hitler, Chamberlain had made a frantic effort to come to some sort of terms with his adversary 'while he was in a way with him'. But Chamberlain was too late. Matters were unexpectedly to come to a head in central Europe.

---

[1] See Chap. 9.

[2] For German reactions to Vansittart's appointment, see DGFP (D), Vol. I, despatches from London of 5 and 14 January, pp. 169–70 and pp. 176–7; to Eden's fall, despatches from London of 25 February, ibid., pp. 218–25.

[3] Ibid., a minute of 4 March, pp. 240–9. See also Henderson, *Failure of a Mission*, pp. 115–8.

CHAPTER 12

The Effects of the Anschluss

It has been seen how at his conference of 5 November 1937 Hitler[1] was thinking in terms of a simultaneous entry of German troops late in 1938 into Czechoslovakia and Austria. No immediate change therefore could be expected in his existing policy, formulated after the murder of Dollfuss, towards the discouragement of revolution in Austria. At the end of September 1937 Hitler had told Göring that 'Germany should cause no explosion of the Austrian problem in the foreseeable future'.[2] Events in Austria, however, which have been described in greater detail elsewhere, got out of control.[3] The illegal Austrian Nazi Party, sharing the aspirations of the Sudetenlanders, became increasingly impatient and hoped to bring the day of their 'deliverance' nearer by violent means and by forcing the hand of the Reich.[4] But, living in a State which was professedly 'German', they were unable to pose as a persecuted national minority. Their riotous behaviour had the mark of insubordination; it involved them in endless squabbles, not only with the Austrian authorities, but with the Reich. Early in July 1937 the Austrian Government learnt of the illegal contacts between the Party in Austria and Germany; and Papen, supported by Seyss-Inquart, a 'respectable' Nazi, protested to Hitler that the policy of capturing the Austrian Government by non-revolutionary means was in jeopardy.[5] Once again Hitler decided to tame the Party men. Later in July he promptly put them under the control of SS *Gruppenführer* Dr. Keppler, a member of Göring's economic staff. This did not prevent them from giving further trouble, and on 25–26 January 1938, the Austrian police were provoked into raid-

---

[1] See Chap. 11.

[2] See a memorandum probably by Keppler of 1 October 1937, DGFP (D), Vol. I, pp. 463–4.

[3] Eichstädt, op. cit.

[4] Papen evidently took this view, see his despatch to Hitler of 4 February 1938, DGFP (D), Vol. I, p. 499.

[5] Abundant documentary material on these disputes can be found in DGFP (D), Vol. I, Chap. II.

ing their headquarters in Teinfaltstrasse, Vienna, where incriminating documentary evidence was found proving that they were banking on armed intervention by the Reich in 1938. Hitler, who always tried to present his policy under the façade of legality, was in a parlous position. Whereas he had taken Henlein into his confidence after a similar incident a few months before, he now dismissed the leader of the Austrian Nazis, Captain Leopold, and angrily told him that his actions were 'insane'.

Immediately after the Teinfaltstrasse raid Schuschnigg was forced to take the initiative. He had no option but to try to conciliate the more moderate section of National Socialist opinion, and accordingly visited Berchtesgaden on 12 February. There he failed to obtain any assurance from Hitler that Germany would continue to abide by the 'Gentleman's Agreement' of 11 July 1936. Although he agreed, under duress, to admit Seyss-Inquart into the Federal Government, and although Mussolini no longer backed him, he had not surrendered. Having attempted to rouse Austrian patriotism by a speech of 24 February he made the desperate decision of 8 March to call a plebiscite for the 13th. Hitler, aware that the plebiscite would probably result in a popular vote in favour of Austrian independence, was determined to forestall Schuschnigg. He hurriedly summoned his military commanders and in a directive of the 11th ordered them to be ready for the invasion of Austria at the latest by noon of the 12th.[1] Schuschnigg's cancellation of the plebiscite on the 11th was of no avail. That day Göring, in Hitler's absence, demanded first Schuschnigg's resignation and later the appointment of Seyss-Inquart as Chancellor. President Miklas refused to comply with the second demand, whereupon Göring ordered Seyss-Inquart to act on the Austrian Government's own behalf and ask the Reich for armed protection. Although Miklas gave way shortly before midnight on the 11th, German troops were already on the march.[2] Hitler was in no mood to cancel the operation at this stage. Earlier on the 11th he had despatched Philip of Hesse, his unofficial emissary to Rome with a long and pompous letter intended as a *pièce justificative* for Mussolini. Hesse phoned Hitler from Rome at 10.25 p.m.

---

[1] Hitler's directive for the invasion, ND: 102-C, was released at 2 a.m. on the 11th but not signed until 1 p.m. See Jodl's Diary for 10 and 11 March.

[2] For Göring's telephone conversation on the 11th, see ND: 249-PS and DGFP (D), Vol. VII, Appendix III.

and said that the Duce 'had accepted the whole thing in a very friendly manner'.[1] Hitler was thrown into transports of joy and said, repeating himself hysterically many times: 'I will never forget him for this.' He was soon to be with his Army on its way to Linz.

Of the great powers Italy was the one most immediately affected by an *Anschluss*, and the French were not likely to take action alone, particularly at a time when they were without a government. On the 11th the French Ambassador in Rome had tried but failed to contact Mussolini on counter-measures.[2] Britain was even less likely to do anything if Italy held aloof, for according to the Anglo-French communiqué of 3 February 1935 she had merely expressed her willingness to join in discussions with other interested powers on the maintenance of Austrian sovereignty.[3] Chamberlain, it seems, was not so much alarmed by the prospect of an *Anschluss* as by the methods Hitler was using to bring it about, and he had no alternative but to register some kind of protest. This, however, did not prevent him from expressing his readiness to continue negotiations on colonial concessions. All in all, Chamberlain wished to be conciliatory, but he had to show righteous indignation.

On 10 March Ribbentrop on his farewell visit to London held an important discussion with Halifax, the new Foreign Secretary. Halifax made no bones about the seriousness of the situation; he was certainly not taken in by Ribbentrop's bombastic banter. Having reminded Ribbentrop that the colonial question could never be treated in isolation, he insisted that Britain had not tried to thwart German ambitions in Austria but had rather tried to 'steady European opinion shaken by the Berchtesgaden interview'. Halifax continued on a warning note, quoting Bismarck. 'The experience of all history went to show that the pressure of facts was sometimes more powerful than the wills of men; and if once war should start in Central Europe it was quite impossible to say where it might not end or who might not be involved.' Later Halifax pointed out that while he personally held little faith in

---

[1] DGFP, Vol. I, pp. 573–6. Bullock, op. cit., p. 389, has incorrectly given the 10th, instead of the 11th, as the date the letter was sent. The letter was subsequently published with the omission of hostile passages concerning Czechoslovakia, see also Ciano's *Diaries*, 12 March. Hitler's answer by phone can be found in ND: 2949-PS.

[2] Ciano's *Diaries*.

[3] See p. 55.

plebiscites Schuschnigg was perfectly entitled to hold one if he wanted to 'without interference or intimidation'.[1]

There can be no gainsaying that this was plain speaking. Halifax, even at this early stage, knew what to expect from Hitler. But the whole immediate impact of his words was lost, for Ribbentrop in his own version of the interview, addressed directly to the Führer, made no mention of Halifax's warning. He had also so watered down and misleadingly phrased Halifax's reference to the plebiscite that he gave the impression that Britain had expressed her *désinteressement* in Austria, albeit with just sufficient reservations to clear her conscience. In describing his impression from this and other interviews in a memorandum for Hitler of the 10th Ribbentrop expressed himself in less cynical terms than he had done on 2 January.[2] 'It looks', he maintained, 'as if Chamberlain and Halifax want to achieve a peaceful understanding among the Four Great Powers of Europe without the Soviet Union.' Ribbentrop added that a solution to the colonial issue was possible. He no longer believed that Britain wanted to negotiate with Germany in order to disrupt the Berlin-Rome Axis, but that she was trying to improve her relations with both Germany and Italy simultaneously. This could only be 'advantageous' to Chamberlain because 'England's primary aim continues to be to gain time in order to complete her armament.' Ribbentrop also raised the question, 'What now will England do if the Austrian question cannot be settled peacefully? Basically, I am convinced that England of her own accord will do nothing in regard to it at present, but that she will exert a moderating influence upon other powers.' Nor was it likely in Ribbentrop's mind that France, Italy and their respective allies would intervene. The prerequisite, however, would be a 'very quick settlement of the Austrian question. If a solution by force should be prolonged for any length of time, there would be danger of complications.'

Ribbentrop was soon given further significant indications of the trend of British policy. At a luncheon party on the 11th Chamberlain told him that 'it had always been his desire to clear up German-British relations, and he now made up his mind to realize

---

[1] DBFP, third series, Vol. I, two despatches from Halifax, pp. 4–6.

[2] DGFP (D), Vol. I, pp. 264–9, cf, ibid., pp. 162–8. See also Kordt's memorandum of 10 March on a conversation with Sir Horace Wilson, ibid., pp. 269 ff.

this aim'. Ribbentrop was requested to tell the Führer that this was his 'sincere wish and firm determination'.[1] Shortly before Ribbentrop left Downing Street that afternoon telegrams on latest developments in Austria were brought to the Prime Minister. It now transpired that Schuschnigg had been given an ultimatum to resign. According to Chamberlain an 'exceedingly serious situation had arisen', and the discussion continued in a 'tense atmosphere'. According to Ribbentrop, 'the usually very calm Halifax was more excited than Chamberlain, who outwardly at least appeared calm and cool-headed'. Ribbentrop, according to Halifax, was 'frankly mystified' by the news from Austria. He had received no instructions and was thus in the embarrassing position of not being able to give a prepared reply.[2]

Halifax recognized that any warnings he made through Ribbentrop were not likely to have much effect. He had therefore instructed Henderson beforehand to convey to Hitler the substance of the warning delivered to Ribbentrop on the 10th. After the lunch party, when the crisis had perceptibly worsened, Henderson received further instructions arising from his government's remonstrances to Ribbentrop.[3] That evening Henderson raised the subject of Britain's reactions with Neurath, still acting Foreign Minister, whom he found to be in a reasonable mood and evidently pleased over the censure his hated rival in London had been given. Later that night Henderson met Göring. Having lodged his Government's protests Henderson 'reluctantly agreed' with Göring, that Schuschnigg had behaved with 'precipitate folly'. The next day Halifax expressed great annoyance with Henderson and told him that the opinions he had expressed to Göring 'diminished the force of the protest'.[4] Ribbentrop, too, instead of stressing the great indignation which Hitler's *fait accompli* had aroused in Britain, merely gave Göring a gushing account of the general atmosphere of friendliness in London and of Chamberlain's goodwill towards the Reich. He had also added so many words of his

[1] DGFP (D), Vol. I, pp. 276–7.
[2] For the German account of the interview see ibid., pp. 273–5; see also Wörmann's note fn. 98, p. 275. For the British account of the interview, see DBFP, third series, Vol. I, pp. 21–3. Halifax here also described a conversation he had with Ribbentrop at 5.15 p.m.
[3] DBFP, third series, Vol. I, p. 8, p. 14 and pp. 18–19 and Henderson's résumé of events, 15 March, pp. 56–9.
[4] Ibid., pp. 15–6, pp. 23–4, and p. 29 and p. 39.

own to the translation for the Führer of the agreed text of his talk with Halifax on the 10th, that the effect of the warning, which in any case had arrived too late, was muffled.[1]

Although the Great Powers of Europe had not time to forestall Hitler, they responded promptly by defining their attitude to any fresh acts of aggression. France, alarmed by what she must have regarded as a Sadowa, reaffirmed her obligations to Czechoslovakia on 14 March, and was supported by Russia. Whether Britain would stand by her if war broke out was now a question the answer to which brooked no delay. Halifax's warning to Ribbentrop of the 10th was to serve as a general formula of British policy for several months ahead, Chamberlain used it in the House of Commons on 24 March when he declared: 'If war broke out it would be unlikely to be confined to those who have assumed such obligations.' Had the declaration been made publicly before the *Anschluss* it might have done some real good. But its terms were too loosely phrased to meet the new situation: it left Britain with the option, rather than with the obligation, of resisting aggression. But if Chamberlain is accused of obscuring issues, it must be said in his favour that he had consulted with both the Foreign Office and the Chiefs of Staff on Churchill's proposal for a grand alliance, but that their response was negative.[2] Even if Chamberlain failed to give France and her allies qualified support his declaration was a definite advance on previous statements of policy and it was open to new and more binding interpretations. Whereas a year earlier the possible victims of German aggression in central Europe

[1] For Ribbentrop's telephone conversation see ND: 2949-PS. For his interpolations to the agreed text of the interview of the 10th see the passages in double parenthesis, DGFP, Vol. I, pp. 253–61. Meanwhile Göring's interception service of the Luftwaffe, the *Forschungsamt*, had deciphered what were evidently circulars to French diplomatic missions abroad from which, he claimed, it could be proved that the French urged intervention but that 'action was frustrated only because Britain declined'. Göring, in describing the contents of these intercepts (*braune Meldungen*) for the Führer over the phone to Bodenschatz, one of his staff, on the 13th, said that Britain's attitude was 'decisive' and that it was in no way represented by her pro-Austrian Minister to Vienna. There is no evidence to suggest that Britain was ever approached by France on immediate military action, and the intercepts probably gave a distorted picture of both British and French intentions. The *braune Meldungen* may have served as additional proof that Britain was averse to assuming fresh commitments on the Continent, DGFP (D), Vol. VII, Appendix iiie, pp. 600–2. Unfortunately the intercepts have not been found.

[2] Wheeler-Bennett, *Munich*, pp. 62–3; Churchill, op. cit., Vol. I, pp. 213–4; Feiling, op. cit., p. 347.

were told that they could not count on British assistance, Germany was now told that she might have to reckon with British intervention. Wörmann, the German Chargé d'Affaires in London, even regarded the Declaration as an implied 'warning' to Germany and an 'emphatic proffer of help to France'.[1]

The *Anschluss* was not only an abrupt check to the movement towards an Anglo-German rapprochement but it encouraged Chamberlain to persevere in conciliating the other partner of the Axis. The opportunity seemed favourable, for despite Mussolini's dramatic *nihil obstat*, Hitler's coup was far from welcome to Italian sentiment. The German minority in the South Tyrol were, according to Ciano, getting 'too uppish'. On 24 April Mussolini told him that if they attempted to move the frontier post 'one single yard' they must 'learn that it cannot be done without the most bitter war, in which I shall combine the whole world into a coalition against Germanism, and we shall crush Germany for at least two centuries'.[2] For a time it was questionable whether the Axis could survive the strain, and it was still open to Italy to look for friends elsewhere. Indeed, if she failed to follow up British overtures for a settlement of disputes in the Mediterranean and East Africa she might find herself isolated and forced to look on helplessly at German expansion towards the Adriatic.[3]

In these perplexing circumstances an Anglo-Italian Agreement was concluded on 16 April, according to which Italy was obliged to withdraw volunteers and material from Spain, at the latest after the Civil War, while Britain promised to facilitate recognition of Italian sovereignty over Abyssinia.[4]

[1] For a convenient account of the declaration see Wheeler-Bennett, *Munich*, pp. 32–40. See also DGFP (D), Vol. II, pp. 192–3.

[2] Ciano's *Diaries*, 3, 17 and 18 and 20 April and a memorandum by Mackensen of 20 April, DGFP, Vol. I, pp. 1082–3. Mackensen recommended that Hitler should allay Italian suspicions about a *Drang nach Südosten* during his forthcoming visit.

[3] See Ciano's *Diaries*, 23 April, where Mussolini even considered an agreement with the French. See also minutes of conversations with the British Ambassador for 22 February, 8 and 12 March, Ciano's *Papers*. Grandi evidently feared that if an agreement were not reached speedily Chamberlain might fall (Ciano's *Diaries*, 4 March). These British approaches were treated cynically by Mussolini because of the probable effect made on him by the steady leakage of documents from the British Embassy at Rome, all of which he read personally. See also Toscano, *Le Origini del Patto d-Acciaio*, Chap. I.

[4] For the text see RIIA, *Docs.*, 1938, Vol. I, pp. 141–8. Mussolini made a very chauvinistic speech at Genoa on 14 May which resulted in a British pro-

Reactions to the Treaty in Germany were hardly uniform. Whereas the Naval High Command and the *Wilhelmstrasse* were relieved because the danger of war with Britain on account of a rash Italian move was reduced,[1] Hitler was evidently thinking on entirely different lines. It has been seen how complications in the Mediterranean were essential for his plans. According to notes by Schmundt on a conversation with Hitler, probably at the time of the Anglo-Italian agreement in April, German action against Czechoslovakia was still dependent on Italian initiative.[2] Hitler claimed that, should Mussolini consider his mission finished, Czechoslovakia would have to wait until the distant future and the German frontier in the West would be fortified. If Mussolini chose to extend his *imperium* in Africa, which would not be possible without German help, 'Czechoslovakia would be in the bag'. If Czechoslovakia were supported by Britain and France, she could be eliminated only by a 'close alliance' of Italy and Germany. The West would then not intervene, as the redeployment of forces from Africa to the French eastern frontier would take four weeks. At the conference of 5 November Hitler had merely hoped to take advantage of an independent Italian warlike enterprise. It seems that now, perhaps under the influence of Ribbentrop, he desired a military alliance.

But his primary concern was to prove to Mussolini that despite the *Anschluss* Italy was safe. Accompanied by Ribbentrop he visited Rome and conferred with Mussolini and Ciano between 3 and 6 May. Ribbentrop sounded Ciano on an alliance, and whereas the Duce was disposed to take up the offer, Ciano gave an evasive answer. Ribbentrop's bellicose utterances were a bit much even for Mussolini who described him as one 'belonging to that category of Germans who are a disaster to their country'. Ribbentrop had

test on the 18th. Thereafter Anglo-Italian relations did not improve. Since the Treaty could not take effect until certain conditions were fulfilled it had little immediate force; and when it was implemented in October there had been no improvement in Anglo-Italian relations.

[1] See also DGFP (D), Vol. I, pp. 1079–80, a despatch from Weizsäcker to the German Legation in Prague of 19 April. See also a memorandum by Mackensen of 25 April on possible future developments in Italian policy, pp. 1097–1001.

[2] ND: 388-PS, item 1. The notes are semi-legible and handwritten. They are not dated but the next item in the file is 21 April. It is also evident from the context that they were written at about the time of the Anglo-Italian Agreement of 16 April.

in fact talked of 'making war right and left', without naming an enemy or defining an objective. 'Sometimes he wants, in collaboration with Japan, to destroy Russia. Sometimes he wants to hurl his thunderbolts against France and England. Occasionally he threatens the United States.' Hitler on the other hand showed remarkable discrimination, and succeeded pretty well in melting the ice round him. After his return the ill feeling evoked by the *Anschluss* was soon forgotten.[1] At a staff conference of 28 May Hitler described tension between Italy and the West as 'extraordinary', and he again talked of an alliance with Italy and Japan.[2] By that time, however, a German attack on Czechoslovakia was no longer dependent on an Italian move, for the assumptions underlying Hitler's plan had changed.

Immediately after the *Anschluss* there were military no less than political reasons for not dealing with the Czech problems immediately. Although Czechoslovakia was now almost fully encompassed, Austria, owing to bad communications was not, according to operational plans drawn up in the summer of 1938, to prove such an effective new strategic vantage point as might be supposed.[3] Moreover, the military organization for the movements of troops was improvised and far from successful. Improvements would have to be made before a real military operation could be contemplated. In these circumstances Hitler was in no hurry to solve the Czech problem: 'Austria would have to be digested first'.[4] Since it was in his interests to allow the general state of tension to calm down, his Government declared that its Arbitration Treaty with Czechoslovakia in 1925 was still valid, and the more moderate German Legation in Prague was allowed to exert a measure of control over the rowdy followers of Henlein.[5] Nevertheless the Sudeten Germans, wild with excitement over events in Austria, were more anxious than ever that their cause should be taken up by the Reich, and on 17 March Henlein wrote to Ribbentrop expressing thanks to 'all those who contributed to the success

[1] Details of the visit are graphically described in Ciano's *Diaries*, 3–9 May. See also the entry for the 12th.

[2] Förster, op. cit., pp. 89–90, see also p. 125.

[3] See p. 130.

[4] See the undated entry in Jodl's *Diary* preceding the first entry for May 1938, p. 46.

[5] See Göring's assurance to Mastny, the Czech Minister to Berlin, of 11 March, DGFP (D), Vol. II, p. 157.

of this great new work of the Führer'. He went on to say: 'the new situation demands an examination of Sudeten German policy. To this end I beg the opportunity of an early personal talk with you.' Henlein duly arrived in Berlin where he conferred with Hitler and other Nazi leaders on 28 March. Hitler complimented him on his previous success in London, and instructed him to make another visit and to 'continue to use his influence with a view to ensuring non-intervention by Britain'. Hitler was doubtless influenced by Chamberlain's Declaration of 24 March, which was not regarded with such equanimity in Germany as might be supposed. Hitler also stated earlier in the conference that he intended to 'settle the Sudeten problem in the not too distant future'. It was agreed, largely on Henlein's own initiative, that the Sudeten Party should not 'drive things to the limit' but always demand 'so much that we can never be satisfied'. On the 29th, when Henlein met Ribbentrop, it was decided that in the future the Sudeten Party, not the Government of the Reich, was to appear to be the negotiating party with Prague.[1]

The decisions reached in Berlin determined Henlein's future conduct, and there is a marked resemblance between the draft proposals drawn up by Ribbentrop and dated 28 March and Henlein's later demands on the Czech Government. But it must not be supposed that the Sudeten Germans responded automatically to directives emanating from either their own party or Berlin. With pent-up ebullience released by the *Anschluss*, and suffering from severe economic hardships, they were more than capable of acting on their own. According to Eisenlohr, they expected possible direct intervention from the Reich after the plebiscite in Austria due to be held on 10 April. Early that month feelings became more violent and they characterized the negotiations which were then taking place between their leaders and the Czechs as 'a betrayal'.[2] Henlein had thus to keep the road open for negotiations without disappointing his turbulent followers, for if he failed to specify his demands the British Government might assume that he did not desire a settlement.[3] On the 24th he put *April* forward eight demands at Karlsbad in which nothing short of full

---

[1] Ibid., pp. 173–4 and pp. 197–9 and pp. 204–5.

[2] See despatch of 31 March, ibid., pp. 208–9 and of 9 April, pp. 226–7.

[3] See Eisenlohr's despatch of 26 April, ibid., p. 245 and a report of 14 April, p. 236.

administrative self-government was declared to be acceptable. The demands themselves were not formulated in precise legal terms: they were extraordinarily elastic, and Henlein could represent them as the basis either for negotiation or for an ultimatum. For instance, he later suggested that if Benes suddenly accepted them he could insist on a change in Czech foreign policy.[1] The Karlsbad demands had their desired effect on British opinion. They reinforced Chamberlain in his view that, provided Benes could be prevailed upon to make concessions, Britain would be saved the necessity of having to take a definite stand. On 3 May Halifax informed Dirksen that his Government intended to exert pressure on Prague 'to show the utmost measure of accommodation to the Sudeten Germans'. An Anglo-French *démarche* was made in Prague on 7 May, and the Czechs agreed to negotiate on the 17th.[2]

Meanwhile from 12 to 14 May Henlein visited London. Despite pronouncements to the contrary he first received instructions from the German Government and was briefed by Ribbentrop and Weizsäcker on the 12th. He was to deny that he was acting under orders and to speak of the progressive disintegration of the Czech political structure, actually taking place, 'in order to discourage' those who 'consider that their intervention on behalf of this political structure may be of use'. On his arrival Henlein met Vansittart as well as certain opponents and supporters of the Prime Minister. He stated clearly that the Karlsbad demands were not an ultimatum but a basis for negotiation. According to Dirksen Henlein created an excellent impression.[3] It is not known what he reported to the Führer on his return, but his account of the general opinion in Britain must have been encouraging. Hitler as a result of Henlein's report may even have been persuaded to force events inside Czechoslovakia where municipal elections were to be held on 22 May and where a serious crisis was brewing.

Despite the Karlsbad demands the Sudeten Germans remained restive. In a despatch of 13 May, while Henlein was still in London, Eisenlohr described how 'hardly anyone thinks any longer of autonomy on however a comprehensive scale. The overwhelming majority, in fact almost the whole population, hopes for *Anschluss*

---

[1] Ibid., pp. 242–3 and a memorandum of 3 June, p. 384.

[2] Ibid., pp. 255–6 and Wheeler-Bennett, *Munich*, pp. 49–52.

[3] See Dirksen's assurances to Halifax of 3 May, DGFP (D), Vol. II, pp. 255–6, and Ribbentrop's statement to Henderson made after his visit to Rome, *Failure of a Mission*, pp. 132–3.

with the German Reich and expects it in the immediate future.'[1]
A few days later a German Press campaign was launched against
Czechoslovakia. In the excited sequel it was rumoured that German troop movements in Saxony and Austria were intended for an
immediate invasion. On 20 May, Czechoslovakia partially mobilized.[2] The next day Halifax delivered a warning to Dirksen, the
wording of which was almost identical with that of Chamberlain's
Declaration of 24 March. Halifax, however, took pains to explain
to the French that they should not take British armed assistance
for granted. At this stage the irresolution of the French government became apparent, for although it reaffirmed its pledges it
urged the Czechs to abstain from military measures.[3]

Hitler had not yet decided on armed action, and the alarm felt
in Prague was unfounded. But he was filled with indignation: he
was now determined to repay the Czechs for what he later described as their 'rascally trick'.[4] On 28 May he again addressed
prominent Army, State and Party leaders and disclosed an even
more drastic plan than that of 5 November 1937. 'In the event of
war between Germany and the Western Powers, the aim of which
is the extension of our coast line (Belgium and Holland), Czechoslovakia, as an enemy in the rear, stands in the way of a certain
German victory. She must be removed.'[5] While Hitler was now
definitely thinking in terms of a war fought exclusively against the
Western Powers the immediate problem, however, was Czechoslovakia. Hitler gave his listeners two reasons why an invasion of that
country could not be attempted immediately: inadequate striking
power for storming the Czech fortifications and slow progress made
on the West Wall. There were, Hitler pointed out, certain advan-
tages to be gained from a longer interval of peace: more could be
learnt about Czech military intentions and the German people

---

[1] DGFP (D), Vol. II, pp. 276–9.

[2] Ibid., p. 289, a despatch from Eisenlohr of 18 May. See also a report by
Canaris, ND: 388-PS, item 9.

[3] DGFP (D), Vol. II, pp. 322–3 and DBFP (third series) Vol. I, pp. 346–57.

[4] DGFP (D), Vol. II, p. 672, an undated memorandum for Mussolini of
September 1938.

[5] Förster, op. cit., pp. 88–90. Beck's notes on the conference are not quoted
by Förster verbatim but are paraphrased. According to Förster the number
of people attending the conference was probably greater than on 5 November
1937. He quotes Kordt, *Wahn und Wirklichkeit*, p. 110, as evidence of this
view. See also Hitler's reference to the conference in a speech of 30 January
1939, Baynes, op. cit., Vol. II, p. 1571.

could be psychologically better prepared. Hitler believed that outside intervention was improbable; British rearmament would only make itself felt in 1941–42, while France and, above all Russia, were inadequately prepared for the offensive.

On 30 May, two days after the conference, a directive was issued for the invasion of Czechoslovakia. It was to be launched at the latest on 1 October.[1] There is a marked contrast between the wording of the preamble to this directive and that to a draft directive produced by OKW on the 20th. It was now Hitler's 'unalterable decision to smash Czechoslovakia in the near future. It is the concern of the political authorities to await or bring about the suitable political and military occasion. Events inside Czechoslovakia and elsewhere which create a favourable opportunity might lead me to take early action. The proper choice and determined use of a favourable moment is the surest guarantee of success. . . .'

[1] See also a covering letter to the directive of 30 May. ND: 388-PS, item 11. Cf. item 5.

CHAPTER 13

Hitler Versus the Generals

On 28 May Hitler had definitely decided on Operation Green, and further protests from his staff were only to be expected. Beck's attempts, first to force Hitler to abandon his plan and later to remove him from office, have been described fully elsewhere.[1] Here prominence is given to the strategic issues which divided Hitler from his Generals.

Hitler's operational intentions, put forward in a draft directive to Keitel of 21 April, and with certain modifications reincorporated in a directive of 30 May, were in certain respects new. In previous plans it was hoped to take Czech forces by surprise and to destroy them before they were properly mobilized.[2] After the May crisis Hitler recognized that an attack out of the blue (*aus heiterem Himmel*) was no longer possible, and he prophetically stated that he would reserve this fate for Germany's last enemy on the Continent. Some ingenious device therefore had to be worked out which would not make Germany appear to be guilty of an unprovoked attack. Two choices were considered: first, Germany could strike after a period of political tension; second, she could avail herself of a diplomatic incident, such as the assassination of the German Minister in Prague.[3] If the first alternative were followed counter-measures might be taken and surprise rendered less effective. Hence the second was favoured but could, if necessary, be combined with the first. By this curious means Hitler hoped to combine military efficiency with political wisdom.

The attack would have to be driven home with utmost ferocity

---

[1] Förster, op. cit., chap. V. Hossbach, op. cit., chap. IX. Wheeler-Bennett, *The Nemesis of Power*, Chap. III. Rothfels, *The German Opposition to Hitler*, pp. 55 et seq.

[2] See p. 89 and p. 109.

[3] Hitler had no objection to removing Eisenlohr, the German Minister in Prague.

127

and speed. Provided that the Czechs could be defeated in about four days, French, and therefore Russian, intervention, which was dependent on the French, would be purposeless. A later OKL appreciation of 25 August shows in greater detail what was expected to happen. First, in contrast with Blomberg's speculations in the previous year, France was likely to declare war only if she were certain that Britain would follow suit. Second, France was obliged to support Czechoslovakia only in the event of an 'unprovoked' attack. The two Western Powers therefore would probably need two days to decide on a legal formula and a third for the resulting ultimatum to expire. For military reasons the French were not expected to fight until 4 to 18 days after the attack, by which time Germany would have deployed forces for a defensive in the West. A lightning four day blitzkrieg would also have resounding effects on Poland and Hungary, who, like 'wolves', wished to be in time for the kill. They were even more likely to take part if France, fearing Italy, held aloof.[1]

Beck heatedly contested the validity of these assumptions in a series of memoranda which he produced in the course of the summer.[2] He maintained that there could be no question of impressing the world with the hopelessness of Czechoslovakia's military situation within a few days; to expect to reach Prague after two days was a 'mad dream'. The Czechs would not be taken unawares but be prepared. Success of a surprise initial blow was, moreover, for tactical reasons, by no means certain. Beck could not predict how long it would take to break Czech resistance, but gave three weeks as a favourable estimate. Not for 14 days could German forces in the West, which from the start were under strength, receive their first reinforcements from the south-east to resist a French offensive.

Beck accepted the view that France was 'the strongest military Power' on the Continent. Even if substantial forces were pinned down by Italy she would still have effective preponderance over the Reich. Already on the fourth day of mobilization, she would have three times the divisional strength of German forces on the

---

[1] ND: 375-PS. An appreciation of 25 August, and ND: 388-PS, item 2.

[2] Beck's memoranda of 5 and 30 May, of 3 June and 16 and 19 July, his conversation with Brauchitsch of 29 July and his military testament, which was intended to be read by Brauchitsch to the other generals early in August, are here all considered in conjunction. They can be found in Förster, op. cit., chap. V.

fifth in the west. He also claimed that the assembly of forces for the two theatres of war could not be carried out simultaneously; and that the air formations should be deployed for defence of the west rather than against Czechoslovakia. Beck had no doubt that France would honour her obligations and that as early as the first day or war Britain would stand by her. Britain realized that time was on her side and that she would gain access to the vast resources of the USA. She would probably decide how the war was to be conducted and select the objectives. At first a limited offensive on land with the aim of occupying the west bank of the Rhine might be attempted. The main effort, however, would be made from the sea and air. Czechoslovakia would not be abandoned if such a course were followed, for, if she were overrun, her independence would be restored at the end of the war, like that of Serbia after World War I. An attack on Czechoslovakia would be the occasion, not the cause, of war; Britain would fight not so much for the preservation of that country as for the defeat of a 'new Germany', which was 'destructive of peace and a threat to the most important elements of English political life: justice, Christianity and tolerance'.

Beck, like most military experts in other countries, certainly exaggerated the dangers to which his own country was exposed. On his reasoning Germany's potential allies were either weak or unreliable; her enemies, resolute and strong. In addition she herself was worse off economically than she had been in 1917–18. One wonders whether he was not deliberately painting an over-pessimistic picture and using the Czech crisis to utter a warning against Hitler's general policy. Even before the May crisis Hitler also discussed waging a separate war with Britain, and although Beck did not allude to it explicitly it may have been at the back of his mind. At any rate Beck repeatedly declared that, irrespective of the outcome of the campaign in Czechoslovakia, 'Germany would lose the war'.

Beck relinquished his post at the end of August and was thereupon succeeded by the less resolute General Halder on 1 September. Thereafter disagreement between Hitler and his staff hinged to a greater degree on technical matters. Was the main objective to be Prague or the point of convergence of two armies slicing Czechoslovakia in half? Should operations start at dawn

9

or noon? How long was the interval to be between the order for the attack and the attack itself?

At a Führer conference on 3 and again on 9–10 September OKH put forward their intentions.[1] The 2nd Army under General von Rundstedt, operating from Silesia, should be heavily reinforced with mobile formations and make contact with the 12th and 14th Armies under Generals von Leeb and List, advancing respectively from Bavaria and Austria. The aim of these thrusts from the north and south was to cut Czechoslovakia at her waist and so prevent a retreat from the western areas into Slovakia. At Hitler's instigation the 10th Army under General von Reichenau, deployed on the extreme western tip of Czechoslovakia, was to be reinforced by one motorized division at the expense of Rundstedt's and Leeb's formations. Hitler's motives were almost certainly political. Reichenau was not only one of his sympathizers, but his army was to operate in an area largely inhabited by Sudeten Germans, and Hitler mentioned making possible use of them in operations. Moreover, Hitler was anxious to capture Prague as soon as possible: on 9–10 September he stated that a political success was necessary and that a far-reaching territorial gain had to be scored in the first eight days.[2]

Differences of opinion were even more deep seated. In post-war accounts of the German opposition, it has been claimed that OKH demanded a clear and prompt advance notice on the date and hour of the attack because their intended coup was to take place between this order and the 'first exchange of shots'.[3] Whatever is to be said in support of this, OKH were moved by technical no less than political considerations. The German armies were deployed in widely dispersed assembly areas and they would have to advance from different directions. Rolling stock would only be available a few days before the attack. It was thus essential that movements should be concerted, and the date and hour of operations known in good time. At an inter-service conference on 24 August the Army leaders argued that mobilization could only proceed smoothly if advance measures were taken three days before the invasion; that the order for attack should not be given

[1] ND: 388-PS, items 18 and 19. The controversy is fully and ably described by Telford Taylor, op. cit., pp. 206–12. See also Jodl's *Diary*, 10 September.

[2] ND: 388-PS, items 18 and 19, the conference of 3 and 9–10 September.

[3] This question is fully described in Wheeler-Bennett, *The Nemesis of Power*, p. 409.

later than at 2 p.m. the day before. The Air Force, on the other hand, anxious to take enemy air formations by surprise, were opposed to all measures planned before the order for attack. It should be given as late as possible on the previous day so as to prevent the fact of German mobilization from becoming known. In Jodl's opinion the 'fixing of the time and hour' for the 'diplomatic incident', which was to be used for opening hostilities, was of the 'utmost importance' and would have to determine the issue.[1] It must be staged when weather conditions were favourable. Authentic news should reach OKW at noon the day before so that the order for the attack could be automatically released at two o'clock. The respective branches of the services should only receive warning two days in advance. On no account should measures be carried out which might create the impression that the incident had been staged. On the 31st the Führer agreed to act on these lines.[2]

Defensive preparations for war against France constituted the most important issue. It has been seen that at the end of May Hitler ordered work on the West Wall to be speeded. General Adam, the Commander-in-Chief of the 2nd Army Group deployed in the west, was not confident that the fortified positions could be held for long. At the close of a long after-dinner speech which Hitler delivered to his staff on the 10th, General Adam, who was not present, was quoted by General Wietersheim as saying that the West Wall could not be held for longer than three weeks. Hitler, on hearing this, flew into a rage and said: 'I tell you, General, the position will not be held for three weeks but for three years.'[3] Yet Hitler, realizing the defectiveness of the West Wall, issued a directive through Keitel to OKH ordering work (henceforward known as the *Limes* plan) to be continued at its existing rate even if mobilization were in force, provided that military action was not made immediately necessary by France. In a directive of 24 August Brauchitsch passed the Führer's instructions to the 2nd Army Group. It was foreseen in this directive that after 20 September the railways could only supply material for *Limes* to the extent that requirements for mobilization and the assembly of

---

[1] See the Führer conference of 3 September, ND: 388-PS, item 18.

[2] Yet no final decision was evidently taken, for on 8 September Stülpnagel, the acting Deputy Chief of Staff, was informed by Jodl that a written assurance would be given five days in advance, but that it would not be considered as final since the weather could only be forecast two days ahead, Jodl's *Diary*.

[3] Jodl's *Diary*.

forces permitted. According to the directive, the fortified installations in the west should, for all practical purposes, be completed by 28 September, the date of the attack. Brauchitsch's directive of 24 August was followed by a tour of inspection by Hitler of the West Wall between 26 and 29 August.[1] The *Limes* programme and possible hostilities in the west, were discussed at three sessions of a conference held between the 27th and 28th. Hitler greatly exaggerated Italy as a power factor. 'Today', he declared, 'France is not in a position to order her entire wartime army to her north-east frontier, for she must maintain strong forces against Italy on her Alpine frontier as well as in North Africa. She will even find it necessary to transfer troops from the mother country to North Africa.' Brauchitsch doubted whether this was correct, but nevertheless believed that France would have to leave forces in North Africa. 'For the time being', Hitler continued, 'England can intervene with five divisions and one armoured brigade. Motorization of these divisions is still not complete.' Contrary to his later convictions of the invincibility of armour, Hitler claimed that as a weapon of attack it had already passed its zenith. Like cavalry charges in the past it could only be relied on to achieve success if the enemy had been taken by surprise or badly shattered. 'We dispose of over 2,000 anti-tank guns on the Western front and we possess in the anti-tank mine an outstanding instrument of defence.' Having pointed out how French mobilization would require five to six days and the assembly of forces an additional period, Hitler stated that France could at most commit forty divisions against Germany. 'France', he declared, 'will therefore not take the risk.' There followed an altercation between Hitler and Brauchitsch on the subject of the twenty divisions constituting the replacement army. Only eight of these divisions would, to Hitler's annoyance, be available in the west at the end of three weeks.

General Adam, conscious of the lack of reserves, argued on the least favourable hypothesis. He believed that Holland and Belgium would support France and attack, in which event the Palatinate would have to be evacuated. He was brought severely to book by

[1] The conference was attended by Generals Brauchitsch, Adam, Keitel and Jodl and Dr. Todt. The Führer's words were only taken down verbatim in certain passages. DGFP (D), Vol. VII, Appendix III (K), pp. 640–3 (Author's own translation).

Hitler[1] who declared that the Palatinate would be held at all costs and that Holland, the weakest enemy, should first be attacked by Germany. Hitler had no idea how forces were to be raised for this audacious operation. Was he, one wonders, thinking in terms of what would be possible after German rearmament had progressed one stage further? The object of the *Limes* programme, he continued, was to intimidate the Belgians as well as to protect the Reich. 'They [the Belgians] must see from the construction of fortifications near their frontier that Belgium will be a battlefield if they attack us, or if they permit the French to march through.'

The rest of the conference was taken up with technical details, and at the end Hitler expressed enthusiasm over the work which had already been achieved. He was convinced that German troops could not be 'shot out' of their positions. He may have formed an exaggerated impression from what he had seen, for on 8 September Stülpnagel confided to Jodl that he no longer believed that the Führer would be deterred by fear of Western intervention. Jodl, who was consistently loyal to Hitler, commented with some concern on the progressive change in emphasis since Blomberg's directive of 24 June 1937.[2]

There can be no doubt that the High Command were unanimously of the opinion that Germany was not yet ready for war, above all if Britain sided with France. Germany possessed no arm capable of delivering a mortal blow to her major antagonists; at sea, even in 1939, she disposed of few ocean going submarines and was prepared for a purely defensive war.[3] Although she had a pronounced preponderance in the air, her air staffs were far from convinced that the Luftwaffe at its existing strength could force a decision against either the British fleet or industrial centres.[4] Finally

[1] According to Jodl Hitler is reported to have exclaimed: 'He who cannot hold this position is a scoundrel [*Hundsfott*] . . . I only regret that I am the Führer and Reich Chancellor and that I cannot be Commander-in-Chief of the West Front'. (*Diary*, 26–29 August).

[2] According to Jodl: 'The impression formed from the attitude of the population as well as from the workers is powerful—that which has been achieved in a short time is grandiose' (*Diary*, 26–29 August).

[3] Raeder, *Mein Leben*, Vol. II, Chap. XII.

[4] See an OKL Appreciation 25 August 1938, ND: 375-PS. See also ND: R-150 and ND: 43-L. The possibility of an attack on the British fleet from the air and an occupation of the Low Countries was discussed at an interservice conference of 20 May 1938, see Note on Sources, p. 195. While possession of the Low Countries was prized by the Air Force, the Navy were more interested in submarine bases on the Atlantic coasts of France and Norway.

in 1938 Germany disposed of few reserve divisions and only two of her famous armoured divisions were ready.

However much these factual considerations weighed against Germany it does not follow that Hitler's reasoning was absurd or that of his Generals fool-proof. The term *balance of strength*, as his generals conceived it, meant calculation of power in terms of such things as war potential, strategic frontiers, trained reserves and even climate, in which all possible contingencies were weighed against each other and from which it could be argued that no power was ready for war. In Hitler's mind it meant calculation of risk in which the one most promising factor, such as the element of surprise or a superior weapon, was considered to the exclusion of all others. Hitler realized that neither Britain nor France was prepared to take the risk. In this respect it must be admitted that his insight was superior to that of his staff. The vital question, as he saw it, was not whether Germany was ready for war but whether the Western democracies would fight. His views are best summarized in a memorandum which was transmitted to the Duce in September.[1] '... it can hardly any longer be doubted, [he claimed], that Great Britain is determined to get rid of one or other of the two totalitarian nations as soon as she has completed her rearmament. The following facts stand in the way of an immediate realization of this plan.' Hitler then tried to prove how the Royal Navy could not meet the defensive needs of the Empire; British anti-aircraft defence was weak; the regular army, ill prepared for operations in a European theatre. The RAF would catch up in a few years, the other Services at a later date.[2] He concluded that Britain was trying to prevent or postpone a European conflict. Germany therefore should fight soon. There was a grain of truth in these words: Hitler had attributed to Chamberlain motives which were his own. But whereas Chamberlain was trying to postpone a conflict, but had to face up to its dreaded possibility, Hitler wanted one, but might be compelled to postpone it. He was deter-

[1] DGFP (D), Vol. II, pp. 671–3. This was evidently the document which Prince Philip of Hesse read to the Duce on 7 September, Ciano's *Diaries*. For other examples of the Führer's views see the handwritten notes made by Schmundt, his *Wehrmacht* adjutant, of April 1938, ND: 388-PS, Item 1, and also his conference of 28 May, Förster, op. cit., pp. 88–90.

[2] Hitler in his letter to Mussolini and elsewhere evidently attached more importance to the possession of a particular weapon and the element of surprise, than to war potential. See also his conference of 23 May 1939, DGFP (D), pp. 574–80.

mined to push things to the limit,[1] and take his chance if not in 1938 then in 1939. If he had to wait he could use the coming crisis to test the stamina of his own people, the loyalty of his generals and Mussolini, the resolution of Chamberlain and Daladier.

[1] Whether Hitler ever wavered on the question of carrying out Operation Green is doubtful. A draft directive of 18 June admittedly reads, 'I will only decide on military action against Czechoslovakia if, as in the case of the occupation of the Demilitarized Zone and the entry into Austria, I am firmly convinced that France will not march and that consequently Britain will not intervene', ND: 388-PS, item 14. This directive, which was only a draft and not signed by Hitler, does not necessarily reflect his views. On 28 July Captain Wiedemann told Beck that Hitler was still resolved on war even if the West intervened, Förster, op. cit., p. 106. Ribbentrop evidently also took this view; see Weizsaäcker's minute of 21 July, DGFP (D), Vol. II, p. 504.

CHAPTER 14

Victory Without Violence

(Munich)

After Hitler's tour of inspection of the West Wall at the end of August a decision was taken of major importance: the *Limes* plan was to be continued until the beginning of winter for both military and political reasons. As rolling stock had also to be made available for the assembly of troops, it was decided by OKH that the loading of trains for *Limes* should cease on 17 September but that those trains already loaded should run until the 20th. The railway timetable for mobilization was to be in full force between 21 September and 30 September and preparations completed by 1 October, the prospective date of attack. These mere technical details of railway timetables may seem tedious and irrelevant, but they did impose certain physical limitations on Hitler's freedom of action. No wonder he regretted that work on the West Wall had not started earlier. Strategic surprise had been one of the underlying conditions, not only for the initial onslaught, but for the success of the campaign as a whole. It had to be completed before the Western Powers had decided on intervention and before their military preparations were complete. If the political crisis in the form of an insurrection in the Sudetenland came to a head before German mobilization was complete Hitler would have to revise his plans.

Until the end of September Hitler had, through Henlein, to continue making fresh demands on the Czech Government without causing any sudden rupture. Although the protracted negotiations carried out in August under the auspices of Lord Runciman were a conspicuous failure, it did not seem at the end of the month that there would be an immediate rupture. On 1–2 September Henlein again conferred with Hitler. According to post-war accounts Henlein was instructed to continue negotiations and to give the impression that they were *bona fide* until the appointed hour. These

136

instructions were to be kept secret even from other members of the Sudeten negotiating committee.[1] On 4 September Henlein discussed his interview with Ashton-Gwatkin, a member of the Runciman mission, and said that his party would agree to accept the Karlsbad points as a basis for negotiation and would not insist on a plebiscite.

After Henlein's return Benes, under pressure from Britain and France, put forward a new plan which embodied the Karlsbad points almost in their entirety.[2] Since Henlein could not reject it without appearing to be in the wrong he could only wreck negotiations by resorting to violence. On the pretext of a minor incident[3] the Sudeten Germans refused to negotiate and they were in full revolt by the 12th. At 4 p.m. on the 13th, after the Czechs had tried to restore order, Henlein issued an ultimatum to Prague demanding that martial law should be suspended and the Czech police be withdrawn from the Sudeten areas.[4] While the revolt and Henlein's ultimatum certainly had Hitler's subsequent approval they do not, for two reasons, seem to have been instigated directly from Berlin. First, Hitler was not ready for technical reasons to march, and his speech at Nuremberg of 12 September, however insulting to Benes, cannot be regarded as a summons to arms.[5] Secondly, in such turbulent times liaison is poor and orders are likely to be overtaken by events before they are received. It is of some interest that the German Legation in Prague had difficulty in keeping pace with Henlein's movements; it may even have been deliberately kept in the dark. But Henlein could not dispense with its services entirely. On the 13th telephone communications between the Sudeten Party Executive and the Reich were cut, and Party officials requested the Legation to pass on the text of the ultimatum to the Reich some hours after it had been delivered to the Czech

---

[1] DGFP (D), Vol. II, 5 September, p. 700. Facts on Henlein's conversation with Ashton-Gwatkin reached the German Legation in Prague through the Italian Legation. See also ibid., pp. 700–4.

[2] DGFP (D), Vol. II, p. 711, a despatch from Hencke, the German Chargé d'Affaires in Prague, of 7 September, despatches of 8 September, pp. 719–20 and pp. 721–2. Wheeler-Bennett, *Munich*, pp. 90–2, gives the wrong date for the Benes offer. It was made on the 7th, not the 4th.

[3] A Sudeten-German deputy alleged that he had been struck with a whip by a Czech police officer at Mährisch-Ostrau on 7 September. See also Wheeler-Bennett, *Munich*, pp. 92–3, and RIIA, *Survey, 1938*, Vol. II, pp. 310–3.

[4] DGFP, Vol. II, pp. 751–2, a telephone message from Prague.

[5] Baynes, *Hitler's Speeches*, Vol. II, pp. 1487–98.

Government.[1] Had the terms of the ultimatum been formulated at Hitler's express command there would have been no need to transmit them back to Germany through the Legation.

After the ultimatum expired Henlein fled to Asch, a town inside the Czech frontier, but not under effective Czech control. Here at 11.30 on the 14th he met members of the Runciman mission, whom he informed that he could no longer negotiate on the basis of the Karlsbad points, but would demand a plebiscite. On the same day Eisenlohr reported that, owing to the helpless situation of the Sudeten Germans, a proclamation should be made demanding a plebiscite, for this would have the effect of isolating the Czechs politically and of undermining their will to fight. On the 15th Henlein duly issued a proclamation in which he insisted that the Sudentenland should be ceded to the Reich.[2] The breakdown in negotiations on the 14th coincided with the introduction of secret mobilization in Czechoslovakia.[3] The political climax had now been reached, and the question arose whether Hitler's forces could be made ready to move earlier than planned. This possibility was discussed on Hitler's orders by OKW on the 15th. But the dates (i.e. 17 and 20 September) for the loading and unloading of trains (for the *Limes* programme) could not be altered. As Jodl observed[4] Hitler had committed himself by his decision to continue work on the West Wall; he had involuntarily given his opponents the chance to define their attitude and forestall him.

On 13 September, the day after Hitler's speech at Nuremberg, Chamberlain asked for a meeting with Hitler.[5] There were certain significant indications of what Chamberlain might agree to. On 7 September *The Times* had declared in its leading article that Czechoslovakia would become a 'more homogeneous state by secession of that fringe of alien population . . .'. Despite official

---

[1] DGFP (D), Vol. II, a despatch of 6 September, pp. 701–2, in which Hencke complained about the way the Legation was kept in the dark, and pp. 751–2. The ultimatum had been delivered to the Czechs at 4 p.m. and transmitted to Berlin. See also RIIA, *Survey, 1938*, Vol. II, p. 261.

[2] See despatches of 14 September, loc. cit., pp. 757–60 and the text of proclamation, pp. 801–2.

[3] Ibid., p. 757. Secret mobilization was reported to have been introduced at 6 p.m. on the 14th. See also Jodl's *Diary* for 14 September and Hassell's Diary for the 17th. The English version of Hassell's Diary incorrectly gives the date as 4 instead of 14 September.

[4] Jodl's *Diary*, 15 September.

[5] DGFP (D), Vol. II, p. 754 and p. 763.

denials that the article was inspired, Th. Kordt, the German Chargé d'Affaires, in a despatch of 8 September, claimed that, whereas it probably did not originate from the Foreign Office itself, it might have been inspired by members of Chamberlain's personal entourage. There were further reasons for believing that this was so. On 10 September Kordt reported that he had learnt from an 'absolutely unimpeachable source' that Halifax had just informed Corbin, the French Ambassador, that Britain could not be expected to take up arms to prevent the fulfilment of the right of self-determination by means of a plebiscite. But Kordt also described what he thought was a contrary trend in British policy, for he made the quite incorrect claim that Halifax in this interview stated that France could 'count on British armed assistance in the event of armed action by Germany against Czechoslovakia'.[1]

The German Embassy dwelt on other indications that Britain had resolved to resist aggression, such as articles in the Press and the assurance that she could rely on the USA.[2] It believed that if Chamberlain decided to adopt a firm attitude he would have little difficulty in enlisting public support. A statement he made to foreign Press representatives on 11 September, in which he merely said that Germany could not resort to force without 'fear of intervention by France and Great Britain', was, for example, considered particularly important, in that it had the full backing of the opposition.[3] Hitler's speech of the 12th added insult to injury. Kordt described on the 13th how German Press correspondents learnt from the Prime Minister's Press secretary that Chamberlain felt 'disappointed and hurt' by the speech and that he 'considered a European war to be unavoidable if matters were allowed to run the same course as hitherto'. Although, according to Kordt, Chamberlain was prepared to consider far-reaching proposals, including the demand for a plebiscite, certain conditions would have to be fulfilled: first, he should be given time; secondly, 'the Sudeten Germans should not take precipitate action'. If these conditions were not observed 'he would be obliged to assume that

---

[1] Ibid., pp. 722–3 and p. 732. Halifax never gave this assurance. See his memorandum on his talk with Corbin of the 9th, DBFP, Third Series, Vol. II, pp. 275–5.

[2] DGFP (D), Vol. II, a despatch of 10 September, pp. 734–5. See also despatches from the USA of 10 September, p. 735 and of 12 September, pp. 743–4.

[3] Ibid., despatches of 12 September, pp. 742–3.

Germany wanted a European war'.[1] In general Kordt seems either to have been misled or to have deliberately painted too bleak a picture. Whereas he was correct in stressing Chamberlain's intention to ensure that the principle of 'self-determination' was fulfilled, he over-rated his resolve to resist aggression. Chamberlain's Government continued to hedge over committing itself until much later in the crisis.[2] In all probability Hitler himself, no less than his diplomats, failed to appreciate Chamberlain's intentions fully. On 20 September he told Lipski, the Polish Ambassador, that he expected Chamberlain was coming 'solemnly to inform him that Britain was ready to take armed action'. In the event Chamberlain's failure to make it clear to Hitler at Berchtesgaden on 15 September that this was so came as a disappointment to Weizsäcker and seems to have been unexpected.[3]

In the course of the discussion with Chamberlain Hitler demanded the 'return' of the three million Germans living in Czechoslovakia.[4] 'He would face any war, and even the risk of world war, for this.' Chamberlain replied that he personally recognized in principle the German claim but that he would have to consult his colleagues, Lord Runciman, and the French, on how the principle could be implemented. Chamberlain asked Hitler for the assurance that force would not be used before the next meeting which was to take place in a few days. Hitler somewhat hesitantly agreed. He could afford to do so as the date of the advance could not in any case be put forward. From Hitler's point of view the meeting progressed most favourably.[5] Chamberlain's reference to consultation with Lord Runciman must have been particularly gratifying, for Hitler knew what kind of advice Runciman was

[1] DGFP (D), Vol. II, pp. 754–5. Weizsäcker noted in the margin 'Telephone through to RM (i.e. Ribbentrop) *immediately*'. Kordt was associated with the moderate opposition to Hitler. See Namier, *Europe in Decay*, pp. 229 et seq. This certainly influenced his reporting.

[2] The idea that Britain should warn Germany was in fact suggested by Halifax to Henderson on the 9th but was at the latter's most earnest insistence withdrawn, DBFP, third series, Vol. II, pp. 277–85. See also *Failure of a Mission*, p. 147.

[3] *Documents and Materials* (USSR) Vol. I, pp. 176–84, a report of the conversation which Lipski sent to Colonel Beck. See also Weizsäcker's conversation with Hassell on 16 September, Hassell's Diary, 17 September.

[4] DGFP (D), Vol. II, pp. 786–98. Hassell, who had been conferring with Wörmann on the 16th, noticed the omission of the word 'plebiscite' in the report he was given on the conference, Diary, 17 September.

[5] See Schmundt's reference to the meeting, Jodl's *Diary*, 15 September.

likely to give. The mission had served as an effective sounding board of British intentions. Its members were informed by Henlein at Asch on the 14th that nothing short of a plebiscite would satisfy the Sudeten Germans. In a letter to Hitler on the 15th, Henlein correctly predicted that Chamberlain would actually propose cession of Sudeten territory. Henlein could only have formed this impression through his contacts with members of the Runciman mission. Henlein also proposed to Hitler that Germany should demand the *immediate* cession of areas with more than fifty percent Germans and that the occupations should be carried out in twenty-four or forty-eight hours.[1] It will be seen how Hitler later tried to act along these lines.

The main difference between the German and British view after 15 September was almost entirely one of procedure. Whereas Chamberlain and his colleagues were anxious that any transfer of territory should take the form of an orderly business-like transaction, Hitler wanted forcible and immediate seizure of the Sudetenland. In this he was unquestionably moved by vengeance against Benes, who had shown such firmness in expelling Sudeten German insurgents and in re-establishing Czech authority over the area of disturbance. While those Germans who remained felt deserted,[2] their leaders craved to return as soon as possible and restore confidence in their flagging leadership. Hitler was willing to take up their cause. On 17 September a number of Sudeten Germans who were expelled were organized into a force on German soil known as the Henlein Free Corps. Their task was to provoke incidents and keep up a state of unrest on the frontier, that is to say, to play the role of picador before the army was ready to deliver the *coup de grâce*. From the professional military point of view the pillaging expeditions undertaken by these armed bands merely had the effect of attracting Czech forces towards the frontier and were of no account. On 20 September these missions were greatly restricted in scope.[3]

There were, however, more lethal forces of disruption which, could in the name of 'self-determination', be let loose against Czechoslovakia. On the 20th, Kundt, one of Henlein's henchmen,

[1] DGFP (D), Vol. II, p. 801.
[2] For descriptions by the German Legation of the situation in the Sudeten areas after Henlein's flight, see ibid., p. 824, p. 826 and pp. 827–8.
[3] ND: 388-PS, item 25 and 30, also Jodl's *Diary* for 17 and 20 September.

met the Slovak leaders and invited them to stake their demands.[1] That day Hitler was also busy with other claimants. The Hungarians had so far remained silent, and the Führer exhorted them through their Minister in Berlin to display more activity. The Poles were more vocal after the Berchtesgaden meeting, and Hitler merely invited them to state 'precisely' what their wishes were.[2] But neither German terrorism, nor the claims of other parties interested in the spoils of Czechoslovakia, were in themselves forces powerful enough to intimidate the Czechs into submission; they were artificially created by Hitler and could never prove effective if the Czechs felt sure of support from their allies.[3] Everything therefore depended, not merely on France, but on the decisions reached in London after Chamberlain's return.

Chamberlain duly consulted Runciman in London and, as Henlein predicted, proposed that the Czechs should transfer to the Reich all territory containing more than fifty percent Sudeten Germans. Since the French also associated themselves with these proposals they were known as the Anglo-French Plan. They were submitted to Prague and, in return for a guarantee of the new frontiers, accepted with extreme reluctance on the 21st. Although the Germans were aware of the existence of these proposals on the 20th their content was not known. The next day at 11.15 a.m. Hitler learnt that the Czechs had accepted unconditionally.[4]

Czech acceptance of the Anglo-French Plan had military consequence of the highest importance. Previously it was assumed that the Czechs would fight and that their resistance would be stiff. By 21 September neither of these assumptions obtained. The effect of this was twofold. First, while preparations for Operation Green were to be continued, plans also had to be improvised for a small

---

[1] DGFP (D), Vol. II, p. 841. See also Kundt's reply of 20 September, ibid., p. 852.

[2] On 23 August at a conference held at Bled, Hungary and the states of the Little Entente, Czechoslovakia, Yugoslavia and Roumania, renounced use of force and in return recognized Hungary's claim for equality of status in armaments. This caused Hitler great annoyance, see DGFP (D), Vol. V, p. 104. For his approaches to the Hungarians see DGFP (D), Vol. II, a minute of 21 September, p. 865. For his contacts with the Poles, p. 819, p. 840, p. 861 and p. 865. See also *Documents and Materials* (USSR) Vol. I, pp. 176–84.

[3] See DGFP (D), Vol. II, a despatch from Hencke of 19 September, p. 838.

[4] Wheeler-Bennett, *Munich*, pp. 111–28 and Appendix E and Jodl's *Diary*, 21 September. At 4 p.m. on the same day (20 September) Hitler told Lipski that he had 'so far no explicit information as to what had been decided in London'. *Documents and Materials* (USSR), Vol. I, p. 179.

scale operation into areas where German was spoken. A detailed
set of demands had also been drawn up on the 21st by OKW in
case the Czechs agreed to cede areas where German was spoken
and to hold a plebiscite where the population was mixed. It was
laid down that Czechs would have to withdraw all forces, surrender
all arms and equipment in the above-mentioned areas, and evacu-
ate fortifications beyond their confines. No arms were to be
produced in Czechoslovakia and the Czech Army was to be
demobilized.[1] Second, even if force were still necessary, less resistance was expected. According to an intelligence report of 22
September, prepared by the Foreign Armies Section of OKH:
'growing difficulties in the Czechoslovak State must affect the
cohesion and striking power of the army in a way that cannot be
foreseen: it would scarcely be capable of taking the field at its
previously estimated strength'.[2] On the morning of the 22nd the
Luftwaffe raised the question whether in view of the 'feeble resistance' now expected the attack might not start at noon instead of
dawn. At 7.20 p.m. that evening, after Hitler's first conference
with Chamberlain, Stülpnagel telephoned Jodl's staff from Godesberg on behalf of Keitel stating that the date of D-Day could not
be determined. It is evident from Jodl's entry that if a full scale
attack, based on Green, was to be carried out the date would not
be before 30 September; if it were decided to attack earlier, a new
and less grandiose operation could be improvised.[3]

Hitler was now from the military point of view in a far more
favourable position for bargaining than he had been at Berchtesgaden the week before. Others were doing his work for him. Instead of thanking them he could afford to raise his demands, and
on the 22nd he told Chamberlain that he was morally bound to
champion the claims of Poland and Hungary. At 10 p.m. the next
day (23 September) Hitler handed Chamberlain the notorious
'memorandum'[4] in which certain demands seem to have been
taken from the list of military proposals of the 21st and from
Henlein's recommendations of the 15th. Hitler also insisted on a
time limit: the Czechs were to start evacuating the German areas

---

[1] ND: 388-PS, item 28, also Jodl's *Diary*, 21 September.
[2] See Note on Sources, p. 195.
[3] Jodl's *Diary*. On the same day an order was given to the Free Corps Henlein to enter the Sudeten areas but was later rescinded. Evidently the Czechs
were erroneously reported to have evacuated the frontier areas.
[4] DGFP, Vol. II, pp. 870–9, pp. 908–10 and *Failure of a Mission*, pp. 154–5.

at 8 a.m. on the 26th and complete the operation by the 28th. Following protests from Chamberlain, the time limit was extended to 1 October.

Contrary to Hitler's expectations, neither the Western Powers nor Czechoslovakia was cowed by the German ultimatum. Czechoslovakia ordered full mobilization on the night of the 23–24th. On the 24th France started partial mobilization and the British fleet was reported to have put to sea.[1] On the 25th Britain, France and Czechoslovakia all rejected the Bad Godesberg memorandum. At 5 p.m. the next day Sir Horace Wilson personally conveyed a letter from Chamberlain in which it was suggested that direct German-Czech negotiations should be opened. Weizsäcker's minute of the conversation records that the Führer described the British proposal as useless so long as the Czechs had not accepted the Bad Godesberg memorandum.[2] On the same day Hitler made a speech at the Sport Palast, the general tone of which was anti-Czech rather than anti-British. This was followed by a Foreign Office statement that, if a German attack were made on Czechoslovakia, the immediate result would be French intervention and Britain and Russia would stand by France. This pronouncement had no immediate result in Germany. At 12.15 p.m. on the 27th Wilson conveyed a further warning from Chamberlain on the certainty of intervention by Britain. The warning, according to Henderson, who was also present, evoked Hitler's comment 'let them do so'.[3] The interview in general, however, was far from unfriendly, and according to the official account of the conversation written by Schmidt, Hitler's interpreter, at the end Hitler told Wilson that England could wish for no better friend than himself.[4]

That evening Hitler wrote to Chamberlain. The letter was couched in conciliatory terms; and in Henderson's view was 'indicative of a certain nervousness'. Hitler laid the onus of blame for unreasonableness on the Czechs but confirmed the promise he made in his speech the previous day that he was willing to give a formal guarantee to the remainder of Czechoslovakia.[5] He was not, however,

[1] DGFP (D), Vol. II, p. 920 and pp. 931–2. See also Jodl's *Diary*, 26 September.

[2] DGFP (D), Vol. II, pp. 934–5 and pp. 944–5.

[3] *Failure of a Mission*, pp. 160–1. For Hitler's Speech, see Baynes, op. cit., Vol. II, pp. 1508–27.

[4] DGFP (D), Vol. II, pp. 963–8, in which Schmidt's record of this interview includes some of the English words alleged to have been spoken.

[5] Ibid., pp. 966–8.

willing to compromise on the question of an 'immediate occupation' which he described as no more than a 'security measure'. Hitler was not wavering. At 1.30 p.m. he agreed that the first assault wave should advance to a line from which they could attack after the 30th. The final decision would be released at noon the day before the invasion. At 6 p.m. five active divisions in the West were mobilized.[1]

On the 27th Hitler had made both a conciliatory and a defiant gesture to the Western Powers. Reactions from the two Governments were received in the course of the night. It is evident from a despatch from Bräuer, the German Chargé d'Affaires in Paris, received at 10.20, that the attitude of the French Cabinet was uncertain but that they might agree to at least some of the German demands. Should, however, the Germans invade Czech territory, France most probably would honour her obligations.[2] Twenty minutes later a further report was received from Kühlenthal, the German Military Attaché, counter-signed by Bräuer. From the military point of view it may well have been cause of some alarm. Kühlenthal believed that the French could produce their first sixty-five divisions on the German frontier on the sixth day of mobilization.[3] Early next morning, after news was received that the British fleet had been mobilized, war seemed inevitable.

But the West had more to offer in the form of concessions than in threats. At 11 p.m. on the 27th Henderson handed Weizsäcker a new Anglo-French Plan, which went a long way towards bridging the gap between the Godesberg memorandum and the original Anglo-French Plan, and it constituted the main basis of the final settlement at Munich. On delivering it to the Reich Chancellery at midnight Weizsäcker found the Führer and Ribbentrop still determined to destroy Czechoslovakia. At 8.30 the next morning François-Poncet informed Weizsäcker that he was instructed to convey a new French proposal which went further than anything so far put forward by the British or French and which was not even known to the Czechs.[4] After a delay which caused him some uneasiness, François-Poncet was invited to present the proposals at the Chancellery. In the middle of his interview with Hitler a

[1] See Jodl's *Diary*, 26 and 27 September, also ND: 388-PS, item 33 of 28 September.
[2] DGFP (D), Vol. II, p. 978 and Wheeler-Bennett, *Munich*, p. 146, describing the French Cabinet meeting of 27 September.
[3] DGFP, Vol. II, p. 977.   [4] Ibid., pp. 987–9, enclosure 2.

EUROPE 1933-39

MILES

0   50   100   150

Annexed by Poland 1938

Annexed by Hungary 1938-39

Areas ceded at Munich

DENMARK

Hamburg

Kiel Canal

EIDE

Weser

Amsterdam

THE HAGUE

LONDON

HOLLAND

Rotterdam

GER

Calais

BRUSSELS

Dortmund

Düsseldorf

Rhine

BELGIUM

Ardennes

Le Havre

Hochst-am-Main

Frankfurt

LUXEMBOURG

SAAR

PARIS

Seine

Stuttgart

Danu

Loire

Vosges

Muni

F R A N C E

Zurich

LIECHTENSTEIN

Innsb

Jura Mts

BERN

SWITZERLAND

P

Lyon

L

A

Rhone

Milan

Turin

I T A L Y

Po

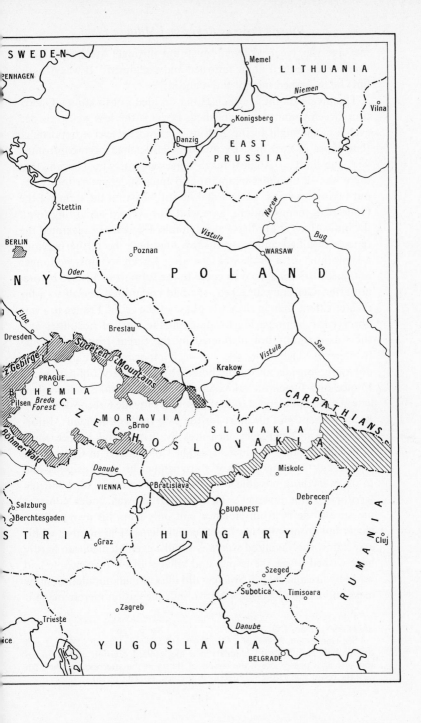

message was received from Mussolini through Attolico. After a short absence the Führer returned and exclaimed: 'It was Mussolini: he too asked me not to go ahead.'[1]

The precise point at which Hitler decided not to launch Operation Green cannot be established. Perhaps the less well recorded events of the night of the 27th were of more decisive importance than those of next day. By midnight Hitler had been confronted with the limit of Anglo-French appeasement, which meant that there was all the more temptation to enter Sudeten territory without taking up arms. Yet, should he still insist on the terms of the Godesberg memorandum, a general war seemed according to all the indications at his disposal inevitable. However exaggerated the reports of allied military measures may have been, the previous assumptions for a successful Operation Green certainly no longer obtained. Britain agreed to come to the support of France before, not after, Germany attacked; she had committed herself to a far greater extent than in the early phase of the crisis. France too was observed to be preparing to attack at the start of hostilities and she was certainly not distracted by the threat from the Alpine frontier, to which Hitler attached such importance. Finally, Russia not only considered herself bound by her treaty obligations to France and Czechoslovakia but threatened to take independent action against Poland should that country invade Czechoslovakia.[2] In the first entry of his diary for the 28th Jodl commented: 'Information about emergency measures by Britain and France equal to partial mobilization increases. The Commander-in-Chief of the Army begs the Chief of OKW to remember his responsibility and to do everything possible with the Führer to make sure Sudeten territory is not invaded'. That day Hitler was under constant pressure to desist from violence, not only from his own military chiefs but from influential German civilians. The number of his associates who favoured war was small—even Henlein can hardly have wished to see the homes and villages of his own people laid waste by fire and sword. Still less did the German population show mass enthusiasm.[3] Perhaps Mussolini's mediation merely made it

[1] François-Poncet, *Souvenirs*, Chap. X, and Celovsky, *Das Münchener Abkommen*, Chap. IX.   [2] See p. 156.

[3] See Henderson, *Failure of a Mission*, p. 163 and also Hassell's Diary, 1 and 10 October. According to Henderson a mechanised division was given no applause as it passed down the streets of Berlin in the afternoon of the 27th with the result that Hitler was deeply impressed, op. cit., p. 161.

easier for Hitler to change his mind without losing face, for Hitler hated having to haggle over a conference table unless the Duce, whom alone he regarded as his peer, was by his side. Unquestionably he would have preferred to have thrashed the Czechs and to have made a processional entry into their capital. Yet in the end he enjoyed the substance of victory without having to fight and so had more reason to be gratified than resentful. In the following January he asked Csaky, the Hungarian Foreign Minister: 'Do you think that I myself would have thought it possible half a year ago that Czechoslovakia, so to speak, would be served up to me by her friends? . . . The way in which everything happened is historically unique. We can offer each other heartfelt congratulations.'[1]

[1] DGFP (D), Vol. V, pp. 361–6.

CHAPTER 15

A Plan for the Invasion of Poland

(April 1939)

The Munich settlement and its sequel created new issues, and until April 1939 German military planning conformed even less with a grand design than it had done.[1] It was not even possible to work out a general plan for mobilization on the lines of the directive issued by Blomberg on 24 June 1937, for the situation at a future date could not be predicted even approximately. For some time there was doubt in Hitler's mind on the timing and extent of Germany's next annexations, on which of the small Powers should be chosen as allies or turned into dependencies. Even at the end of 1938 Weizsäcker was of the opinion that, while Hitler's policy aimed at war, it had not been decided whether to proceed 'right away against England and for this purpose to continue to keep Poland neutral, or to move against the East first in order to solve the question of Poland, the Ukraine (i.e. the Carpatho-Ukraine) and Memel'. Weizsäcker implied that Hitler had freedom of action; that he could proceed either against the north-east, the south-east or the west.[2]

After Munich one thing is certain: Hitler was determined on complete political and economic mastery of Czechoslovakia. His central problem was to achieve this without having to divide the spoils with other claimants. He had certainly not abandoned the idea of a military occupation.[3] Early in October Weizsäcker informed Hassell that the Führer 'had again expressed himself to the effect that within a few months the Czech problem must still be liquidated totally' by means of an operation cutting Czechoslovakia at her waist. On 21 October, after the Sudeten areas had

---

[1] See Hassell's Diary, 24 October 1938.
[2] Hassell's Diary, 20 December 1938.
[3] For German economic interest in Czechoslovakia see ND: 1303-PS and ND: 33-R. See also Hassell's Diary for 22 March 1939.

been occupied, OKW issued a directive for this operation.[1] Although it was only to be put into effect if the Government of Prague reverted to the policy of Benes, Czech provocation could easily be 'arranged' at some convenient time. Further reduction of Czech military strength was the most immediate concern. Despite the lacerations of Munich, Czechoslovakia was still a power factor of some importance. Early in October Keitel believed that if Germany were involved in a war with the West, Czech forces could still contain twenty-five divisions. The construction of new fortifications opposite the German frontier on the south-east should not therefore be tolerated. Germany for her part had no intention of fortifying this area: to secure herself completely, only three Czech divisions should be permitted.[2]

There were, however, strong objections against reducing Czechoslovakia's strength to negligible proportions. Munich had caused a displacement of power in central Europe with political consequences, and the new Czech Government which succeeded that of Benes, far from persisting in the old policy, was now even prepared to atone for the past. It virtually severed its ties with Russia, and no longer regarded its treaty obligations with France as operative. Fearing further dismemberment from its smaller neighbours it even sought the protection of the Reich.[3] Since, moreover, the Slovak element, which had never been so markedly anti-German as the Czech, carried more weight, there was some reason for allowing the now hyphenated state a brief and grudging respite of peace. German interests could be threatened from Budapest no less than from Prague. Formerly, the Carpatho-Ukraine (Ruthenia), an unruly province in the east had, together with Slovakia, belonged to the Hungarian half of the Habsburg Empire. However much Hitler hated the Czechs he had no desire to restore the *Ausgleich* with the Magyars by giving them back their lost possessions. Nor did he wish to allow the Poles a privileged place in his new *Mittel Europa*. OKW pointed out—the *Wilhelmstrasse* and Hitler

[1] Hassell's Diary, 10 October. The English translation of this passage is faulty. The text of the directive can be found in ND: 135-C.
[2] See a memorandum of 12 October by Wörmann, head of the Political Department of the German Foreign Office, DGFP (D), Vol. IV, pp. 56–9. For further material on OKW's views on future Czech military strength, see a memorandum of 21 November, ibid., pp. 167–8.
[3] See Ribbentrop's conversations with Chvalkovsky on 13 October, ibid., pp. 60–3.

endorsed their views[1]—that, rather than allow Slovakia and the Carpatho-Ukraine to merge with either Poland or Hungary, they should both be granted, at least provisionally, home-rule under Prague. It was argued that by preserving Slovakia and the Carpatho-Ukraine, Poland and Hungary would be denied a common frontier, for such a frontier, if established, might act as a screen against German expansion beyond the Carpathians, control of which was of great strategic value.

By the middle of October both Slovakia and the Carpatho-Ukraine were granted independence within the framework of Czechoslovakia. Hitler had political, no less than military, reasons for sponsoring the national consciousness, recently awakened in these territories. Having declared that Germany herself had no further territorial claims in Europe, he deemed it inexpedient to allow racial Germans in foreign countries to demand changes in the *status quo*. He did, however, keep the road open for future expansion with greater effect by appealing to the watchword of self-determination on behalf of non-German nationalities. For example, he refused to satisfy Hungarian ambitions in Slovakia by claiming that he was bound to consult the wishes of the inhabitants. Above all he realized that more was to be gained by appealing to the Ukrainians, who could always win a sympathetic hearing in the Reich, than to the Germans living in Poland.[2] The former were a larger minority, numbering over six million, and the Poles feared nothing more than the contagion of Ukrainian nationalism spreading to Eastern Galicia. With headstrong persistence they demanded that the Carpatho-Ukraine, that hotbed of Ukrainian discontent, should come under Hungarian domination.[5]

[1] DGFP (D), Vol. IV, p. 40, an OKW memorandum of 6 October, and a Foreign Office memorandum of 7 October, pp. 46–9. The Führer's views are contained in a memorandum by Erich Kordt, head of the Foreign Minister's Secretariat, of 8 October, p. 49, and also in a memorandum prepared for Weizsäcker of 12 October, pp. 54–6. See also a telephone conversation between Göring and Weizsäcker of 4 October, ibid., p. 31.

[2] Early in October Hitler ordered racial Germans living in other states to abstain from 'irredentist activities'. See a German Foreign Office memorandum of 3 October, DGFP (D), Vol. IV, pp. 20–1. See also a circular sent to German missions abroad from Weizsäcker of 10 October, p. 52 and p. 93. The general watchword in German policy was to be 'self-determination'; anti-Polish and anti-Hungarian slogans were not to be used.

[3] Colonel Beck unsuccessfully tried to win Roumanian acceptance for a Hungarian occupation. See a despatch from the German Legation at Bucharest of 6 October, DGFP, Vol. V, pp. 312–3. See also despatches from Moltke of 19 and 22 October, ibid., pp. 98–100 and p. 102.

Hitler could not ignore the claims of Poland and Hungary altogether. He had supported them before Munich, and while he was disappointed by the lack of vigour displayed by the Hungarians against Czechoslovakia he had no reason to quarrel with the Poles. They had taken a strong, though independent, line in the last phase of the September crisis,[1] and thus he was prepared to tolerate their ultimatum of 1 October for the prompt cession of the Teschen area. He even allowed them to take possession of Oderburg, a town containing many racial Germans who strongly resented the transaction.[2] Poland and Hungary could also look for support elsewhere. Even before the *Anschluss* Mussolini toyed with the idea of counter-balancing German strength by what he called a 'horizontal Axis' of Italy, Yugoslavia, Hungary and Poland. Although he was forced to recognize the impracticability of this scheme in the autumn of 1938, he was prepared to sponsor Hungary's ambitions in at least the purely Magyar areas of both Slovakia and the Carpatho-Ukraine to a greater extent than his German partner.[3] Towards the end of October Ribbentrop rejected Ciano's proposal for Axis arbitration in the dispute between Czechoslovakia and Hungary, but since Ribbentrop was also angling for a military alliance with Italy he eventually deferred to Italian wishes and, by the Vienna Award of 2 November 1938, Czechoslovakia was made to surrender rather more territory to Hungary than Hitler originally intended.[4]

Connected with the territorial changes in the south-east were those of the Baltic. Hitler never regarded his frontier with Poland as more than provisional, but was prepared to overlook the problem during the Czech crisis. He probably believed that he could persuade the Poles to relinquish Danzig and the Corridor by offering them compensation elsewhere. This would explain why in a memorandum of 17 March 1938 Ribbentrop claimed that, if Lithuania were annexed by Poland, she would cease to be of value

[1] See a conversation between Hitler and Daranyi, the ex-Prime Minister of Hungary, of 14 October, DGFP, Vol. IV, pp. 73–7. For a detailed account of Poland's attitude to Czechoslovakia before and after Munich, see despatch from Moltke of 6 October, DGFP(D), Vol. V, pp. 85–8.

[2] See Moltke's despatch of 1 October, Ribbentrop's memorandum of the same date, ibid., pp. 78–80.

[3] See Ciano's *Diaries*, 3–15 October. For a convenient discussion on this subject, see Namier, *Europe in Decay*, p. 20 and p. 126.

[4] Ciano's *Diaries*, 22–3 October and 2 November. For the German documents on the Award, see DGFP (D), Vol. IV, pp. 118–27.

as an object for compensation.[1] The Carpatho-Ukraine and Slovakia were even of greater value as bargaining counters. On 4 October Göring told Wiezsäcker that if a dispute should arise on account of these areas, a deal might be made with Poland over Danzig. Towards the end of the month bargaining with Poland became a practical issue[2] and in a memorandum for Ribbentrop of the 22nd Weizsäcker suggested that it would be a 'great gesture' if, contrary to the precedent of Munich, Poland were included as one of the adjudicators in the dispute between Czechoslovakia and Hungary. As opposed to OKW he believed that if Poland and Hungary were offered a common frontier on the Carpathians, Poland's interests in the south-east would be recognized and Germany might demand 'compensation' in Danzig and Memel.[3]

On the 24th Ribbentrop met Lipski and presented him with secret proposals for Colonel Beck. Danzig should return to the Reich, and Germany be allowed an extra-territorial rail and motor road across the Corridor. Poland for her part would be given similar facilities for access to the sea. Besides these quasi-territorial provisions the German-Polish treaty of 1934 was to be extended and Poland was to be invited to join the Anti-Comintern Pact. In his reply Lipski stated as his own personal opinion that union of Danzig with the Reich was not possible, if only on account of public opinion in Poland: 'Beck could never prevail upon people to accept it.' Ribbentrop said later in the conversation that Poland would like to have the support of Germany in ensuring that the Carpatho-Ukraine went to Hungary. He promised to think carefully over this 'complex of questions'.[4] Ribbentrop had given a hint but made no promise, and he was no more willing to support Hungary's claims after the meeting with Beck than before.[5] Lipski returned with Beck's reply and again met Ribbentrop on 19 November. Besides covering much the same ground as in the previous conversation, Lipski pointed out that if 'the Danzig question were

[1] DGFP(D), Vol. V, pp. 433–4.

[2] Ibid., pp. 81–2. On 18 October 1938 Lipski called on Weizsäcker and stated that Colonel Beck would like to remain in friendly consultation with Germany in regard to the Hungarian-Slovak question, ibid., pp. 96–8.

[3] DGFP (D), Vol. IV, pp. 102–3.

[4] DGFP (D), Vol. V, pp. 104–7. See also Polish White Book, No. 44.

[5] On 28 October Ciano noted in his *Diaries*: 'Ribbentrop now speaks with hostility, not only about the Magyar leaders, but about the whole people. An ugly sign. Very ugly.'

opened German-Polish relations would be seriously endangered'. Ribbentrop 'regretted' the position taken by Beck.

Hitler's ill-feeling towards the Poles was already aggravated by a number of factors, and the atmosphere was already charged with tension. Early in November the *Volksdeutsche Mittelstelle* (the Party Office for questions pertaining to racial Germans) presented Ribbentrop with a memorandum describing the 'intolerable situation' of the German minority in Poland and requesting intervention on their behalf. The question was brought to the notice of Hitler who commented that he 'did not intend to put up any longer with the conduct of our eastern neighbours towards his fellow Germans'.[1] But Poland was only one of Germany's eastern neighbours, and the question arises, which of them did Hitler tolerate least? The answer is perhaps to be found in his attitude to Poland's aims in the Carpatho-Ukraine. It was believed in Germany that by concentrating forces the Poles were inciting the Hungarians to seize the province.[2] This suspicion was justified by events; on 20 November the Hungarians, having mendaciously informed the Duce that they had been given permission by Berlin to occupy the Carpatho-Ukraine, attempted to do so. Before the operation could start, however, they were brought to book by Hitler for playing a 'frivolous game'.[3] Yet Hitler had made no final decision on the Carpatho-Ukraine, and his attitude to the problem is uncertain.[4] Although he had restrained Hungary and was angry with the Poles he told Ribbentrop a few days later that he would refuse a Roumanian request against cession of the area to Hungary.[5] His aim was to keep both 'irons in the fire' and 'to shape matters in the German interest according to the way the situation develops'. Hitler also made the revealing remark that his future policy towards the Carpatho-Ukraine would be largely determined 'by the manner in which Prague in future developed its relations with Germany'. For the moment the acquisition of Bohemia rather than the Corridor was his immediate object. So long as he seriously

[1] DGFP (D), Vol. V, pp. 127–9 and a note by Twardowski of 12 November. ibid., p. 125.

[2] See Wörmann's memorandum of 12 November, ibid., pp. 125–7.

[3] See Ciano's *Diaries*, 20 November and also DGFP (D), Vol. IV, pp. 148–9. pp. 152–3, pp. 162–3. See also DGFP (D), Vol. V, pp. 134–6.

[4] See p. 152.

[5] See a minute of Hitler's conversation with King Carol of Roumania on 24 November and Ribbentrop's addendum on the Führer's personal views, which is given separately, DGFP, Vol. V. pp. 338–42.

had to reckon with Prague there was no great danger of a sudden rupture with Warsaw.

The Poles, were, however, haunted by the fear that it was their turn next. Their anxiety over the Carpatho-Ukraine made possible a new approach to Russia, who also strongly resented German propaganda in Ukranian territories. The resulting rapprochement between Poland and Russia was something of a diplomatic revolution. During the Czech crisis a rupture between the two countries seemed possible; there were clashes on the frontier, and the Soviet Union threatened to abrogate her non-aggression pact with Poland of 1932 if that country threatened Czechoslovakia.[1] Friendship was soon restored. According to Schulenburg, the German Ambassador in Moscow, both Poland and Russia not only felt 'spurned' at Munich, but shared the belief that German penetration in the Carpatho-Ukraine constituted a threat.[2] On 26 November Russia and Poland re-affirmed their non-aggression pact: negotiations were evidently stimulated by the pending Franco-German Declaration and by economic factors.[2] Once more Hitler had to reprimand the Poles. On 2 December Ribbentrop informed Lipski that the German Government was 'surprised' that Poland had not informed it beforehand of the agreement with Russia. This was 'not quite in keeping with our friendly relations. . . .'[3] The consequences were serious. Until then Poland's existence was justified in Hitler's eyes by the need for a firm barrier against the Bolshevist East. With her refusal to join the Anti-Comintern Pact in January 1939 Poland's mission was drawing to an end. But, even at this stage, the Entente of 1934, though strained, was not dead. By a combination of threats and promises, Hitler still hoped to bring his obstinate, erring hireling to her senses.[4]

[1] According to Schulenburg, the German Ambassador in Moscow, the Poles made the first advance on or about 10 November, DGFP, Vol. V, pp. 138–40. Frontier clashes were described by Lipski to Ribbentrop on 2 December, ibid., p. 137; see also Schulenburg's comments on a note delivered by Potemkin, the Soviet Deputy-Commissar for Foreign Affairs, of 23 September, DGFP (D), Vol. II, pp. 948–9.

[2] DGFP(D), Vol. V, a despatch of 3 December, pp. 138–40.

[3] Ibid, p. 137. See also a despatch from Moltke of 27 November, DGFP (D), Vol. V, p. 136 and from Welczeck, the German Ambassador in Paris, of 30 November, DGFP (D), Vol. IV, pp. 467–9.

[4] See the conversations between Ribbentrop and Colonel Beck of 6 January DGFP (D), Vol. V, pp. 159–61, and between Hitler and Beck of 5 January 1939, ibid., pp. 152–8, cf. pp. 167–8.

Plans to destroy her matured more slowly than those against Czechoslovakia of the previous year. German staffs had always paid attention to the Baltic, and, during the Polish-Lithuanian crisis of March 1938,[1] OKW considered that in the event of war between Poland and Lithuania, Memel should be seized in order to prevent its falling into Polish hands. In the autumn of 1938 there had been a Polish-Lithuanian *détente*,[2] but the military order of the previous March was reincorporated into the directive of 21 October for the invasion of Czechoslovakia. For geographical reasons alone, the problems of Memel and Danzig were inseparable. On 24 November, two days before the Russo-Polish non-aggression pact was re-affirmed, Keitel issued a directive for a possible occupation of Danzig. Military formations were to be made available in such a way that this operation could be carried out at the same time as an assault on Memel; they were evidently to support an internal *coup de main*. It will be seen how Hitler later believed the Poles might be made to acquiesce in a *fait accompli*. Perhaps this explains why it was specially laid down in the directive that war with Poland was not intended.[3]

Of far greater immediate importance were Hitler's plans for the annexation of what was left of Czechoslovakia. The directive of 21 October was superseded on 17 December by a new directive, in which no mention was made of Czech provocation as a *casus belli*. Whereas previously a high and continuous state of preparation had been considered necessary, but not full mobilization, no appreciable resistance was now expected. Troops would leave their quarters on the previous night and were not, as previously planned, to be deployed along the frontier. That the operation was to have the appearance of a peaceful and not a warlike undertaking is in itself an indication both of the extent and of the limitation of what could be achieved by political pressure alone. However much Czechoslovakia had been weakened by successive cessions of territory,[4] there remained a hard core of resistance, represented

---

[1] For the German attitude during the Lithuanian crisis, see DGFP (D), Vol. V, pp. 433–4.

[2] See a German Foreign Office memorandum of 25 November, ibid., pp. 487–90.

[3] ND: 136–138–C.

[4] For the internal changes in Czechoslovakia and its transformation into 'Czecho-Slovakia', see Wheeler-Bennett, *Munich*, p. 337.

by those who refused to barter away their national independence. Their hopes could only be destroyed by a military occupation. Whereas the new Czech Government nervously tried to come to terms with the Reich and so protract its moribund existence, the legacy of Benes was too strong to be eradicated entirely.[1] According to Hencke, in a survey of internal conditions on 24 October, only a 'thorough reorganisation which would establish the *Führer prinzip* could in time effect a change here. . . . The weak central government can obviously prevail only with difficulty in face of the feeling against everything German which was somewhat intensified after the cession of the Sudeten-German areas.'[2] It is not surprising that those Germans who remained in Bohemia and Moravia were far from popular with the Czechs. Indeed they envied the lot of their fellow nationals who were now citizens of the Reich, and there can be little doubt that reports exaggerating their economic plight, were calculated to persuade Hitler to 'liberate' them.[3] The future status of the German minority came up for discussion at a conference of 7 November 1938 between members of the German Foreign Office and the Volksdeutsche Mittelstelle.[4] A Foreign Office plan for a long-term treaty with Czechoslovakia for the protection of ethnic groups on either side of the frontier was rejected on the grounds that the Czechs now living in Germany must not be given the same civic rights as Germans in Czechoslovakia. This meant that a situation had arisen in which the alternative to extending the principles of the Karlsbad demands to foreign minorities living on German soil was the complete subjugation of Czechoslovakia. Hitler may have reached his final decision before he met Chvalkovsky, the Czech Foreign Minister, on 21 January, for he made no concrete proposals for the future. He certainly had no doubts after the meeting. On 26 January Weizsäcker told Hassell that Hitler's programme still demanded 'a complete settlement of the Czech issue'. Weizsäcker also stated

[1] See a despatch from Hencke of 15 December, DGFP (D), Vol. IV., pp. 182–3 and ibid., pp. 190–5.

[2] Ibid., pp. 104–8. Further amputations added to the ill-feeling in November. See a conversation between the Czech Minister and Wörmann of 11 November, p. 143.

[3] See Hencke's despatch of 10 December, ibid., pp. 179–81. Cf. a report from Funck, the spokesman of the German minority, of 16 December, pp. 183–5.

[4] Ibid., pp. 140–2. See also the unsigned proposals of SS *Oberführer* Behrends of the Volksdeutsche Mittelstelle of 4 November, pp. 133–4.

that 'the barometer indicated peace even in the East where at most some sort of undertaking is desired against Poland'.[1]

Weizsäcker was widely off the mark, and the evidence for Hitler's attitude towards a general war after Munich is abundant. On 29 September, the day before he signed his famous 'peace' declaration with Chamberlain, he told Mussolini that 'the time will come when we will have to fight side by side against France and England'.[2] Feeling at once triumphant and thwarted, he was determined to prepare his own people for the inevitable conflict. 'Previously', he declared at a secret conference to German press representatives on 10 November, 'circumstances have compelled me for decades to speak almost only of peace'.[3] There could now be only one choice: 'to speak nothing more nor less than the brutal truth. . . .' He claimed that, according to intelligence reports, German propaganda had broken the nerves of the men of Prague. He had since met Chamberlain and Daladier, and while he did not mention them by name, he most certainly hinted that they would be easy victims of strong words.

A new strident note was already sounded in German propaganda. In his Saarbrücken speech of 9 October he made a personal attack on British statesmen: Duff Cooper, Eden and Churchill.[4] Hitler had gravely miscalculated: intimidation did not have its desired effect, and the speech was to be followed by a 'strong forward surge for invigorated [British] rearmament'.[5]

Dirksen, now German Ambassador in London, backed by Dr. Fritz Hesse, the German News Agency representative attached to the Embassy, registered firm protests.[6] Contrary to his advice, British rearmament was to be vigorously attacked. The campaign was ordered directly by Ribbentrop, who was convinced that, since Britain was rearming in any case, German propaganda could not provide her with an additional stimulus to do so. The campaign, he thought, would cause a rift between those who on no account wanted war and those who demanded an increase of

---

[1] Ibid., pp. 190–5 and Hassell's Diary.

[2] DGFP (D), Vol. II, p. 1617 and Vol. IV, pp. 287–93.

[3] The address, preserved on a tape recorder, is reproduced in full in *Vierteljahrshefte für Zeitgeschichte*, April 1958, together with a commentary by Professor W. Treue.

[4] Baynes, *Hitler's Speeches*, Vol. II, pp. 1532–7.

[5] Churchill, *The Second World War*, Vol. 1, pp. 257–8.

[6] DGFP (D), Vol. IV, despatch of 11 October, p. 303 and p. 307.

armaments 'to face up squarely to Germany "next time". . .'[1] The German Embassy attempted without success to prove that the spate of British rearmament should not be exaggerated; and that, provided the prospect of an agreement was kept alive, Chamberlain's position was secure. On 31 October Dirksen reported that Hoare and Burgin, the Minister of Transport, had informed him that Chamberlain had complete confidence in the Führer, and that 'no time is so favourable as the present' for an Anglo-German settlement.[2]

Although failure to respond to the British proposals, as well as the great indignation aroused by the November pogroms, diminished Chamberlain's prestige, Dirksen later described how Britain was still attempting to improve commercial relations with Germany and to supplement the Naval Treaty of 1935 with a protocol for the exchange of information. On 14 December Halifax again approached Dirksen on the possibility of a general understanding but without success.[3]

Halifax's attempt was made at a time when Britain was considered the more 'dangerous' but France the more 'certain' enemy.[4] Hitler therefore, playing for quick returns from Czechoslovakia and Poland, was more ready to listen to overtures from France. On 6 December after some delay a declaration of non-aggression, modelled on the Anglo-German Agreement of Munich, was signed in Paris.[5] The next day Bonnet admitted to Ribbentrop that the Franco-Russian pact was no longer effective and, despite his later statements to the contrary, he seems to have created the impression that France had tacitly abandoned Eastern Europe. Bonnet, however, spoke of the 'fundamental and unshakeable character of Franco-British solidarity'.[6] He could afford to do so as he still had no reason to suppose that Britain would later commit herself to defend Eastern Europe. He failed to realize that France remained threatened even when she was no longer the mainspring of a group of powers pledged to halt German expan-

[1] See letters exchanged between Weizsäcker and Dirksen on 17 October, ibid., pp. 311–2.
[2] See Dr. Hesse's despatch of 18 October, ibid., p. 313 and pp. 319–23.
[3] See Dirksen's despatch of 17 November, ibid., pp. 333–4.
[4] See a memorandum by Weizsäcker of 20 June 1938, DGFP (D), Vol. II, p. 420.
[5] For the text see DGFP (D), Vol. IV, p. 470.
[6] Ibid., p. 471.

sion, for Hitler also needed French territory for air and naval bases in a war with Britain.[1] On 26 November 1938, before Ribbentrop left for Paris, Keitel had submitted to him a memorandum on the possible form operations by Germany and Italy against France might take. In it the entire emphasis was on the offensive, and the underlying assumptions of previous directives were superseded.[2] The Franco-German Declaration was thus the last pathetic link in a security system that had already crumbled—it was a guarantee against German aggression from Hitler himself.

Lack of sympathy on the part of Britain for both Poland and Russia at the end of 1938 certainly encouraged the belief that not only France but also Britain had written off Eastern Europe. Dirksen described British opinion in two comprehensive despatches of 3 and 4 January.[3] He believed that interest in Czechoslovakia had waned and that Britain was piqued because of Poland's hostility to Czechoslovakia. 'It is noted without feelings of sympathy, that Germany will now present her [Poland] with a bill for Teschen.' Later Germany would make further claims on the Corridor and Danzig and cut her off from her Ukrainian territories. The British public, convinced of the impotence of Russia, was more hostile to both Russia and Poland than it had been in the previous year. Dirksen even believed that further German penetration towards the Ukraine, 'whose conquest by Germany is firmly believed to be timed for the spring of 1939', would be accepted. He concluded that even if military force were used by Germany in the creation of an independent Ukraine, the psychological appeal to the 'slogan' of self-determination should be skilfully exploited, for Britain would not allow a conflict to arise provided that this principle were respected.

This was the Indian summer of appeasement, and Dirksen's optimism was shared by Henderson, who arrived back in Berlin after sick leave in the middle of February. There were, Henderson thought, unmistakable signs of what he described as a return to 'normalcy'. Economic relations were improving, and both he and Dirksen tried to cement friendship by arranging return visits of Stanley, President of the Board of Trade, Hudson, Secretary of Overseas Trade, and Funk, the German Minister of Economics.

---

[1] See p. 173.
[2] DGFP (D), Vol. IV, pp. 529–32.
[3] loc. cit., pp. 357–67. The two despatches are analysed in conjunction above.

Finally on 8 February the British Government approached the Reich on the Four Power guarantee of Czechoslovakia, which had been agreed to in principle at Munich.[1] Between 11 and 14 January Chamberlain and Halifax had, however, failed to persuade Mussolini that the moment was opportune and, fondly believing that no German action against Czechoslovakia was imminent, remained rather half-hearted about the guarantee.[2]

Prague

Illusions were to be shattered quite unexpectedly by Hitler's entry into Prague on 15 March, an event which need only be summarized here.[3] Early in the month President Hacha of Czechoslovakia was informed that the local governments of the Carpatho-Ukraine and Slovakia were, with German connivance, striving to sever their connections with Prague. Hacha was not prepared to acquiesce in the dismemberment of his country. He dismissed the leaders of the Carpatho-Ukraine on the 6th and the leaders of Slovakia on the 9th.[4] On 13 March Hitler virtually ordered Tiso, the ex-Prime Minister of Slovakia, to proclaim the independence of his country. Tiso complied on the 14th and sought the protection of the Reich.[5] Although the Carpatho-Ukraine followed suit, Hitler had already on 12 March given the Hungarians a free hand: on the 15th they marched into the province. Hitler had a different fate in store for Bohemia and Moravia. On 14 March Hacha was summoned to Berlin, where in the early hours of the 15th he was 'persuaded' into signing the death warrant of his country.[6] On the same day Hitler's forces entered Prague.

The moral shock of the 'Ides of March' reverberated across Europe.[7] Hitler could no longer justify his action even on the extremely elastic principle of 'self-determination' which had

---

[1] See *Failure of a Mission*, Part II, Chaps. VIII and XI, also a conversation between Henderson and Ribbentrop of 16 February, DGFP (D), Vol. IV, pp. 402–3. See also *Documents and Materials* (USSR), Vol. II, pp. 164–7. Dirksen's final report and Dirksen's *Moscow, Tokyo, London*, pp. 226–8.

[2] DGFP (D), Vol. IV, pp. 207–8.

[3] See *The Bulletin of the Institute of Historical Research*, No. 47, November 1953, in which a despatch from Attolico summarizing his experiences in March 1939 is printed by M. Toscano.

[4] See Hencke's despatch of 9 March, DGFP (D), Vol. IV, pp. 230–1 and a German Foreign Office memorandum of 10 March, pp. 233–4.

[5] Ibid., pp. 243–5, an undated telegram from the Slovak Prime Minister to Hitler, p. 250.

[6] Ibid., pp. 240–1 and pp. 263–9. For the text of the ultimatum drawn up by OKW on 12 March, ibid., pp. 234–5.

[7] See Wheeler-Bennett, *Munich*, pp. 349–59.

yielded so much and promised more. The attitude of the British public was transformed, and Dirksen commented that the event would have 'deep and lasting repercussions'. 'We thus', he wrote mistakenly in his final report, 'had the converse of the developments of 1936 ... when it was the Government and Parliament who were at first in favour of war but who under the moderating influence of the electorate had to declare in favour of greater restraint'.[1] New alignments were to follow. In the previous year, Hitler had regarded the eastern section of Czechoslovakia, the Carpatho-Ukraine, as a possible salient for further German expansion. By occupying the western areas, and by allowing the Carpatho-Ukraine to pass to Hungary, he antagonized the signatories of Munich rather than Russia. Even Mussolini sank into a fit of depression and for a time hesitated about an alliance.[2]

The country most immediately affected was Poland. It might be thought that the Hungarian seizure of the Carpatho-Ukraine would silence her protests, for this had been her demand in the previous autumn. But at that time she had assumed that Slovakia, once independent, would become her ally. Since Slovakia was now under German control, a common frontier with Hungary on the Carpathians was of no practical value. Indeed Hitler was in a better position to turn on the screw than before.[3] On 21 March Ribbentrop in a conversation with Lipski again broached the question of Danzig and the Corridor. He reminded him that the settlement in the Carpatho-Ukraine 'had caused the greatest satisfaction in Poland'. Lipski expressed anxiety over the fact that Germany had assumed the protection of Slovakia and stated: 'this news had hit Poland hard'. Ribbentrop then 'gave a slight hint' that the question of Slovakia 'could perhaps be the subject of joint discussions if German-Polish relations developed satisfactorily'.[4] Although Ribbentrop gave no specific assurance concerning Slovakia, Hitler may still have been prepared to negotiate on the future of the province, for on 25 March Brauchitsch formed

---

[1] *Documents and Materials*, (USSR), Vol. II, p. 171 and DGFP (D), Vol. VI, pp. 36–9, a despatch of 18 March.

[2] Ciano's *Diaries*, 15–19 March.

[3] See a political report from Moltke of 8 October 1938, DGFP (D), Vol. V, pp. 90–1, and a despatch of 27 October, p. 115.

[4] DGFP (D), Vol. VI, pp. 70–2. In Doc. No. 203 of the German White Book the words 'I gave a slight hint' have been altered to 'I let it be clearly understood'.

the impression from a conversation with the Führer that Slovakia might be used as a bargaining counter with Hungary and Poland.[1] Hitler also told Brauchitsch that he did not wish to solve the Danzig problem by force as this would drive Poland into the arms of Britain. A seizure of the town would be considered only if, as Hitler supposed, the Polish Government hinted that a *fait accompli* would be easier for their people to accept than a voluntary cession of the town.[2] Hitler evidently believed that the Poles might yet be persuaded to take a 'realistic' view of the German proposals, for he did not wish to prejudice negotiations by taking part in them personally. He therefore left Berlin.

Memel

Before Lipski returned, German-Polish relations received yet a fresh shock from which they were never to recover. On 23 March Hitler seized Memel. According to Moltke, the German Ambassador in Warsaw, this added to the general excitement in Poland: military and political circles were now certain that a German coup against Danzig was imminent.[3] Beck reacted vigorously and ordered partial mobilization. On 26 March, when Lipski returned with Beck's reply, in which a compromise was suggested, Ribbentrop told him that the Reich would only accept the definite reincorporation of Danzig and an extra-territorial link with East Prussia as the basis for a final settlement. In warning Lipski of the possible consequences of Polish troop concentrations, he said that a violation of the sovereignty of Danzig would be regarded in the same way as a violation of the frontier of the Reich. Although tempers were on edge the interview was not so negative as might be supposed: Ribbentrop formed the impression that the military measures taken by Poland were of a defensive character, and that the Polish Government's compromise proposals might not represent their last word.[4] But Beck refused to be browbeaten. On the

[1] ND: 100-R.

[2] Hitler probably formed this impression from Lipski's reference to public opinion in Poland on 24 October 1938, see p. 154.

[3] On 22 August Hitler himself described the seizure of Memel as a turning point; ND: 798-PS. See Moltke's despatch of 28 March, DGFP, Vol. VI, pp. 144–5. The passage concerning Memel and Danzig is not included in Doc. No. 210 of the German White Book.

[4] DGFP (D), Vol. VI, pp. 121–2. *The German White Book*, Doc. No. 208 has inserted an additional sentence to the early part of the text which reads: 'M. Lipski replied that it was his painful duty to point out that any further prosecution of these German plans [i.e. the German proposals], especially as far as the return of Danzig to the Reich, meant war with Poland.' Ribbentrop's own impressions are omitted from Doc. No. 208 of the German White Book.

28th he told Moltke that, since Germany had just stated that she would regard a unilateral Polish attempt to alter the *status quo* of Danzig as a *casus belli*, Poland would take an identical view towards an attempted German coup. Nevertheless Beck persisted in his hope that a solution could be found 'satisfactory to both sides'.[1] Beck had not only turned down Hitler's proposals but made it abundantly clear that he would not acquiesce in a *fait accompli*. Hitler was filled with indignation and later attributed Polish intransigence to British backing.[2] In fact the Poles neither approached the British for help nor kept them informed of the nature of the German proposals. Hence the origins of Chamberlain's guarantee to Poland of 31 March are to be sought elsewhere.

After Hitler entered Prague all sorts of rumours reached London: it was feared among other things that Roumania was immediately threatened. On 17 March Tilea, the Roumanian Minister in London, erroneously informed Lord Halifax that a virtual German ultimatum was to be expected within the next few days. The British Government, alarmed by the prospect of Germany's gaining control over the resources of Roumania, considered counter-measures. They recognized that no practical assistance could be given to Roumania unless other Powers, above all Russia and Poland, were included among the guarantors, and unless Poland were the first to take military action. But the Poles were not prepared to participate in an agreement which included Russia, and since they had every reason to demand that the West should do as much for them as for Roumania, Chamberlain was persuaded that the threat to Poland constituted the real and immediate problem; that she herself should be given a unilateral guarantee.[3] His decision, which was announced in the House of Commons on the 31st, was followed by Beck's visit to London and by the conclusion of the Anglo-Polish treaty of alliance of 6 April. Meanwhile Axis domination over South-East Europe was making still further headway. A far-reaching commercial treaty between

---

[1] DGFP (D), Vol. VI, a despatch of 29 March, pp. 147–8. The sentence containing these words has been omitted from Doc. No. 211 of the German White Book.

[2] See his staff conference of 27 August 1939, ND: Raeder 27.

[3] See Kordt's telegram of 20 March describing events in London, DGFP (D), Vol. VI, pp. 50–1, also an article by Professor Desmond Williams on the negotiations leading to the Anglo-Polish Agreement, reprinted from *Irish Historical Studies*, Nos. 37–8, March–September 1956.

Germany and Roumania was concluded on 23 March. Mussolini seized Albania on 7 April. As a result Britain concluded treaties of mutual assistance with Greece and Roumania on 13 April and Turkey on 12 May. Far from having abandoned eastern Europe, she had reversed her policy and was now, without weighing the military consequences, showering the small states with guarantees.

(Bullock p. 497)

Until the beginning of April Hitler had in fact issued no directive for an invasion of Poland or any other country. When he met Brauchitsch on 25 March he still hoped to win Danzig by peaceful means. He nevertheless said that plans for war with Poland would have to be examined; that if war were decided, the new frontier of the Reich would run from the eastern border of East Prussia to the eastern tip of Silesia. He did not wish to enter the Ukraine. He was prepared to leave open the question of establishing an independent Ukraine. Stimulated by events at the end of March, which had been brought about by his own action in Czechoslovakia, Hitler got down to practical business. On 3 April he ordered OKW to draw up a plan for the invasion of Poland (Operation White): 1 September was given as the earliest date when it might be necessary to put it into force. Operational aims were laid down by OKW in a general directive of the 11th. Although it was stated in the preamble that Germany would continue to avoid a conflict, Poland was to be smashed if she reversed her policy. The final frontiers in the East and the Baltic would be determined by Germany's military needs. In spite of the prominence given to Poland in the directive it does not follow that Hitler had abandoned the ultimate aim of fighting Britain and France, for it was also stated that the final goal of German armaments was war with the West: Operation White was merely to be regarded as a broadening of the scope of preparations, not as a prerequisite of war elsewhere: the Naval High Command laid particular stress on this ruling.[1]

[1] ND: 100-R and 120–6–C.

CHAPTER 16

Russia and Hitler's Final Decision

(22 August 1939)

After Hitler ordered Operation White on 3 April he brought his general policy into line with his military intentions. In a speech of 28 April he repudiated what were the two mainstays of his foreign policy, the Non-Aggression Pact with Poland of 26 January 1934 and the Anglo-German Naval Agreement of 18 June 1935.[1] He also refrained from hurling his customary oratorical insults against the Soviet Union: a community of interests with the sworn enemy of his political faith was soon to emerge.

Although Russian propaganda at the time of the Czech crisis had been strong in its condemnation of 'Fascist aggression', it seemed to German observers even before Munich that Stalin was less than whole-hearted in his support of the West.[2] There had been little military activity inside his country and, according to the German Embassy, preliminary preparations for mobilization were neglected.[3] After Munich there were certain sinister portents of a change in Germany's favour. Early in October Potemkin, the Deputy-Commissar for Foreign Affairs, allegedly told Coulondre, the French Ambassador: '*Mon pauvre ami . . . Pour nous je n'aperçois plus d'autre issue qu'un quatrième partage de la Pologne.*' It seemed that the stage was set for a revival of Rapallo, for at that time Hitler was in fact giving serious thought to the questions of Danzig and the Corridor.[4] But it would be a mistake to interpret German-Soviet relations in the autumn of 1938 too much in the light of later events. Admittedly the Soviet Union felt slighted at Munich, and watched with growing resentment the collapse of collective security. She was prepared, moreover, to talk about the removal of certain minor irritants in her relations with Germany, and she even came to a tacit understanding with her on refraining

[1] Baynes, *Hitler's Speeches*, Vol. II, pp. 1606–56.
[2] See P. W. Fabry, *Der Hitler Stalin Pakt*, Chap. I.
[3] DGFP (D), Vol. IV, pp. 604–7, a despatch from Moscow of 10 October.
[4] Coulondre, *De Stalin à Hitler*, p. 165 and p. 157.

from personal abuse in propaganda.[1] Despite this the Russians had more to fear than before from Germany, now that Czechoslovakia had been cowed into submission. According to Schulenburg in a despatch of 3 December 1938 German influence in the Carpatho-Ukraine was regarded in Moscow as a 'major threat'.[2] Russia was now even prepared to make common cause with the country which was later to be sacrificed on the altar of friendship with Germany; on 26 November she had reaffirmed her non-aggression pact of 1932 with Poland. It can be contended that German-Soviet relations were so bad after Munich that almost any change would have been for the good. No new risk was therefore involved if Hitler continued to adhere to the anti-Bolshevik thesis of his foreign policy. Much was to be gained if others could be persuaded to associate themselves with it.

By accident rather than design Russia's potential allies, above all France, not her enemies, were held responsible for her exclusion at Munich and for the declarations of non-aggression made afterwards. Worse was to follow: in January Soviet leaders suspected that Chamberlain had expressed British disinterestedness to Mussolini concerning German intentions in the Ukraine.[3] Stalin had now every reason to believe that the democracies were not only placating but egging on the dictators, and in his speech to the 18th Congress of the Communist Party of 10 March he vented his wrath in public.[4] Schulenburg, in analysing the speech, three days later, made no mention of any new developments in Soviet policy, but regarded Stalin's accusations as significant.[5] On 18

[1] See despatches from Moscow of 3 and 10 October, DGFP, Vol. IV, pp. 602–7. At the end of October 1938 Schulenburg intended approaching Soviet authorities in order to solve questions disturbing German-Soviet relations; see his despatch of 26 October, ibid., pp. 607–8. For the Press truce, see Hilger, *The Incompatible Allies*, pp. 288–91. A change in German propaganda on the Ukrainian issue was noticed by the Poles who claimed that since it attacked the 'so-called Stalin system' rather than the 'Soviet Union in general', Germany might be inclined to make a pact with another regime in Russia. Moltke's despatch of 25 October, DGFP (D), Vol. V, pp. 107–9.

[2] DGFP (D), Vol. V, pp. 138–40.

[3] Rosso, the Italian Ambassador in Moscow, learnt this from a Polish colleague who heard it from Litvinov. See Toscano, *L'Italia e gli Accordi Tedesco-Sovietici del Agosto 1939*, pp. 9–15.

[4] For the text see RIIA, *Docs.* 1939, pp. 361–70. See also E. H. Carr, *German-Soviet Relations*, pp. 126–7; the last passage has, according to Carr, been rendered less accurately, with the metaphor 'pull her chestnuts out of the fire for her'.

[5] DGFP, Vol. VI, pp. 1–3.

March Russia, incensed by the German occupation of Prague, and still not knowing the extent or direction of future German expansion, rather half-heartedly proposed a six power conference to counter further aggression. The offer was declined. Chamberlain, instead, negotiated treaties with Poland and Roumania. Stalin now knew that even if the Soviet Union assumed no new commitments fresh German action would be resisted automatically by Great Britain; he could thus let others act first and fix his own price for Soviet support.[1]

While the Russians continued negotiations with the West, they simultaneously explored the possibility of a deal with the Reich.[2] Opinion in Berlin was already ripe for a Soviet approach. On 16 April Göring, who in conversation was often disarmingly frank, told Mussolini that he would ask the Führer whether it would not be possible to put out feelers cautiously to Russia through certain intermediaries with a view to a rapprochement so as to cause Poland anxiety over Russia as well. Göring also described how the open antagonism between Russia and Germany had abated.[3] He was interested in improving trade with Russia and may have been influenced by his personal jealousy of Ribbentrop, who at that time was taking pains to transform the Anti-Comintern Pact into a triple alliance. Before Göring returned the Russians had taken the initiative. On 17 April Merekalov, the Soviet Ambassador, told Weizsäcker that ideological differences need not jeopardize a 'normalization of German-Soviet relations'. Later, on 3 May, Molotov was appointed Soviet Foreign Minister in the place of Litvinov. This was regarded as a favourable augury enabling Hitler to compete against the West in a bid for Stalin's favours.[4]

Whereas the subsequent talks between Molotov and representatives of Britain and France were drawn out—it seemed interminably—and were for the greater part conducted in the official and rather stifling atmosphere of the Kremlin, exchanges between Germany and Russia were at first intermittent and surreptitious.

---

[1] Coulondre, op. cit., p. 263.

[2] Dr. Peter Kleist, a member of Ribbentrop's Dienststelle, a private bureau independent of the Foreign Office, states that he was ordered to make contact with members of the Soviet Embassy on 7 April (*Zwischen Hitler und Stalin*, pp. 26–9). Unfortunately no documents of Ribbentrop's personal bureau are available to check his account.

[3] DGFP (D), Vol. VI, pp. 258–63. Göring also told Mussolini that Germany had little interest in the Ukraine.

[4] DGFP (D), Vol. VI, pp. 419–20.

If mutual suspicion brought discussions with the West to a standstill, it seemed that definite negotiations with Germany would never take place.[1] But whereas the number of problems which were likely to stand in the way of a treaty with the West multiplied, even in the course of negotiations, those in the way of a Russo-German agreement dwindled before serious negotiations were started. By the end of March Hitler, instead of occupying the Carpatho-Ukraine, had allowed the province to be absorbed by Hungary. This was, from the Soviet point of view, by far the lesser of two evils. Contrary to British predictions he had shown no great interest in the remaining Ukrainian territories, nor in the Baltic.[2] Hitler had instead decided on Operation White.

An agreement with Russia was now Hitler's most logical course, but it involved a complete reversal of existing German policy in one important respect. It has been seen how before 7 November 1937 the Anti-Comintern Pact was developing into something more than an ideological manifesto.[3] During the Czech crisis Mussolini had agreed to march beside Germany 'with everything', but staff conferences had not been held and there was no Italian mobilization. On 29 September, during the Munich crisis, Ribbentrop handed Ciano a draft treaty for a triple alliance between Germany, Italy and Japan and described it as the 'biggest thing in the world'. Later there was to be much confusion, for Göring, behind Ribbentrop's back, proposed that Italy should put her signature to a Four Power Pact of consultation.[4] Ribbentrop was at first to make greater headway with the Japanese. They had recently launched an offensive against Canton and occupied a large strip of the east coast of China where British interests were at stake. Sympathy in Japan for Germany was growing, and in October Oshima, a staunch advocate of the Axis, was appointed

---

[1] For a convenient account of German-Soviet relations in the summer of 1939, see Weinberg, *Germany and the Soviet Union 1939–1941* (Leiden, E. J. Brill, 1954) and E. H. Carr, *German-Soviet Relations*, pp. 128–37.

[2] In his directive of April Hitler mentioned a possible entry into the Baltic States as far as the frontier of old Courland (ND: 120-C). Hitler also approached the Baltic States with non-aggression pacts in May. See the German communique of the 19th in RIIA, *Docs. 1939*, pp. 256–7.

[3] See p. 102.

[4] For German-Italian relations during the Czech crisis, see entries in Ciano's *Diaries* for 11 August and for September. See also Mackensen's despatch of 6 October and Weizsäcker's reply of the 11th, DGFP (D), Vol. IV, p. 435 and pp. 436–7.

Ambassador in Berlin.[1] On 27 October the Japanese Ambassador in Rome handed Ciano the text of an alliance. Ribbentrop was exultant, and the next day described in glowing terms for Ciano and Mussolini the military prospects of the Axis. Mussolini however remained hesitant. He had recently been approached by Britain on implementing the agreement of April 1938, and he told Ribbentrop that he was against the alliance if only because the Italian people were not spiritually prepared. At that time there had also been serious differences of opinion between Italy and Germany over Hungary's claims on the Carpatho-Ukraine.[2] Towards the end of December the Duce changed his mind. He had recently insulted the French over Nice and Corsica and was turning covetous eyes on Albania. On 3 January Ciano informed Ribbentrop of the Duce's desire to resume discussions, and he suggested that if possible the treaty should be signed as early as 28 January.[3] The pourparlers with Chamberlain and Halifax in Rome on 11 to 14 January were described as a 'fiasco' and Mussolini became progressively more in favour of a dual alliance with Germany. On 10 March he was gratified to learn that Hitler agreed that the two countries should march together and that staff talks should begin. On the fateful 14th of March Attolico, the Italian Ambassador in Berlin, asked that they should be started soon.[4]

While Mussolini was showing impatience the Japanese were reluctant about concluding the alliance with undue haste. It was, they thought, manifestly directed against the Western Powers rather than Russia, whom they regarded as the real enemy. Although they were prepared to modify the anti-Russian emphasis of their own proposals early in April, Hitler did not feel that they had gone far enough[5] but hoped that he could, if necessary, win

---

[1] DGFP (D), Vol. IV, a despatch from Tokyo, 29 October, p. 684 of 1 November, p. 685. See also Ciano's description of Oshima, 15 December (*Diaries*).

[2] Ibid., pp. 515–20 and Ciano's *Diaries* and *Papers*. There are some minor divergences between the German and Italian accounts of the meetings of 28 October.

[3] See Ciano's *Diaries*, 23 December 1938 and 1 and 2 January 1939. See also DGFP (D), Vol. IV, pp. 543–5 and pp. 545–6, a despatch from Mackensen of 4 January.

[4] Ciano's *Diaries*, 12 January, 8 February and 3 March. See also DGFP (D), Vol. IV, 10 March, p. 588 and p. 590.

[5] For a summary of the Japanese attitude, see a report of Ribbentrop of 25 April 1939, RIIA, *Docs.* 1939, pp. 157–9.

them over to an alliance—albeit against Russia alone—whenever it suited him.[1] In the meantime he concentrated on negotiations for a dual offensive military alliance with Italy. He straight away encountered one serious obstacle. Public opinion in Italy was outraged over the events of 15 March, and it was feared that the Croats, as well as the Germans in the south Tyrol, would follow the lead of the Slovaks and appeal to the Reich.[2] The annexation of Albania by Italy on 7 April gave Mussolini a spurious sense of security. Göring was sent to Italy to pour oil on the troubled waters. He was told by Mussolini on the 15th that Italy was not yet ready for war and hoped that it would not break out over Poland. On 6–7 May Ribbentrop met Ciano in Milan for further negotiations on the alliance, and staff discussions were opened. They were duly held but merely had the effect of exposing Italy's military weakness. On 22 May a treaty, later known as the Pact of Steel, was concluded. In the event of war Italy was pledged to support Germany with all her military forces on land, sea and air. Since in a secret memorandum of 30 May Mussolini expressed the reservation that Italy was not ready for war for some four years,[3] the Treaty was merely a propaganda victory for Hitler whose estimate of Italy as a power factor was entirely false.

The effect of the Treaty was to encourage Hitler to go ahead with his plans. After General Keitel had issued the directive of 11 April for Operation White, German planning proceeded on two lines: operations for a localized war against Poland[4]; for a blockade against Britain. The relation between these two theatres was discussed at length by Hitler at a staff conference of 23 May. After the invariable harangue on *Lebensraum* he gave, rather confusedly, his reasons for attacking Poland.[5] Poland could no longer be considered an effective barrier to Russia. Her internal resistance to Communism was doubtful. Despite treaties of friendship 'Poland will always stand on the side of our enemies' and she had 'the

---

[1] See Hitler's staff conference of 23 May 1939, DGFP (D), Vol. VI, pp. 574–80.

[2] See Toscano, *Le Origini del Patto d'Acciaio*, pp. 143–4 and Ciano's *Papers* and *Diary*. For the German account see DGFP (D), Vol. VI, pp. 444–52 and Appendix I.

[3] Toscano, op. cit.

[4] One draft Plan for the invasion of Poland had been drawn up by a working party under General von Rundstedt on 7 May and a second on the 20th.

[5] ND: 079-L. The minutes of the conference were taken by Schmundt, Hitler's Wehrmacht Adjutant.

intention of doing us harm'. Since a quick victory was not expected in the west, her attitude was a cause of particular anxiety. There were, too, economic reasons for invading Poland; the acquisition of surplus food areas bordering Germany in the east was of utmost importance in the event of war with the West. A repetition of the Czech affair was not to be expected. Hitler said there 'will be fighting'.[1] This does not mean that he believed there would be a general war, for he went on to say: 'There must be no simultaneous conflict with the Western Powers. Germany must not "slither" into war on account of Poland. Should such a conflict arise it would be better to attack in the West and treat the Polish campaign as a subsidiary issue.' Hitler spoke at length on operational conceptions, which had been maturing steadily since his conference of 5 November 1937, for War with Britain.[2] He discussed the relative merits of an air attack on her fleet and a long distance blockade. He did not consider it necessary to land forces in Britain, and he spoke gleefully of the time when German expenditure need no longer be poured into the 'bottomless pit' of the army but could go into naval and air expansion. His natural preference for the junior branches of the armed forces, which were capable of striking Britain, rather than for the pedestrian and conservative army, may also have been an additional inducement to plan for a war with Britain. At the end of the conference it was decided that the years 1943–1944 were to be the new target date for the completion of armaments. By that time the ship building programme would have been complete. Although Hitler expressed his preference for a short war, Germany would have to prepare for a long one of perhaps ten or fifteen years.[3]

[1] This passage has been misleadingly translated 'There will be war.' According to a Naval Directive of 16 May the government was to do everything to restrict the war to Poland, ND: 126-C.

[2] There is abundant evidence on plans for war with Britain. In March 1938 Raeder addressed German ship builders on a new naval construction programme, ND: 23-C. In naval staff studies for April 1938, war with Britain was taken for granted, and *Blitzkrieg* tactics for an attack on the British fleet were discussed at an inter-service conference of 20 May 1938. While the Air Force were in favour the Navy were against an occupation of the Low Countries. The Naval High Command was, however, anxious to secure submarine bases off the west coast of France and Norway. See Note on Sources, p. 195. See also ND: 123-C and ND: 375-PS and Räder, *Mein Leben*, Vol. II, Chap XI.

[3] On 24 May General Thomas in an address to German Foreign Ministry officials made an exhaustive survey of Germany's war potential, ND (IMT): EC-28.

On 23 May Hitler adopted the paradoxical position that the conquest of Poland was necessary for a successful war with Britain; British neutrality for war against Poland. The emphasis was to switch slowly from the first to the second of these assumptions as a result of changes in British policy.

After 15 March, despite a rearguard action in favour of appeasement, there could be <u>no going back</u> on the British guarantee to Poland of 6 April. Although the Treaty had not yet been ratified, Halifax in a speech at Chatham House on 29 June emphasized once more Britain's resolve to 'stop aggression', and on 10 July Chamberlain told the House of Commons that a seizure of Danzig by surreptitious methods could not be regarded as a local matter but as a threat to Poland's independence. He also drew his listeners' attention to the British guarantee which, he said, his Government were determined to fulfil.[1]

There were, however, serious difficulties in the way of implementing the guarantee. On 19 July General Ironside visited Warsaw to discuss military co-operation. The failure of his mission was fully appreciated in Germany. According to an OKH (Army High Command) situation report of 12 August, he told the Poles that, contrary to previous promises, Britain could scarcely equip them with armaments by the autumn. Negotiations for a British loan were no more successful, and the agreement of 2 August, by which the Poles were to receive £8,163,300, was much less than that originally envisaged by the Press. That the <u>French</u> would live up to their promises also seemed improbable. They had concluded a military convention with Poland on 19 May and had agreed to start air attacks on Germany immediately after the outbreak of war: minor operations were to open on the third day of mobilization and a full-scale offensive with 35 to 38 divisions on the sixteenth day. The French later tried to back out of their assurances. They denied that they could be fulfilled. Nor were they likely to aid the Poles in other respects. According to the situation report of the 12th French aircraft were not expected to operate from Polish soil; direct assistance would be confined to delivery of material such as fighter aircraft, anti-aircraft and tank guns. Finally, in spite of the decision to send an <u>Anglo-French military mission to Moscow</u>, which was announced on 25 July, negotiations made little progress. A treaty with the West would have required

[1] Namier, *Diplomatic Prelude*, pp. 224–5 and pp. 236–7.

Russia to provide Poland with material aid. But the Poles, far from expecting any assistance, even suspected that their eastern neighbour might prove positively hostile. According to the situation report of 12 August they had placed two army corps near their eastern frontier to resist a Russian invasion.

The difficulties in rendering assistance to Poland were fully recognized in Britain. It was only to be expected that Chamberlain or those who stood close to him would seek an opportunity to disembarrass themselves from commitments hastily made. In the third week of July conditions were favourable for such a step. There had been a slight *détente* over Danzig and the public mood, which according to Dirksen had been stiffening earlier in the month, became 'more tranquil'.[1] The question remained how overtures could be conveyed to those circles in Germany which were most likely to give them a sympathetic hearing. During the summer of 1939 there were differences of opinion among Hitler's own lieutenants. While Ribbentrop remained uncompromisingly hostile to the West and now sought his personal advancement in a rapprochement with Russia, Göring was prepared to start negotiations behind his back.[2] On 18 July Dr. Wohltat, a prominent member of his economic staff, arrived in London to take part in a whaling conference. Between 18 and 21 July he met Robert Hudson, Parliamentary Secretary for Overseas Trade, as well as Sir Horace Wilson, the Chief Industrial Adviser to HM Government. Wohltat described these talks after his return in a memorandum prepared for Göring on the 24th.[3] While the talks were mainly on economic questions Wilson proposed a 'joint Anglo-German declaration not to use aggression'. Such a declaration, Wilson claimed, would render Britain's guarantee to Poland and Roumania 'superfluous'.

Although certain facts concerning Wohltat's activities leaked out to the Press and sent the Opposition and the French into an uproar, the proposals were not withdrawn. It is evident from a

---

[1] Compare his despatch of 10 with 24 July, DGFP (D), Vol. VI, pp. 891–3 and pp. 859–71. See also his final report, *Documents and Materials* (USSR), p. 182.

[2] It is of some interest that already on 6 July Dahlerus, a Swedish citizen, discussed Anglo-German relations with Göring. Namier, *Diplomatic Prelude*, pp. 418–9.

[3] DGFP (D), Vol. VI, pp. 977–83. See also Dirksen's despatch of 22 July, ibid., p. 954, also *Documents and Materials* (USSR) Vol. II, pp. 67–72.

report from Dirksen of 1 August that the desire for an under-standing was even strengthened.[1] On 3 August Dirksen met Wilson and asked him for a more precise statement of the British plan. Apart from going over in rather 'clearer' terms what he had told Wohltat, Wilson drew Dirksen's attention to the risk which Chamberlain would incur by coming into the open, and he expressed the desire that the Führer, who had less to fear from public opinion at home, would make the next move. Dirksen received no further instructions, and when he arrived to report in Berlin on 13 August he was unable, much to his annoyance, to contact either Hitler or Ribbentrop. Dirksen afterwards claimed that no great significance was attached to the proposals in Germany, but that they were regarded as a further symptom of British weakness.[2] He had in fact judged the Führer's attitude correctly. At a staff conference of 14 August and again on 22 August Hitler described trends in British policy, among them unmistakably the Wohltat-Wilson negotiations, as evidence that Britain was trying to wriggle out of her commitments.[3] Although he had as yet no interest in negotiations, the object of which was to oblige him to desist from violence, the contacts established were to prove valuable at a later stage.

In the second week of August a fresh crisis had broken out over Danzig. On the 14th Polish customs officials were informed that they would be obstructed from carrying out their duties. This resulted in a vehemently hostile exchange of notes. According to Henderson, German propaganda, which had previously concentrated on British encirclement, was turned full blast on to stories of Polish atrocities.[4] Hitler was now, as Ciano observed, determined to strike but he had not fixed a date for the attack. He had, first, to galvanize Mussolini and persuade him to drop his reser-

[1] *Documents and Materials* (USSR) Vol. II, pp. 201–4. Kordt also had a talk with C. R. Buxton, a Labour politician, on 29 July, ibid., pp. 105–12.

[2] Ibid., pp. 116–25. See also Dirksen's letter to Weizsäcker of 19 August, pp. 136–7 and his final report, pp. 190–2. See also Dirksen, *Moscow, Tokyo, London*, pp. 242–4.

[3] E.g., the Ironside report, the British loan to Poland, and the moderate position adopted by Britain during the recent exchange of German-Polish notes over Danzig. It is of some interest that early on the 15th Weizsäcker in conversation with Halder concurred in the Führer's analysis and believed above all that Chamberlain and Halifax were trying to avoid bloodshed. Halder's *Diary* for the conference of the 14th. For the conference of 22 August see ND: Raeder 28.

[4] See *Failure of a Mission*, p. 250.

vations and, secondly, to agree with Stalin on the future of Poland.

Ciano had arrived in Germany on the 11th. The next day Hitler told him that the attack on Poland would probably begin at the end of August and that the Western Powers would not intervene. Hitler dangled the bait of acquisitions in Croatia and Dalmatia before his guest's eyes and explained that, by going to war, Germany would render Italy a great service. Ciano argued that it had previously been agreed to allow a period of two or three years to pass before taking steps which might entail war. He produced facts for the Führer regarding Italy's military weakness. The meeting was a dismal failure. The two parties could not even agree on the text of a communiqué. Ciano was fully aware that Hitler merely intended using Italy to contain enemy divisions. On his return he pressed the Duce not to take part in a war 'which we have neither wanted nor provoked'.[1] Hitler for his part could not conceal his disappointment. At the staff conference on 14 August he admitted that Italy was not interested in a major conflict but would merely seek minor adjustments. He yet persisted in his belief that Italy was ruled by a 'man' and that when the time came Mussolini would not let him down.[2]

Hitler realized that Italy was more likely to take part in a conflict if she had nothing to fear from Turkey and Roumania, and the prospect of an agreement with Russia, which would have had the effect of neutralizing these countries, was used to instil a little enthusiasm into his ally.[3] During his discussion with Ciano on the 12th he had already disclosed the contents of a communication which he had just received from Moscow, stating that the Russians had agreed to accept a German negotiator. That morning Astakhov, the Soviet Chargé d'Affaires, who had also received his instructions, told Schnurre, the economic expert of the German Foreign Ministry, that his Government agreed to discussions in Moscow on all issues. He added that the question whether the German Ambassador or a special envoy should be sent could

[1] See Ciano's *Papers* and *Diaries*, 11–13 August. See also Ciano's reference to his talk with Ribbentrop on the 11th (*Diary*, 23 December 1943).

[2] Halder devotes a special entry to a conference at Obersalzberg and describes the morning and afternoon sessions separately; he also gives a summary. The conference is mentioned in Hassell's Diary, 15 August. Hassell correctly learnt what had taken place from Gisevius.

[3] This is evident from Hitler's letter to Mussolini of 25 August, NSR, pp. 80–1. See also Hassell's Diary, 1 August.

remain open.[1] Surprisingly Hitler did not take up the proposal immediately. In the morning session of the conference of the 14th Halder noted that he was favourably disposed towards giving Russia the assurance asked for (concerning the Baltic and other areas) but that he had not decided whether to despatch a negotiator or whether the negotiator should be a prominent figure.[2] Perhaps Hitler thought that because an Anglo-French military mission had arrived in Moscow on the 11th the Russians would drive a harder bargain. He may also have believed that there was no need to partition Poland and that he would get off cheaply in a short and purely local war.

On the evening of the 14th Hitler was to make up his mind about the Russian proposals and there is every reason to suppose that he was persuaded to do so by military considerations. The campaign against Poland had to be completed by the middle of October before the autumn rains: delay after 1 September entailed risks.[3] On the other hand owing to logistical difficulties it could not be launched at short notice. It has been seen that, because of the strain imposed on rolling stock by work on the West Wall, Hitler could not invade Czechoslovakia before the end of September 1938.[4] Improvements on fortifications were continued in 1939 and were to be completed by 25 August, the date considered by OKW to be the most favourable for the start of operations. Troops had to be moved in unprecedented numbers to widely dispersed assembly areas in eastern Germany. According to Gercke, Chief of Army Transport, the Armed Forces could fulfil their requirements but not the transport system. In the previous year troops were assembled well in advance and under camouflage. This, Gercke pointed out, would be impossible in the present situation unless the orders were issued well in advance.[5] In the

---

[1] DGFP (D), Vol. VII, pp. 58–9.

[2] Halder's *Diary*, 14 August. Hitler had evidently contemplated sending Frank, the party legal expert, and Schnurre, a Foreign Ministry economist, to Moscow. DGFP (D), Vol. VII, pp. 68–9.

[3] Hitler told Ciano on 12 August that from the end of September to May Poland was 'one big swamp', and that if the Poles tried to seize Danzig in the middle of October only minor retaliatory measures were possible. The Luftwaffe would encounter particular difficulties. DGFP (D), Vol. VI, pp. 53–6 and Ciano's *Papers*. Hitler also assured the High Command on 30 August that 'there would be no fighting after 2 September'. (Halder's *Diary*).

[4] See p. 125 and p. 138.

[5] See ND: 13136-NIK, Military Tribunals, and ND: 3787-PS, a meeting of the National Defence Council of 23 June 1939. For a convenient summary see Telford Taylor, *Sword and Swastika*, p. 272.

middle of July OKW prepared a timetable of dates on which the decision would have to be either given or confirmed; it was based on the assumption that 25 August would be the date. OKW wanted to know by the 12th whether a certain manoeuvre on the Weser was to be cancelled, as it could not take place if it were decided to attack Poland. The Party Rally could be held only if Operation White were cancelled, and a decision was requested by the 15th. It was also necessary to know by the same date whether merchant raiders were to be despatched to the Atlantic. The final decision would have to be made on the 23rd with confirmation 24 hours later. Cancellation at this stage would mean that the mobilization already in force could scarcely be camouflaged as 'manoevures'. It is not surprising that General Halder opened his Diary of 14 August with the words *Weser Exercise* and *Party Rally* followed by question marks.

At the conference of 14 August Hitler had not yet decided on the date but he declared that, since future developments could not be predicted with certainty, he would withhold the order for the attack until 48 hours beforehand (the minimum period allowed by OKW). But important decisions were taken in other respects. On that day Hitler concluded a military convention with Slovakia: on the 15th the Party Rally was cancelled; disturbances were instigated in Upper Silesia and ships were ordered to put to sea. So far Hitler had in all essentials complied with the request of his staffs. One adjustment had to be made to the German timetable. The Poles accelerated the call up of troops. On the 15th Halder noted that to keep abreast Germany would have to start mobilizing on the 21st.[1] Everything was to be gained if the Poles could be subjected to an immediate threat from the east. Perhaps this explains why, late on the 14th, Hitler agreed to send Ribbentrop to Moscow.[2] In his despatch arranging for the visit, Ribbentrop instructed Schulenburg to remind Molotov that if agreement were not soon reached matters 'might take a turn which would deprive both governments of the possibility of restoring German-Soviet friendship and of clearing up jointly the territorial questions of

[1] Diary 15 and 16 August.

[2] DGFP (D), Vol. VII, p. 59 and pp. 62–4. The American Embassy in Moscow had acquired very accurate intelligence concerning the German *démarche* at Moscow of the 15th. It was transmitted to London on the 17th but was not received in the central office of the Foreign Office until the 22nd. See DBFP (third series), pp. 41–2.

Eastern Europe'. Speed was again emphasized by Ribbentrop on the 16th and 18th. On the 19th Molotov, apparently after consultation with Stalin, agreed to receive Ribbentrop, but suggested that he should arrive on the 26th or 27th.[1] These dates were too late: the deal had to be clinched and its less sinister clauses made public before, not after, German troops crossed the frontier of Poland. Hence Hitler accepted a Soviet draft treaty, without reservations, on the 20th, but again insisted on speed, and proposed that Ribbentrop should arrive on the 22nd or at the latest on the 23rd. Stalin agreed on the 21st.[2] Important military decisions could now be taken. On the 22nd, a draft directive was issued for the invasion of Poland. That morning and evening Hitler again addressed his staff.[3] Britain, he declared, could no longer hope that, after the defeat of Poland, Russia would become Germany's next enemy. Hitler could thus speak with even greater confidence than on 14 August. He covered much the same ground. On 23 August, the day after the conference, he gave the order to prepare for the attack at 4.15 or 4.30 a.m. on 26 August: the final order was to be given on the 25th.[4] Military preparations were now complete. Unless Hitler had made some grave miscalculation, he would not be deprived of his war.

[1] DGFP (D), Vol. VII, p. 134.

[2] DGFP (D), Vol. VII, p. 168.

[3] There are altogether six versions of this conference: (*a*) a short account given by Greiner, the OKW war historian, from which it is evident that Hitler spoke in the morning and afternoon. Greiner was provided with his information by Warlimont, Jodl's Deputy, and by Canaris, see *Die Oberste Wehrmachtführung 1939–1943*, pp. 38–43; (*b*) Halder's *Diary* which contains passages verbatim; (*c*) ND:798-PS; (*d*) ND: 1014-PS; (*e*) ND: Raeder 27 (IMT), which is a record by Admiral Böhm who was present. A textual analysis of the last mentioned and the previous two is given in ND: 876 and 877-D (NCE Supp. A). At Nuremberg Admiral Böhm denied that Hitler used certain ungentlemanly expressions in ND:798-PS, IMT Vol. XVII, pp. 407–8 and Vol. XIV, pp. 43–8; (*f*) ND: 3-L. This is a highly coloured account of more than doubtful authenticity (see IMT Vol. XIV, p. 45 and Vol. XIX, p. 374). It was, however that version of the speech which, through an American journalist, fell into British hands, DBFP, third series, Vol. VII, 25 August, pp. 257–60. See also ibid., pp. 316 and 317, a letter from Forbes of 27 August.

[4] Halder and Jodl's *Diaries*, 23 August. 26 August was given as the probable date in the conference of 22 August (Halder's *Diary*). In using these documents it should be borne in mind that the letter designating the assembly was 'A' for 'Aufmarsch'; the day of attack was known as 'Y-Tag'; the hour of attack as 'X-Zeit'; the order for concealed mobilization as 'X-Befehl'; the order for attack, 'Fall Weiss'. The last two mentioned were to take effect simultaneously. The days were counted as from 'Mob-Tag', i.e. 26 August, when the 'X-Befehl' took effect.

CHAPTER 17

The Postponement and the Attack

(23 August–September 1939)

Operation White, which Hitler intended launching at dawn on 26 August, was based on certain assumptions: that the Non-Aggression Pact with Russia would deter the West from intervention; that Italy would stand by the Pact of Steel of 22 May. In the last days of August, because both these assumptions proved wrong, the entire issue of peace or war hung in the balance. No greater mistake could therefore be made than to assume that war was inevitable, and although much has been written on the subject, unpublished or recently published German military documents throw new light on some of the major issues.[1]

Immediate British and Italian reactions to the 'bombshell' of the Russian Pact, news of which was made public late on the 21st, were quite unexpectedly disappointing. Henderson who advocated 'some immediate mediatory action', which was precisely what Hitler did not want, arrived at Berchtesgaden at 1 p.m. on the 23rd with a letter from Chamberlain in which Hitler was warned that no greater mistake could be made than to believe that because of a German-Soviet Agreement 'intervention by Great Britain on behalf of Poland is no longer a contingency that need be reckoned with'.[2] On the same day (23 August) concealed mobilization was reported to be in force in Britain and increased military activity in both Britain and France. At 3 p.m. on the 24th Chamberlain re-affirmed the British guarantee to Poland in the House of Commons. Hitler could hardly ignore the more rigid stand Chamberlain was now taking, particularly since 650 German ships (totalling three million tons) were on the high seas. At 5.30 Schmundt, Hitler's

[1] Walther Hofer's *War Premeditated* is the best best general study, and A. J. P. Taylor, *The Origins of the Second World War*, Chap XI. Hofer has had access to some valuable German documents, not published, but has not used Halder's Diary.

[2] *Failure of a Mission*, p. 253. For the text see DGFP (D), Vol. VII, pp. 215–16.

adjutant, who had just returned from Obersalzberg, informed Jodl that the Führer was not quite certain whether the British would not act in earnest this time: 'but he does not want war with England'.[1]

The Russo-German Non-Aggression Pact, which was signed at 2 a.m. on the 24th and back-dated to the 23rd, did not even have the desired effect on Italy, Although Mussolini considered himself bound by 'honour' to 'march blindly' with Germany he was dissuaded by Ciano and others from taking any definite stand. On the 21st it was merely proposed that Ciano should confer with Ribbentrop. The meeting could not take place until Ribbentrop returned from Moscow. At 1 a.m. on the 25th, shortly after his arrival in Germany, Ribbentrop phoned Ciano to say that German action was imminent. He misrepresented the effects of the Pact with Russia and expressed his certainty that participation of the West was impossible. Ribbentrop gave an evasive answer to Ciano's suggestion that they should meet. For a time there was complete confusion in Rome. That morning Ciano used his influence with the King to prevent Mussolini from declaring his readiness to stand by Germany. Mussolini for a time agreed but later changed his mind and no immediate reply was received in Berlin.[2]

Early on the 25th, when there was much uncertainty, Halder was informed that the time for releasing the order for the attack would depend on whether the Western Powers intervened: in fact Canaris believed that they would certainly do so. At noon Halder learnt that the order would be given at 3 p.m. instead of at 2 as previously planned.[3] Hitler made full use of the delay. At 1.30 he met Henderson. The tone of the interview suggests that he still hoped to persuade Britain to stand aloof. After the Polish problem was solved, he would, he stated, approach Britain with a 'generous and comprehensive offer'. According to Halder, Hitler even gave the impression that he would not take it amiss if Britain decided

[1] See the first entry in Halder's *Diary* for 25 August, extracts of which are published in DGFP (D), Vol. VII, Appendix I. Jodl's *Diary* and Hofer, *War Premeditated*, Chap. V.

[2] See Ciano's *Diaries*, 13–22 August. Canaris also referred to the uncertainty of Italian policy in a talk with Keitel on 17 August, ND: 795-PS and to Halder on 21 August, *Diary*. See also the sequence of events given by with Halder on 21 August, Diary. See also the sequence of events given by a prominent member of the *Abwehr* (German military intelligence). See also entry for 26 August concerning Italy.

[3] *Diary*.

to wage a 'sham war'.[1] Hitler also hoped to profit by the short interval by urging Mussolini; and before the interview was over Ribbentrop evidently disclosed to Attolico, the Italian Ambassador, the contents of a communication to the Duce received in Rome at 3.20 p.m. in which Hitler tactfully hinted that Italy should support him. On his own initiative Attolico said that Italy was not prepared for war and that Britain would fight. The order for the attack was nevertheless released at two minutes past 3, before a reply was received from Rome.[2]

Later in the afternoon, Hitler had cause for real anxiety. At 4.30 news reached Berlin that the Anglo-Polish Treaty of 6 April was about to be ratified.[3] The order for the attack was not, however, withdrawn. Nor does it seem that Hitler was already considering whittling down his demands on Poland. At 5.30 he held a conciliatory interview with Coulondre, but it is evident from a letter, which Coulondre was to deliver to Daladier, that Hitler's decision still stood.[4] While news from London might have caused Hitler to waver, the balance of peace and war still, it seems, rested with the Duce. Two messages were received from Rome. Mackensen, the German Ambassador, who was present when the Führer's letter was read, was told 'emphatically' by Mussolini that he would support Hitler 'unconditionally and with all his resources'. This reply was sent to Berlin at 10.25 p.m. and arrived at 4 a.m. (26 August). Ciano succeeded in dissuading Mussolini after Mackensen left. The negative reply was phoned to Berlin at 6 p.m. on the 25th and reached Hitler first. In it Mussolini said that Italy could not intervene immediately unless she were supplied with raw materials on a most generous scale. Hitler was severely shaken. At 7.30, immediately after Ciano's reply, Brauchitsch, who had been conferring with the Führer, informed Halder that the attack must be postponed: Keitel confirmed this at 8.35. No alternative date was given.[5]

[1] DGFP (D), Vol. VII, pp. 279–81, and Halder's sequence of events, *Diary*, 28 August.

[2] Halder's *Diary*, 26 August. There is some uncertainty from the text as to what Attolico actually said.

[3] Ibid. According to Greiner, *Die Oberste Wehrmachtführung*, p. 46, news was received at 5.00 p.m. Ratifications were actually exchanged at 5.35 p.m. See also Hofer, op. cit., pp. 59 et seq.

[4] *Le Livre Jaune Francais: Documents Diplomatiques, 1938–1939*, No. 242, and Coulondre, *De Staline à Hitler*, pp. 287 et seq.

[5] DGFP (D), Vol. VII, pp. 291–3 and pp. 285–6 and pp. 366–7. Halder's *Diary*, 25 and 28 August, and Ciano's *Diaries*, 25 August.

Even the contemporary evidence in a day so crowded with events is conflicting, and it is not possible to decide whether British or Italian action was decisive. Admiral Assmann's contention that the postponement was due to the additional time needed to reinforce the Western front because the French, relieved from pressure on the Italian frontier, were redeploying their forces, cannot be substantiated.[1] On the previous day Italy brought the army of the Po and other commands up to war strength, and so demonstrated her hostility to France. Italy's attitude, however, was more equivocal than that of Britain and may have turned the scales. Whereas on the morning of the 25th both British and Italian reactions were entirely unpredictable, in the evening there was a certainty that Britain would intervene and an equal certainty that Italy would not. The coincidence of bad news from both London and Rome was too much for Hitler. On the 24th he learnt that the British knew of what took place during Ciano's visit (11–13 August) and that they were 'not convinced that Italy would afford Germany military assistance. . . .' Hitler evidently drew the conclusion that Ciano had maliciously communicated with the British, which was not true.[2]

Apart from minor incidents the postponement was successfully put into effect. The assembly for east and west, together with concealed mobilization, was, however, to continue, and it was even believed that the extra time would provide an opportunity for securing an additional springboard for the attack. Indeed, when Hitler gave his orders on the 25th, 'German mobilization proceeded undisturbed' (*läuft in aller Stille*).[3] Yet the postponement had two serious consequences. First, it has been seen that OKW believed that if the operation were called off at the last moment it could not then be disguised as a manoeuvre. Henderson recognized with a considerable degree of accuracy the significance of the 'various orders and arrangements' which, in connection with German mobilization, came into force on the 26th. What is more, the German General Staff discovered that accurate information on the postponement had leaked out.[4] This meant that the 'bombshell' of the ratification of the Anglo-Polish Treaty had caused a

---

[1] Assmann, *Deutsche Schicksalsjahre*, p. 75 and Jodl's *Diary*, 25 August.

[2] DGFP (D), Vol. VII, p. 269. News of the leakage evidently occurred through a journalist. See also Halder's *Diary*, 26 August.

[3] See Note on Sources, p. 195.

[4] See a passage in Halder's *Diary* of 28 August, on an evidently intercepted conversation between Forbes and Coulondre, and *Failure of a Mission*, pp. 254–8.

bigger shock in Berlin than the much vaunted Russo-German Pact had caused in London. Indeed, the British Foreign Office was fully aware that Hitler was 'wobbling' and that, provided they remained firm, they held an 'unexpectedly strong hand'.[1] Secondly, the postponement meant that it would no longer be possible to disrupt Polish mobilization. Hence military pressure from Russia on Poland's eastern frontier assumed greater importance.

In these changed circumstances, Hitler was forced to adopt new tactics. On 14 and 22 August his one nightmare had been that some 'swine' would cheat him of the fruits of victory by a last minute show of mediation.[2] He was then under the illusion that Britain was not seriously interested in the fate of her ally. After ratification of the Anglo-Polish Treaty, when Britain was fully committed, her mediation acquired a very different meaning. She could now only be induced to leave the Poles in the lurch if she were presented with a clear-cut case proving that they, not the Germans, were in the wrong. Hitler had to set to work on some device which, while encouraging Britain to assume the role of honest broker, would make failure a foregone conclusion. He had only a limited time to reach a final decision. 31 August was now assumed by the High Command to be the date on which the attack was to begin, and the Army Group commanders insisted that it should remain so. Hence when Hitler later told Henderson 'my soldiers are asking me yes or no', he was speaking the truth.[3] At 7.30 a.m. on the 26th, before leaving for London with Hitler's proposals, Henderson wrote to Ribbentrop explaining that he would not play for time.[4] He was due to return at 5 p.m. on the 27th. Subsequently, according to a report by an official of the Dienststelle Ribbentrop, an American journalist in Berlin, who had been in contact with one of the British Embassy staff, had given it as his opinion that Henderson personally would make every attempt to persuade his Government to satisfy the German demands.[5] That morning (26 August) Weizsäcker thought that the

---

[1] DBFP (Third series) Vol. VII, a minute by Kirkpatrick and a letter from Forbes, 27 August, ibid., pp. 314–7.

[2] See pp. 179–80.

[3] Halder's *Diary*, 26 and 28 August and *Failure of a Mission*, p. 267.

[4] For the text of the letter see DGFP (D), Vol. VII, p. 305.

[5] DGFP (D), Vol. VII, pp. 366–7, a minute of 27 August 1939. See also Halder's *Diary*, 26 August, where an offer by Henderson to solve the Corridor problem is referred to, and Hassell's Diary, 26 August.

chances for peace were somewhat better and that Germany might after all 'tone down' her demands. For a time this seemed to be correct: no fresh decision was taken at a meeting at the Reich Chancellery in the afternoon. Halder learnt that feelers were taken up but without result.

Halder may have been alluding to an exciting diplomatic adventure which was carried out behind Ribbentrop's back. On the 23rd, the day Ribbentrop negotiated the Russian Pact, Dahlerus, a Swedish citizen, was invited by Göring to act as a liaison for achieving an understanding with Britain. On the 26th Hitler presented Dahlerus with six proposals.[1] Unlike the demands which were given to Henderson on the 25th, they laid greater emphasis on Britain's assisting Germany in solving the Polish problem. They were moderate and, since memorized, brief. According to Halder, Hitler now hoped that Britain might accept certain claims which Poland would reject.

While he was eagerly awaiting the reply to the two sets of proposals, Hitler once more turned to Italy and Russia. Mussolini was asked what supplies Italy needed if she decided on war. During the morning of the 26th a list was prepared: 'It's enough to kill a bull', commented Ciano, 'if a bull could read it.' The list reached Berlin at 1.30 p.m. Neither Göring nor Brauchitsch was in favour of promising Italy the aid she required. Hitler accordingly sent the Duce a negative reply, but asked him to assist Germany by non-military action. He would, he claimed, welcome additional workers from Italy, a propaganda campaign against the West and the concentration of troops on the Franco-Italian frontiers. Hitler also claimed: 'I have no doubt that I can solve the Eastern question even at the risk of complications in the West.' It was, however, of the utmost importance that the world should have no inkling of Italy's real position. He also claimed that by the winter or spring Germany would deploy as many forces in the west as Britain and France.[2] Although the Duce agreed to act on these lines on the 27th, he was not yet over his troubles. If, he declared, Germany failed to take immediate military action in the west, France and Britain might launch a mass attack on Italy, which by 'exhausting [her] limited resources could have serious

[1] Dahlerus, *The Last Attempt.*
[2] DGFP (D), Vol. VII, pp. 313–4 and Ciano's *Diaries*, 26 August. See also Halder's *Diary* (the sequence of events) 28 August.

consequences. . . .'[1] Italy had in fact made extensive preparations; the results were worrying. According to an Italian situation report of the 25th, which fell into German hands, it was expected that France, in response to these preparations, might remain on the defensive against Germany and, instead, attack Italy. A possible allied offensive against Italy would have had no *raison d'être* if Italy herself had openly declared her neutrality. Hence Mussolini's hostile show of force, despite Italy's military weakness, diverted Allied land, air and naval forces to the Mediterranean theatre.

While the Italians were pinning down French and British forces, Russian military pressure against Poland would prove advantageous to Germany. In an operational plan drawn up by General von Rundstedt's staff in May, a withdrawal behind the San, Narew and Vistula rivers was deemed the best defensive possibility open to the Poles.[2] Such action would be rendered impossible if the Russians marched, for, by the Treaty of 23 August, these rivers were to form the boundary between the Russian and German spheres of influence.[3] Although two Polish Army Corps were left in the east to resist a Russian invasion, it was later rumoured that the Russians were easing pressure with the deliberate aim of enabling the Poles to concentrate more forces against Germany. On the 27th Schulenburg was asked to establish whether these rumours were true. He was reminded that if Poland were threatened from the east, the democracies would be less likely to intervene. The next day the question was brought to the notice of Molotov, who denied the rumours and laughed at their absurdity.[4] Although Russian mobilization was not confirmed, considerable military activity in western Russia was observed before the outbreak of war. It was also believed by OKH that since 26 August the Poles were transferring certain army formations to the Russian and perhaps the Lithuanian frontiers.[5] Thus, with prompting from Germany, the Non-Aggression Pact acquired not merely psychological but practical and immediate significance.

Hitler, forced as he was to plead with both Mussolini and the

---

[1] Letters of 26 and 27 August, DGFP (D), Vol. VIII, pp. 353–4.
[2] See Note on Sources, p. 195.
[3] Situation report of 12 August and other intelligence reports. See Note on Sources, p. 195.
[4] DGFP (D), Vol. VII, a despatch of 27 August, pp. 362–3 and pp. 379–80. See also a despatch of 28 August, p. 380 and of 30 August, pp. 438–9.
[5] See also Halder's *Diary* for 31 August.

Soviet rulers, could no longer display his usual intoxicated self-confidence, and, when he addressed officials in the Reich Chancellery on 27 August, created a poor impression. He claimed in the speech which followed that Italy's attitude served Germany's best interests and that he was using the pact with Russia merely to drive out 'Beelzebub with Beelzebub'.[1] There was also a new note in his approach to the Polish problem. He distinguished between 'minor demands', which included the return of Danzig, and a solution of the Corridor by stages, and the 'maximum demands', which depended on the military situation. If the former were not satisfied there would be war.[2] The minimum demands bear a distinct resemblance to the second of the six proposals Dahlerus took with him to Britain. Dahlerus returned in the evening of the 27th with an unofficial and not a final reply: Göring presented it to Hitler, whom he found in a reasonable mood.[3]

The improved atmosphere of the 27th was more apparent than real. Henderson did not return to Berlin as soon as expected. This may have aroused Hitler's suspicions for it was learnt in official German circles that Forbes, Henderson's deputy, told Coulondre that Henderson was working to gain time.[4] The next morning (28 August) Weizsäcker was again pessimistic, and Hitler told Brauchitsch: 'If the worst comes to the worst I will fight a war on two fronts.' That afternoon Halder was informed by Brauchitsch that the attack would start probably on 1 September. The Führer, Brauchitsch continued, intended to put Poland in an unfavourable position for negotiations and so achieve the maximum objective. There were 'rumours', Hitler declared, that Britain would accept a proposal favourable to Germany (a course to which Henderson stood closest) and contrary 'rumours' that Britain believed Poland's vital interests to be threatened. In France attempts to urge the Government not to go to war were on the increase. The Führer next outlined a political stratagem: 'We will demand a corridor through the Corridor and a plebiscite on the basis of the one held in the Saar. England will perhaps accept, Poland possibly

---

[1] In *Mein Kampf*, p. 539, Hitler said this was impossible.

[2] Halder's *Diary*, 28 August and Hassell's Diary, 29 August. Hitler evidently gave the impression in his speech that he ultimately intended to attack Russia (Hassell's Diary, 11 October 1939).

[3] Namier, *Diplomatic Prelude*, pp. 424–5.

[4] Halder's *Diary*, 27–8 August. Henderson was expected to return at 5 p.m. on the 27th.

not.' *Divide them!* Hitler was reported to be 'very calm and clear';[1] and thus in a good humour to receive Henderson.

Henderson returned on the 28th, and at 10.30 p.m. handed Hitler the British reply. HM Government had obligations to Poland 'which they intend to honour'. But they also believed that differences between Germany and Poland should and could be overcome. They advocated direct negotiations between the two countries. If an agreement was reached, 'the way would be open to the negotiation of that wider and more complete understanding between Germany and Great Britain. . . .' Hitler seemed gratified. On this occasion he was even polite to Henderson and allowed him to do most of the talking. Henderson was described by the German Director of Military Intelligence as having expressed himself in a tortuous fashion. He did not deny the Führer's contention that Danzig and the Corridor were not problems. He even suggested that populations might be exchanged. No time limit had been set for the German reply.[2] After the interview the Führer commented: 'I like that. From now on I shall act only on an international basis. International troops, including Russians, can come in.' In this way the rift between England, France and Poland could be widened. On the 29th, the British, in a response to a German request, would persuade the Poles to negotiate. He would receive them on the 30th. The negotiations would break down on the 31st. On 1 September the attack would start.[3]

On the evening of the 28th when Hitler was merely sounding Henderson he could afford to appear reasonable, and Chamberlain's letter was used as the basis for the German counter-proposals. The impression was formed, according to Jodl, that Britain was 'soft' on the question of war. This may have been supported by observations on military preparations. British mobilization on the 23rd was confined to the regular army, and was completed on the 25th. According to the Military Attaché in London in a report on the 26th, it had not been followed by general mobilization.

[1] Hassell's Diary, 29 August. Brauchitsch also claimed that, according to the Roumanian Minister, Henderson brought back little with him and that war was unavoidable (Halder's *Diary*, 28 August)

[2] DGFP (D), Vol. VII, pp. 381–2. The letter was in reply to the German communications of the 23rd and 25th. See also *Failure of a Mission*, p. 262.

[3] Halder's *Diary*, 29 August, a conversation with the Director of Military Intelligence at 4.20 p.m., also telephone conversation with Jodl, in which the text of Hitler's letter to the British Government of 29 August was outlined.

There was also evidence that British forces allocated to the Continent had not embarked. Britain and France, moreover, despite Gamelin's misgivings, assured the Low Countries and Luxembourg that their neutrality would be respected. Hitler was thus certain that, if there were to be a war, it would be a 'phoney' war. Hence he made German action in the west dependent on enemy initiative.[1] Since Britain was showing signs of weakness it is not surprising that when Henderson visited Hitler on the evening of the 29th, nothing again was left undone 'to enhance or emphasize' the solemnity of the occasion. Hitler presented Henderson with a written reply to Chamberlain's letter of the 28th, in which he promised to draw up proposals for negotiation. On reading the passage, 'the German Government count on the arrival' of a Polish plenipotentiary on the 30th, Henderson commented that this 'sounded very much like an ultimatum'. It has been seen that Hitler expected that the British would force the Poles to despatch a negotiator. Henderson's reply may have come as a surprise and a heated interview followed. Although Henderson gave Hitler no assurances, he contacted Lipski immediately afterwards and implored him to urge his government to despatch a negotiator. Henderson also informed London of Hitler's new demand. The first British reply was delivered at 4 a.m.: it would be unreasonable to expect a Polish negotiator to arrive in 24 hours. Needless to say the Poles also objected.[2]

The same day (30 August) Hitler ordered the *Wilhelmstrasse* to draft a further letter to London containing his 'precise' demands on Poland. The proposals in themselves were moderate and have been described as 'a real League of Nations' document.[3] Despite their professional wording they bear an unmistakable resemblance to the plan Hitler outlined to Brauchitsch on the 28th and 29th. In the afternoon of the 30th he made one small concession, which is perhaps an indication of the extent to which he took them seriously. Everything was to be ready for the attack on the 1st, but, should negotiations in London require a postponement, the attack was to be launched on the 2nd. Nothing was to be undertaken after this date, and the Commander-in-Chief of the Army

---

[1] Directive No. 1 of 31 August, ND: 126-C and Halder's *Diary*, 29 August.
[2] DGFP (D), Vol. VII, pp. 413–5.
[3] *Failure of a Mission*, pp. 263–5 and pp. 311–3, and Schmidt, *Hitler's Interpreter*, p. 150.

would be informed by 3 p.m. on the 31st. In the event no negotiator appeared; if Hitler originally hoped to use the proposals as
a basis for negotiation he later changed his mind. On the 31st
he told Brauchitsch that they were only to be forwarded on condition that the Poles arrived, but that intercepted conversations
proved how the Poles were adopting dilatory tactics.[1] Evidently
the proposals were intended to be studied in London while Ribbentrop was 'grilling' the Poles in Berlin. Henderson was received
by Ribbentrop at midnight instead of at 11.30 p.m. on 30 August,
for it had taken quite a time to decode the British Government's
considered reply. An undignified scene followed; according to
Henderson, Ribbentrop portrayed 'intense hostility'. Henderson
was told that since no Polish negotiator had arrived the proposals
were out of date. Yet to prove the sincerity of his Government's
intentions, Ribbentrop 'gabbled through' the contents of the
document in German, but refused to hand it over for Henderson's
perusal. Even on the following day Ribbentrop turned down
Weizsäcker's request to give it to Henderson who, in spite of this,
acquired a copy from Dahlerus.[2]

Hitler most probably abandoned the stratagem for detaching
Britain on the evening of the 30th. At 6.30 a.m. on the 31st the
order for taking up positions was given. At 4 p.m. OKW released
the order for attack. About the same time Admiral Canaris, head
of the OKW Intelligence Service, learnt that Lipski was trying to
contact Hitler.[3] Hitler refused to see Lipski, and OKH were informed that the order for the attack remained in force. In the
middle of this feverish activity Hitler exclaimed to Brauchitsch:
'I cannot carry on much longer in this situation; a decision is
imperative.'[4] Despite the efforts he had made after the 25th to

---

[1] Halder's *Diary*, 30 August. The expression used is: 'the Poles are not there,
England implicated [*eingeschaltet*]'. Halifax in fact could not advise the Poles
to comply. See his instructions to Henderson, which were sent at 6.50 p.m.,
DBFP (third series), Vol. VII, pp. 451–2. The intercepted message was probably a communication from Beck to Lipski of 12.40 p.m., 31 August.

[2] *Failure of a Mission*, pp. 269–72. See also Hassell's Diary, 30 August.

[3] Halder's *Diary*. Lipski was eventually received at 6.30 p.m. by Ribbentrop.
DGFP (D), Vol. VII, p. 462.

[4] Halder's *Diary*, 31 August. That spurious or partially true reports of
Polish atrocities had enraged him to such a degree that he could not hold himself back is more than uncertain. He never mentioned this subject to Brauchitsch and was reported on 31 August to be 'calm' and to have had a good
night's sleep. Besides, at least the frontier incidents complained of in the German
Press were deliberately manufactured. Namier, *Diplomatic Prelude*, pp. 314–5.

detach the Western democracies from Poland there was still no certainty, even on the day before the attack, how they would react. According to Stülpnagel, Deputy Chief of the General Staff, action by the Western Powers was unavoidable, but the Führer was still determined to strike. Later in the day Hitler was reported by Brauchitsch to be optimistic, for he believed that failure to authorize evacuations in the frontier areas of France meant that the West would not intervene. Hitler also told Brauchitsch that he believed the Italian concentration of troops, which were now in full force, would reduce the likelihood of a general conflict.[1]

Yet he can hardly have failed to realize that the Duce's grand manoeuvre of deception would sooner or later be exposed. Italy's defection in 1915 had never been forgotten. It seemed in Rome that the West were responding promptly to Mussolini's sabre-rattling, for that evening (31 August) the British, instead of answering Ciano's proposal for a Five Power conference to be held on 5 September, for reasons of security, cut telephone communications with Rome. Misinterpreting this move and fearing war with the West Ciano, with the Duce's approval, committed an 'indiscretion'. He frankly told Sir Percy Loraine, the British Ambassador: 'Can't you understand that we shall never start a war against you and the French?' Loraine was reported to be on the verge of tears with joy (British diplomats weep only in the presence of Italians) and replied: 'I have known this for fifteen days, but the measures of the last few days have shaken my faith.'[2]

Ciano's 'indiscretion', in a sense, came too late; by 6.30 a.m. on 1 September German troops had crossed the Polish frontier at all points. Mussolini, released from his obligations to Germany, and no longer fearing an attack by the West, continued with his final and fruitless attempt at mediation, embodied in proposals for a cease fire of 2 September. To Ciano's surprise Hitler did not reject Mussolini's proposals out of hand, but asked whether the warning notes, presented by Britain and France on the previous night, had the character of ultimata. At 6.30 he ordered OKH to occupy Posen with strong forces as soon as possible and perhaps also the industrial area of Upper Silesia.[3] No doubt he hoped to provide

[1] Halder's *Diary*.

[2] Ciano's *Diaries*, 31 August. Italy agreed to mediate if Germany were given a 'fat prize' (Danzig). Halifax turned down the proposal concerning Danzig.

[3] DGFP (D), Vol. VII, pp. 492–3 and Ciano's and Halder's *Diaries* for 2 and 3 September.

himself with a handsome slice of Polish territory before an armistice was concluded in accordance with the *uti possidetis* principle. Although it was learnt in Berlin through Rome that the British warning did not constitute an ultimatum, Halifax informed Ciano that negotiations could start only if German forces withdrew from Poland. Halifax correctly feared that Hitler was delaying his reply in order to extend his hold over Polish territory, and that he would then make a magnanimous peace offer. At 9 a.m. on 3 September Henderson arrived at the *Wilhelmstrasse* with the British ultimatum. In the tragi-comedy that followed he was received by Schmidt, Hitler's interpreter, instead of by Ribbentrop.[1] By 11 a.m. the British ultimatum expired, and Britain and Germany were in a state of war. By 5 o'clock that evening France, who had delayed because of Italian mediation for a cease fire, was at war. The delays had provided Hitler with three valuable days in which he could break the back of Polish initial resistance and consider strengthening his Western frontier.

Within a month Poland was laid low. Yet before 27 September Hitler made no definite plans for an offensive against France.[2] It seems that he still hoped to gain recognition of the new *status quo* in the east, but he could no longer ignore Soviet ambitions. According to the secret articles of the Non-Aggression Pact of 23 August the Narew, Vistula and San rivers were to divide Poland into German and Soviet spheres of interest. Whether an independent Polish state should be established could be decided jointly by the two parties.[3] The Russians were asked to stake their claims as soon as possible. On 31 August Hitler believed that they would march immediately after the German initial successes.[4] Although the Russians were again urged to move on the 3rd they delayed. On the 12th Hitler told Brauchitsch that, because of their passivity, he would try to establish an independent Ukraine.[5] On the 17th, after further promptings from Ribbentrop, the Russian advance began. Stalin could now show his hand; the next day Molotov informed Schulenburg that 'contrary to the original inclination' to permit the existence of a rump Poland, the whole country should

[1] *Hitler's Interpreter*, pp. 150 et seq.
[2] Notes by Halder on a conference of 27 September. See Note on Sources, p. 195.
[3] DGFP (D), Vol. VII, pp. 245–6.
[4] Conversation with Brauchitsch, Halder's *Diary*, 31 August.
[5] Ibid., 7, 11 and 12 September.

be partitioned. Hitler consented. The final frontier was settled by the Treaty of 28 September. Lithuania was now to fall to Russia instead of Germany; the province of Lublin and parts of the province of Warsaw to Germany. Since the Treaty of 28 September could only result in the complete elimination of Poland, it had the effect, which Stalin no doubt hoped for, of embroiling Germany even more deeply in war with the West. On the 27th, while negotiations were still in progress, Hitler formulated operational plans which were to bear fruit in May 1940.[1]

As a result of his new policy with Russia, Hitler had temporarily renounced the much coveted field of expansion in the Baltic and the Ukraine, for which territorial gains at the expense of France and the British Empire were a poor substitute. He had embarked on a war in which the fruits of victory were not enough. He fought less for profit than for the destruction of a centre of opposition. What if there were stalemate in the west? In September 1939 Hitler gave no consideration either to this problem or to the consequences of intervention by the United States. But on 22 June 1941 he decided to adjust his military objectives to his final political aim. In so doing he violated the principle of limited liability to which he had owed his original success. From September 1939 he had on his hands a war which he could not win; from June 1941, a war he was certain to lose.

[1] Notes by Halder. See Note on Sources, p. 195.

Note on Sources

In accordance with official practice I am not permitted to give the reference numbers of any documents as yet unpublished, with the result that certain statements in my text are not provided with references to the authorities which I have used; but sources referring indirectly to these statements are quoted. Many of the documents, in particular those in the diplomatic sphere, have now been printed and I have accordingly given them appropriate references, though in some cases I have preferred to retain my own translations. Full references to unpublished documents have been given in the text of the earlier study which was prepared for official use.

BIBLIOGRAPHY

A. Published Documents

Documents on British Foreign Policy, 1919–1939 (abbr. DBFP). Edited by E. L. Woodward and Rohan Butler, second and third series, HM Stationery Office, 1947–1954.

Documenti diplomatici italiani, ottava serie 1935–1939, vol. XII, 23 May–11 August 1939 and vol. XIII, 12 August–3 September 1939. Istituto Poligrafo dello Stato, 1952–1953.

Documents on German Foreign Policy. Published by HM Stationery Office, abbr. DGFP. Series C, vols. I–IV and Series D, vols. I–VII.

Documents and Materials Relating to the Eve of the Second World War, 2 Vols. Vol. II, Dirksen Papers. Foreign Languages Publishing House, Moscow, 1948 (abbr. Documents and Materials, USSR).

Dokumente zur Vorgeschichte des Krieges (Deutsches Weissbuch), herausgegeben vom Auswärtigen Amt, Berlin, 1939.

Führer Conferences on Naval Affairs. Admiralty edition reproduced in Brassey's Naval Annual for 1948.

Hitler's Speeches, edited by N. Baynes. OUP for RIIA, 1942.

Nuremberg Documents (abbr. ND)

    (i)   The trial of the Major War Criminals. The official verbatim report* of the trial and the documents** produced both by the prosecution and by the defence for the International Military Tribunal and published in Nuremberg, 1947–1949 (abbr. IMT). The serial number either of the documents or of the case has been given in the text.

    (ii) Nazi Conspiracy and Aggression, published by US Government Printing Office, 1946 (abbr. NCA). This publication consists of documents assembled for the Nuremberg Trial but not necessarily used in court. The German version in IMT has been used whenever the same document occurs in both series. Where a document appears in only one or other of the series this has been indicated in the text.

    (iii) Nuremberg Military Tribunals, USGPO, Washington, 1951. This series of 15 volumes contains a number of useful documents which were used at the subsequent war crimes trials.

Polish Ministry of Foreign Affairs: Official Documents concerning Polish–Soviet Relations, 1933–1939. Polish White Book. Translated and published by authority of the Polish Government.

The Royal Institute of International Affairs, abbr. RIIA. Annual surveys and companion volumes of documents, published yearly from 1924 to 1937 and after the outbreak of war.

* in English; ** in German.

Thomas, G. Grundlagen für eine Geschichte der deutschen Wehr-und Rüstungswirtschaft (Basic Facts) reproduced in part in ND: 2353-PS. See Nuremberg Documents.

Vierteljahrshefte für Zeitgeschichte, edited by Professor Hans Rothfels and Theodor Eschenburg, Munich, in which many documents have been published for the first time.

B. Private Diaries and Papers

Ciano
  (i) Diaries, 23 August 1937–31 December 1938, translated with notes by Andreas Mayor and an introduction by Malcolm Muggeridge. Methuen, 1952.
  1 January 1939–23 December 1943. Edited by Malcolm Muggeridge. William Heinemann, 1947.
  (ii) Diplomatic Papers, 12 June 1936–30 April 1942. Translated by Stuart Hood and edited by Malcolm Muggeridge. Odhams, 1948.

Ambassador W. E. Dodd's Diary 1933–1938. Edited by W. E. Dodd, Jr. and M. Dodd with an introduction by C. A. Beard, Harcourt Brace and Company, New York, 1941.

Förster, W. Ein General kämpft gegen den Krieg. Aus den nachgelassenen Papieren des Generalstabchefs Ludwig Beck. Münchener Dom Verlag, 1949. This contains memoranda written by General Beck between 1934 and August 1938. (abbr. Förster.)

Halder's Diary. Written between 14 August 1939 and 24 September 1942 by General Halder, Chief of the Army General Staff. The quotations have been taken directly from the German version but the American translation has also been consulted. The diary is a careful day-to-day record of military and political events. Since in its original form it consisted of shorthand notes the meaning of certain passages is far from clear unless their general context is understood. Extracts of the Diary have been reproduced in DGFP Series (D) Vol. VII, appendix I. It is now published by the Kohlhamer Verlag, Stuttgart, 1962.

Hassell, Ulrich von, Diaries. Vom Andern Deutschland. Aus den nachgelassenen Tagebüchern 1938–1944. Atlantis Verlag, Zürich, 1947. The Diaries have also been published in English, Hamish, Hamilton, 1948.

Jodl's Diary (fragments), January 1937–August 1939, reproduced in ND: 1780-PS, described in Nuremberg Documents.

Das Politische Tagebuch Alfred Rosenberg aus den Jahren 1934–1935 und 1939–1940, edited by Hans Günther Seraphim, Mustersmidt Verlag, Göttingen, 1956.

C. General Works and Memoirs

Assmann, K. Deutsche Schicksalsjahre, Eberhard Brockhaus, Wiesbaden, 1950.

Baumont, M. La Faillite de la Paix 1918–1939, Presses Universitaires de France, 1951.

Beloff, M. The Foreign Policy of the Soviet Union, 2 vols. RIIA, 1947–1949 (abbr. Beloff).

Bracher, K. D. Die Auflösung der Weimarer Republik. Eine Studie zum Problem des Machtverfalles in der Demokratie. Ring Verlag, Stuttgart, 1957.

Braubach, M. Der Einmarsch deutscher Truppen in die Entmilitarisierte Zone am Rhein im März 1936. Ein Beitrag zur Vorgeschichte des zweiten Weltkrieges. Westdeutscher Verlag, 1956.

Broszat, M. Der Nationalsozialismus, Weltanschauung, Programm und Wirklichkeit. Deutsche Verlagsanstalt, Stuttgart, 1960.

Bullock, A. Hitler, A Study in Tyranny, Odhams, 1952 (abbr. Bullock).

Carr, E. H.
    (i) German–Soviet Relations between the Wars, Oxford University Press, 1952.
    (ii) The Bolshevik Revolution, Vol. III, Macmillan, 1953.

Castellan, G. Le Réarmement Clandestin du Reich, 1930–1935, vu par le 2e Bureau de L'Etat Major Français, Plon, Paris, 1954.

Celovsky, B. Das Münchener Abkommen 1938. Deutsche Verlagsanstalt, Stuttgart, 1958.

Churchill, W. S. The Second World War, Vol. I. The Gathering Storm, Cassell, 1948.

Coulondre, R. De Staline à Hitler, 1936–1939: Souvenirs d'une Ambassade à Berlin, Hachette, Paris, 1950.

Craig, G. and Gilbert, F. The Diplomats 1919–1939, Princeton University Press, 1953.

Dahlerus, B. The Last Attempt, Hutchinson, 1948.

Dirksen, H. von. Moscow-Tokyo-London, Hutchinson, 1951.

Eichstädt, U. Von Dollfuss zu Hitler, Geschichte des Anschlusses Österreichs 1933–1938. Stein, Wiesbaden, 1955.

Eyck, E. Geschichte der Weimarer Republik in two vols. Eugen Rentsch Verlag Erlenbach-Zürich, 1954–1956.

Fabry, P. W. Der Hitler–Stalin Pakt 1934–1941, Fundus Verlag, Darmstadt, 1962.

Falls, C. A Hundred Years of War, Duckworth, 1953.

Fieling, K. Life of Neville Chamberlain, Macmillan, 1947.

Förtsch, H. Schuld und Verhängnis. Die Fritsch Krise im Frühjahr 1938 als Wendepunkt in der Nationalsozialistischen Zeit. Deutsche Verlagsanstalt, Stuttgart, 1951.

François-Poncet, A. Souvenirs d'une ambassade à Berlin, Septembre 1931–Octobre 1938. Paris, 1946.

Freund, G. Unholy Alliance. Russian–German Relations from the Treaty of Brest Litovsk to the Treaty of Berlin, with an introduction by J. Wheeler-Bennett, Chatto and Windus, 1957.

Gamelin, M. G. Servir, Plon, Paris, 1946–1947.

Gathorne-Hardy, G. M. A. A Short History of International Affairs 1920–1938, (RIIA), second impression, May 1939.

Geyr von Schweppenburg, L. The Critical Years, Allen Wingate, London, 1952. Translated from Erinnerungen eines Militärattacéhs. London, 1933–1937. Deutsche Verlagsanstalt, Stuttgart, 1949.

Görlitz, W. The German General Staff: Its History and Structure, with a preface by Cyril Falls. Hollis and Carter, 1953.

Greiner, E. Die Oberste Wehrmachtführung 1939–1943. Limes Verlag, Wiesbaden, 1951.

Halifax, Earl of. Fulness of Days. Collins, 1957.

Henderson, N. Failure of a Mission, Berlin 1937–1939. Readers Union, 1939.

Hilger, G. and Meyer, A. G. The Incompatible Allies. Macmillan, New York, 1953.

Hitler, A.

(i) Mein Kampf. The Jubilee edition issued by the Nazi Publication Office, 1939; also the English version, Murphy edition (Hurst and Blackett, 1939). Page references have been given to the English version.

(ii) Hitlers Zweites Buch. A publication of the Institut für Zeitgeschichte Munich, edited by G. L. Weinberg, Deutsche Verlagsanstalt, Stuttgart, 1961.

Hofer, W. War Premeditated, Thames and Hudson, 1955. Translated from Die Entfesselung des zweiten Weltkrieges, Deutsche Verlagsanstalt, Stuttgart, 1955.

Hossbach, F. Zwischen Wehrmacht und Hitler 1934–1938, Wolfenbüttel and Hannover, 1949 (abbr. Hossbach).

Jedlicka. Ein Heer im Schatten der Parteien. Die militärpolitische Lage Österreichs, 1919–1938. Verlag Hermann Böhlaus, Graz-Köln, 1955.

Ludendorff, E. Der Totale Krieg, Ludendorff Verlag, Munich, 1936.

Kleist, P. Zwischen Hitler und Stalin, 1939–1945, Athenäum Verlag, Bonn, 1950.

Kochan, L. Russia and the Weimar Republic, Bowes and Bowes, 1954.

Kordt, Erich.

(i) Wahn und Wirklichkeit, Union Deutsche Verlag, Stuttgart, 1948 (abbr. Kordt).

(ii) Nicht aus den Akten. Die Wilhelmstrasse in Frieden und Krieg. Erlebnisse, Begegnungen und Eindrücke. Deutscher Verlagsanstalt, Stuttgart 1950.

Mau, H. and Krausnick, H. Deutsche Geschichte der jüngsten Vergangenheit 1933–1945, Bundeszentrale für Heimatdienst, Bonn, 1960.

Meinck, G. Hitler und die deutsche Aufrüstung, 1933–1939, Franz Steiner Verlag GmbH, Wiesbaden, 1959.

Mowat, C. L. Britain between the Wars, 1918–1940, Methuen, 1955.

Müller-Hillebrand, B. Das Heer, 1933–1945. E. S. Mittler, Darmstadt 1954.

Nadolny, R. Mein Beitrag, Limes Verlag, Wiesbaden, 1955.

Namier, L. B.

(i) Diplomatic Prelude, 1938–1939, Macmillan, 1948.

(ii) Europe in Decay, A Study in Disintegration 1936–1940. Macmillan, 1950.

(iii) In the Nazi Era, Macmillan, 1952.

Papen, F. Memoirs, André Deutsch, 1952.

Reynolds, P. A. British Foreign Policy in the Inter-War Years, Longmans, Green, 1954.

Ribbentrop, J. The Memoirs of, with an introduction by A. Bullock and translated by Oliver Watson from the German, Zwischen London und Moskau. Weidenfeld and Nicolson, 1954.

Roos, H. Polen und Europa, Studien zur polnischen Aussenpolitik 1931–1939, Mohr, Tübingen, 1957.

Rothfels, H. The German Opposition to Hitler, translated by Lawrence Wilson, Oswald Wolff, 1961.

Salvemini, G., Prelude to World War II, Gollancz, 1953.

Schacht, Dr. H. Account Settled, Weidenfeld and Nicolson 1949, translated from Abrechnung mit Hitler, Rowohlt, Hamburg Stuttgart, 1948.

Schmidt, Dr. P. Hitler's Interpreter, Heinemann, 1951, translated from Statist auf Diplomatischer Bühne 1923–1945, Athenäum Verlag, Bonn, 1949.

Seabury, P. The Wilhelmstrasse, A Study of German Diplomats under the Nazi Regime, Cambridge University Press, 1955.

Seton-Watson, H. Eastern Europe Between the Wars, 1918–1941, Cambridge University Press, 1945.

Shepherd, A. Austrian Odyssey, Macmillan, 1957.

Shirer, W. L. The Rise and Fall of the Third Reich, A History of Nazi Germany, Secker and Warburg, 1960.

Siegler, F. Die höheren Dienststellen der deutschen Wehrmacht 1933–1945, Deutsche Verlagsanstalt, Stuttgart, 1953.

Simon, J. Retrospect: the Memoirs of the Rt. Hon. Viscount Simon, Hutchinson, 1952

Taylor, A. J. P. The Origins of the Second World War, Hamish Hamilton, 1961.

Taylor, Telford. Sword and Swastika, Gollancz, 1953.

Templewood, Viscount (Sir Samuel Hoare). Nine Troubled Years, Collins, 1954.

Toscano, M. Le Origini del Patto d'Acciaio. Sansoni. Firenze, 1948. L'Italia e Gli Accordi Tedesco Sovietici dell 'Agosto 1939. Sansoni. Firenze, 1952.

Waite, R. Vanguard of Nazism, The Free Corps Movement in Post-War Germany, Harvard University Press, 1952.

Weizsäcker, E. von. Erinnerungen. List Verlag, Munich 1950.

Wheeler-Bennett, J. W.

(i) Disarmament Deadlock. Oxford University Press, 1934.

(ii) Munich, Prologue to Tragedy. Macmillan, 1948.

(iii) The Nemesis of Power. The German Army in Politics, Macmillan, 1953.

Wiskemann, E. The Rome–Berlin Axis. A History of the Relations between Hitler and Mussolini. Oxford University Press, 1949.

Index

crisis, 79 *et seq.*; system of alliances (after March 1936), 93; as a power factor (1935–7), 44–5, 91, 108; effects of *Anschluss* on, 116; General Beck and, 128; as a power factor (Sept. 1938), 132, 145, 148; German operational plans against (1937), 90–2; (1938), 160–1; concludes declaration with Germany (Dec. 1938), 160–1; obligations to Poland (1939), 174; Hitler plans attack on (Sept. 1939), 193

François-Poncet, A., French Ambassador in Berlin: protests against SA, 30–1; and ratification of the Franco-Russian alliance, 65, 69, 77; and Munich, 145

Franco-Russian alliance (1935), 59–60, 65; ratification of 69, 93

Frank, H., 13, 96

Frick, W., Minister of Interior, 38

Fritsch, General W. Freiherr von; conversation with General Muff, 38; on military expansion (1936), 85, 91; opposition to Hitler's plans (5 Nov. 1937), 108, 110; dismissal of, 112

Fromm, General F., 33, 84

Gaus, Dr., 60

Gentleman's Agreement, 95

Gerckl, General, 178

George V, King, 14

Germany:
  colonies, return of, 113
  conscription, reintroduction of, 34, 56; extended to two years, 82–5
  military directives and operational plans (March 1933), 10; (Oct. 1933), 26; (Oct. 1943), 43; (18 March 1935), 57; (5 March 1936), 78; *Schulung* (May 1935), 90; (June 1937), 90–2, 97; (Dec. 1937), 109. *See also relevant names and subjects*
  operation *Green*, 126, 127; operation *White* (April 1939), 166, 180; (25 Aug. 1939), 183; for an invasion of France, 193–4
  Rearmament, (1932), 5, 49; progress within limits of the MacDonald plan, 20–1; and intelli-

gence reports on Russia, 22–3; the SA and, 28–9, 31; war economy adapted to, 32–4; development of new weapons, 45; British learn of scope of (Nov. 1934), 52–3; Hitler exaggerates level reached (March 1935), 56–7; slow progress (after 1936), 82–3; Hitler's programme criticized, 84 *et seq.*; four-year plan and, 87–8; and mobile formations, 125, 132; the balance of strength and (1938), 134, 159; (1939), 173

Godesberg, memorandum of, 143, 148

Goebbels, J., Reich Minister of Propaganda; xi, 11

Göring, General, later Field Marshal, H., xi and the Rhineland, 72; made responsible for the four-year plan, 86; and the fall of Fritsch, 112; orders resignation of President Miklas, 115; discusses Danzig with Weizsäcker, 154; and negotiations with Russia, 169; negotiates with Italians behind Ribbentrop's back, 113, 170; 175; sends Dahlerus to London, 186

Grandi, Count, 96

Great Britain: attitude to Germany (1934), 49; re-affirms treaty obligations (1935), 55; opposes Italy (1935), 64; not prepared to specify obligations under Locarno, 69 *et seq.*, as a power factor (Sept. 1938), 133–5, 148; (Aug. 1939), 189–90; lack of sympathy towards Poland (Jan. 1939), 160–1; public opinion in (15 March 1939), 163; German operational plans against (1939), 172–3, fn., 173

Habicht, leader of the Austrian Nazis, 14, 16, 35

Hacha, President of Czechoslovakia, 162

Halder, General F., xiii, appointed chief of army General Staff, 129; and the non-aggression pact with Russia, 178; and intervention by Britain and France (Aug. 1939), 182

Index